Multicultural Politics

Racism, Ethnicity and Muslims in Britain

Tariq Modood

Foreword by Craig Calhoun

Edinburgh University Press

See pages 233–4 for copyright information for previously published material in this book.

© the Regents of the University of Minnesota, 2005

First published in the United States of America by the University of Minnesota Press, 2005

Printed and bound in Great Britain by MPG Books Ltd, Bodmin

A CIP record for this book is available from the British Library

ISBN 0 7486 2171 7 (hardback)
ISBN 0 7486 2172 5 (paperback)

The right of Tariq Modood to be identified as author of this work has been asserted in accordance with the Copyright, Designs and Patents Act 1988.

To the memory of my father

Contents

Foreword

Craig Calhoun

In the last few years, Britain's Muslim minority has found increasing public recognition, continued to suffer old sorts of harassment, and been challenged by the both the British state and international pressures in the context of the "war on terror." Even positive media attention has sometimes the mixed character of extolling assimilation more than virtues of Muslims as such, and thus plays into ambivalences within Muslim communities. But in Britain as in America, intensified surveillance, the suspicions of neighbors, various forms of discrimination, and sometimes physical attacks continue to be visited on Muslims.

Britain did not respond to terrorist actions with quite the same focus on Islamic fundamentalism that made "Muslim" the operative focus American anxieties and state action. But Britain did impose new surveillance and did join the US in its invasion of Iraq. Even more importantly, Britain's Islamic populations were larger than America's and the issue was more clearly "internal" as well as "external." If Americans tended to demonize Muslims—or at least "Islamic fundamentalists"—as threats from abroad, in the UK the new concerns came on the heels of decades of difficult adjustment to the presence of a sizeable and visible Islamic minority. Moreover, though Britain like the US came to rely on the apparently religious identity "Muslim," it was harder for a country with an established church to approach Islam as simply one religious denomination entitled to equal recognition alongside others.

Understanding this complex pattern is both intellectually and practically important. It is crucial to sustaining multicultural democracy and crucial to minimizing racism. Understanding must come both from insight into the experience of Britain's Muslims and from analysis of the public context they face. And one of the best guides to both this experience and the public issues is Tariq Modood.

A distinguished sociologist who holds a chair at Bristol University, Modood is one of the founding editors of the journal, *Ethnicities*. Modood is also a veteran of years of practical work on race relations. And as he demonstrates, both of these analytic frames are necessary. There is a tendency to oppose the analysis of race and ethnicity as though they were sharply distinct, but clearly the case of British Muslims shows their complex interrelationship.

Britain has since the 1970s seen a substantial growth in its Muslim population, most of it composed of South Asians from former British imperial dominions. Initially mostly termed "Pakistanis" (or more abusively, "Pakis"), these were recategorized first as Asians and then as Muslims. Some commentators suggested that the shift reflected a move away from racialization towards a cultural identification of the population. But if this is in some sense partially true, Modood shows clearly that race—and racism—remained inextricably intertwined in the way British Muslims were understood. The cultural attributes associated with Muslims were not merely stereotypes, they were understood to be more or less inherent, blocks to assimilation, essentially related to race. And they became the focus of discrimination and outright attacks, from the "Paki-bashing" of the 1970s to the police violence of recent years, some of which has led not just to protests but to street-fighting.

At the same time, many antiracists suggested (despite the seeming contradiction) both that Asians should think of themselves as "black," joining in an anti-racist struggle for which the primary referents were Caribbean immigrants and their descendants, and that race should be understood on the model of class and be the basis for solidarity with white English workers. Both suggestions subordinated the specific concerns of British Muslims (or Asians, or Pakistanis). Both suggested that "ethnicity" was of relatively minimal significance compared to class or race (and that the latter should be understood overwhelmingly as a matter of color). And both represented attempts to make older categories of analysis and struggle work in new situations, attempts to "save" simplistic models or race or class rather than develop more complex analyses of each.

More generally, the fight against racism isn't quite what it used to be. Among the well-intentioned but experientially chastened it's easy to be nostalgic for days when the terms of debate and denunciation were clearer. In those paradoxically golden bad old days, racists insisted that races were real, that basic differences distinguished them, and that these formed a sound basis for social inequality. At a minimum, antiracists challenged the last of these. It seemed clear that the basic evil of racism was social inequality. This implied an egalitarian solution. Sometimes it was argued that equality was more political, sometimes more economic. Questions of equal social status—like an end to discrimination in housing or schooling—consistently loomed large. Only occasionally were questions of equal cultural status raised.

All this changed, for better or worse, in the mid-twentieth century and especially during the 1960s and '70s. The more old-fashioned sort of antiracists faced a series of confusing reversals. Liberal integrationism was challenged over the cultural violence of its assimilationist impulse. The slogan "black is beautiful" was only one of a thousand ways in which racial difference was made a source of pride rather than denied into insignificance. The struggle to value difference rather than bracket or end it was arguably a predictable outgrowth of the antiracist struggle, but it was a shift that spelled trouble for the conceptual coherence of the very project.[1]

Perhaps above all, the effort to think the antiracist struggle in its classical terms of Black and White began to impose identities—and sometimes so too did the attempt to fit race into class terms. British Muslims were largely forced into working class occupations, but they had aspirations for education-led mobility—and over generations showed actual mobility—that set them apart. As Modood shows, not least with loving reference to his own father, many idealized the British and sought to preserve aspects of British civilization they saw as threatened by contemporary declines. This did not stop many from embracing a renewed piety as a basic source of identity and orientation in a new and difficult cultural context. Nor did it stop racist responses to British Muslims. These racist responses were shaped by phenotype, but they were not based on appearance alone. As Modood says, "a culture of a group that is already racialized can be the basis of a more elaborate racism."

It is this situation that Modood examines. He argues for the importance of ethnicity, and of seeing and resisting racism when it is reorganized partially in terms of culture as well as color. He argues for diversity as a positive value. With this in mind, he resists suggests that overcoming material inequalities can in and of itself replace the struggle against racism. British Muslims do suffer discrimination in employment, education, housing and other settings. But it would be not only an irony but an injustice to suggest that in order to avoid these they should surrender their identities or communities.

Modood advocates a multicultural politics, but a more clearheaded one than the soft relativism that often underpins such claims. More than liberalism is required, he suggests, not least because part of the challenge is to work out how non-liberal cultures can fit into mostly liberal societies. More than liberalism is required also because of the pervasive individualism that makes liberal approaches tend to suggest that the ideal of race relations must be voluntary ethnicity—if any. Not all culture can be chosen, and not all people are in equal positions to choose. An adequate multicultural politics seeks to deal with (not deny the relevance of) sharp cultural differences that make working out the applications of justice as fairness truly difficult. Take for example the resistance of many Muslim communities to the liberal individualistic hedonism of the larger culture and society. Claims to "our way of life" do not justify familial or communal repression of individuals and their choices, but neither do the rights of individuals obviously justify eradicating cultural solidarities in tension with liberal hedonism. It is important to see that this is a hard question, one that requires a thoughtful politics, and not one to be swept under the carpet of a more simplistic antiracism focused on individuals, overt phenotypical discrimination, or class analysis.

Modood's arguments have clear relevance for the contemporary U.S. and other settings outside the specific historical context of contemporary Britain. In the U.S., "Asian" has more often meant "East Asian" and South Asians have been sometimes an "invisible minority." Certainly they do not dominate the category of Muslims in America.

But for both Asians and Muslims the issues Modood raises are directly relevant. Race and culture intertwine in discrimination and group identities. The racial politics (and sociology) modeled overwhelmingly on the experience and situation of African-Americans fits poorly. The portrayal of Asians as a "model minority" is perhaps meant to include praise but it also essentializes, underwrites stereotypes that are not all flattering, and often creates a pressure on individuals seeking to find their own balance of cultural belonging and personal choices.

Recent clashes over affirmative action in university admissions have often pitted African-Americans against Asians—notably in California. Emphasizing the benefits one racialized group may reap from changed admissions policies, though, has often been a cover for whites seeking to maximize their own opportunities and retain a challenged class and ethnic position. More generally, holding out the example of Asian success by contrast to African-American lack of social mobility is in fact a reproduction of racism not an overcoming of it. But at the same time, Asian-Americans are clearly not in the same situation as African-Americans (and indeed not all in the same situation as each other, despite partially racialized panethnic constructions). Not least, in the affirmative actions debates and other settings, Americans have lately found it difficult to articulate the positive public good of diversity very well. Instead, the arguments have been conducted overwhelmingly in terms of fairness in the distribution of individual benefits.[2] That is, university admission is treated entirely as an individual good, and the question is how to weigh individual demonstrations of merit against possible difficulties individuals have had to overcome—rather than to see university admission as a public good, and to ask how the well-being of the whole society is shaped by specific policies.

Modood's analyses potentially illuminate not only the situations of Asian-Americans and American Muslims, but also Hispanic or Latino Americans. Consider for example Samuel Huntington's recent arguments about the dangers to American society of continuing Latin American immigration.[3] They are in many ways paradigmatic examples of the pattern Modood identifies. The attributes of Latin Americans that worry Huntington are cultural, but he identifies them in a group constituted as such partly by virtue of an initial racialization, and treats them as at least partially inherent. Whether he is right or wrong about dangers to the American polity, he participates in an argument of just the same kind that Modood considers in the context of British anxieties about immigration. And Huntington is hardly the only analyst to take up Hispanic American identities in this way. But more positively, Hispanic American identities point to the importance of thinking in terms of ethnicities and multicultural politics as well as a struggle against racism.

Not least, we should consider the implications of Modood's arguments for the widespread fantasy that we stand on the brink of a postracial society. A 1993 *Time* magazine cover gave canonical representation of this by morphing several pictures seeming to reveal different racial identities into each other. The 2000 U.S. Census and the celebrity of the golfer Tiger Woods each gave new recognition to biracial or multiracial identities. A wide range of commentators suggested that mixing meant an end to race. Of course this neglected the many ways in which racial categorizations were being reproduced and redeployed. And it was probably an extreme overstatement of a trend. What it meant, perhaps, was that for a time, at least among members of a cosmopolitan middle class, Americans embraced the kind of refusal of sharp racial boundaries long associated in the sociological literature with Brazil. Ironically, this came at the same time as a renewal of racialized identity formation and politics in Brazil (and it was not as though Brazil had ever been quite as completely free of racism as the attractive, mostly elite self-image suggested). But in addition to simply being an exaggeration, the *Time* cover and broader discussion implicitly tried to tie race to its seemingly more manageable and more readily transcendable physical dimensions. As a result, they prepared Americans poorly for the challenge of grasping Muslim identities and racist responses to them in the early twenty-first century—and more generally for thinking through the relationship between race and culture. And Americans were not alone. Longstanding French attempts to deny a public significance to race and also struggle against racism ran into sharp challenges in coming to terms with Muslim, mainly Arab, immigration. The issue is among those most troubling to the European Union as it seeks not only a common immigration policy but common approaches to citizenship more generally.

Modood's arguments in this book gain clarity from addressing one specific context: Britain over the last three decades. But they have widespread relevance and importance.

Notes

1. In *The Force of Prejudice* (Minneapolis: University of Minnesota Press, 2001), Pierre-André Taguieff traces both the story of antiracism and theory and polemical practice and the reversals of value that sparked this crisis.

2. In the Supreme Court decision on one of the most famous of the cases, involving the University of Michigan, Justice Sandra Day O'Connor did assert a compelling public interest in diversity. Such analysis is challenged, however, by the widespread assumption that distributional fairness is the primary (if not the only) good at stake. The same issue appears, in different form, in debates over reparations—for example, in relation to a history of slavery. The dominant frame of discussion privileges the idea of redressing an inequity rather than providing positively for the diverse needs of contemporary citizens.

3. Samuel P. Huntington, *Who Are We? The Challenges to America's National Identity* (New York: Simon and Schuster, 2004).

Acknowledgments

I appreciate that at this point in my career I am in a fortunate position, not least in being read. During the first years in which I worked on the topics of this book (the late 1980s and early 1990s), it was very different: being "unknown" did not help, but the content of what I was arguing—highlighting racism while at the same time opposing political blackness and arguing that Muslims had a right to protest against literary insults—was not welcomed. This book was first conceived as an outline in 1992 but was rejected by more than fifteen publishers, and as it happened pressures of different jobs meant that it was first published as a series of separate essays. The essays were an ongoing response to unfolding sociopolitical developments but were always part of a broader perspective. This opportunity to bring the writings together and enable readers to engage with the larger view is very pleasing.

In this context, I would like to thank those whose support and encouragement were material to the pursuit of my project. First and foremost, Bhikhu Parekh, who from very early days has generously given guidance and mentoring and whose prolific and cutting-edge intellect, ethical vision, and public service have been exemplary. Robin Richardson, who as director of Runnymede Trust sought me out with the wish to publish some of my writings; the result was *Not*

Easy Being British, to which this present book is a sequel. And David Smith, who, knowing that I had no experience of primary research, took the big gamble of appointing me as principal researcher on the Policy Studies Institute Fourth National Survey and so allowed me to work with a skilled and supportive team to give empirical substance to what otherwise might have been just off-stage mutterings.

I have had much support in diverse ways from colleagues in the Department of Sociology at the University of Bristol and senior managers of the university. Gregor McLennan's headship during 2000–2003 created a friendly and productive environment. Notwithstanding a reputation for argumentative robustness, he was a valuable interlocutor, not least for his skills of engaged listening and collegial support for views he disagreed with. To Jackie West, my current head of department, I owe, among other things, the title of this volume.

The book certainly would not have been produced without the deep support of my wife, Glynthea, who saw our family and personal time invested in this project and had to put up with a disproportionate share of the chores of maintaining home and family while I went off to Malmö (as my daughters designated my office on evenings and weekends, following a compromise in which I turned down a visiting post at the university in that Swedish city in exchange for being able to spend more time at my office).

The book is dedicated to the memory of my father, who gave me my Muslim background and taught me to value thought and the importance of interaction between the two.

Introduction

Racism, Asian Muslims, and the Politics of Difference

Origins

Many things influence the development of a point of view. I am very conscious that the essays in this book are not simply focused on a British experience but are shaped by it. The process of thinking about events, of conceptualizing and framing issues, can vary across countries. This is particularly so for the topics of this book. Disciplinary approach is also significant. Most people who study the presence of the new social formations consequent on the postimperial migrations of non-European people into European metropolises are sociologists and social anthropologists and, latterly, students of contemporary culture. My own background is political philosophy. While I cannot be said to have brought this background to bear on the study of race and ethnicity, it would be accurate to say I knew relatively little about the field of study as it had been constructed. The limitations thus created are easy to imagine, but there have been advantages, too, such as a freshness of approach and the direct and inadvertent questioning of established and dominant positions. Another is an attempt to make sense of things without trying to fit them into a certain model of what counts as an explanation—whether the model aspired to is Marxist, Weberian, positivist, Foucauldian, or another. Relatedly, it meant a conception of theory that was highly flexible and assumed that what

1

is theory is contested and so one should not be distracted from pursuing an effort to make sense of contemporary developments by those who ask for the theoretical basis of one's analyses.

Influenced by an interpretation of the philosophy of the later Wittgenstein, I was given the courage to pursue what I thought were urgent questions without first having to define my terms, postulate hypotheses, or review the state of the subject. Contrary to the advice most PhD students receive, I did not feel obliged to review the literature but instead engaged with what I thought was happening in the bit of the world that was my concern. My questions were not based on an evaluation of where the discipline had got to, of what had been achieved by the studies to date, as a basis for deriving what ought to be researched next; it was not the internal flow of a discipline I was interested in, but the flow of events. I thought—perhaps quite mistakenly—that I had learned from Wittgenstein that one does not start from theory, but that theory emerges in how one works through a series of puzzles and problems; theory flows in intellectual activity rather than precedes it. It seems in retrospect—and perhaps at the time—a highly risky and potentially anti-intellectual strategy for me to adopt. To enter the field of "race relations" with a sense of urgency, but with such a cavalier attitude to existing scholarship, theoretical frameworks, and explanatory models, is hardly to be recommended.

In my own judgment, personal location and experience have proved more of a determinant in the development of my views than (the absence of) disciplinary orientation. As a British Asian I had an ambivalent position in British society, so my actual starting point was not British society per se but what racial equality had come to mean by its advocates in the 1980s. My goal was to make my experience, my sense of identity and exclusion speak to the subject of race and equality. While this meant challenging existing ways of thinking about these subjects and unsettling certain political understandings, it was done without a clear intellectual framework—just a certain view of conceptual clarity, a determination to introduce a set of subjectivities and to identify certain social trends. These subjectivities and trends in particular consisted of a greater focus on the British Asian experience than had been given up to that time. This was in the late 1980s; unlike most scholars in this field I entered it at the point of policy formulation and implementation, not scholarship. So my first and perhaps abiding concern has been the constitution of public policy, in particular the education of opinion by which an existing political climate can be shifted through evidence, argument, and rhetoric.

Having mentioned my philosophical, Wittgensteinian background and my entry into the field at a policy rather than a theoretical level, I should briefly say something about my South Asian background. Some of my family, having been part of Mughal Delhi for several hundreds of years, including the period in which it had been thoroughly eclipsed by the British Raj, were prominent in the politics of the 1930s and 1940s that led to the creation of Pakistan as a homeland for and a means to restore the fortunes of Indian Muslims. Their families having migrated to Pakistan at the time of its foundation in 1947, my parents came to London with their small children in 1961 in the hope they would benefit from its civilization, especially from the educational opportunities for their children. Coming from a disrupted, privileged middle-class life, we found ourselves experiencing a combination of middle- and working-class London. My schooling is an example. From ages eight to eleven I was at a mainly middle-class junior school, whose intake was disproportionately Jewish. Having failed the eleven-plus exam[1] due to not quite good enough English, I went to a working-class secondary school whose intake in 1964 was predominantly white, but by the time I left in 1971 pupils of West Indian origin were a majority. This reflected the changing character of this part of London, Willesden in the borough of Brent in northwest London (a borough for which the 2001 census recorded a majority of people as not categorizing themselves as white). It was a period of "Paki-bashing," of white young male skinheads harassing, violently attacking, and even murdering Asians in the streets and other public places. This was not too serious an anxiety in my middle-class neighborhood, but at my secondary school bullying was rife. The black boys excelled at most of the things that the white boys wanted to be good at—including fighting—but most of us Asians did not and so as a group were at the bottom of the school pecking order and the natural victims of racialized bullying.

We did not talk much about racism at home. There was a shame about talking about such things, and we did not see ourselves as victims. There was a strong expectation that we would work hard at school and excel, and this expectation was not easily dented by the business failures that my father experienced that reduced him to manual work or by the calamity of my failing the eleven-plus exam

and ending up in a patently nonacademic, even anti-academic school.
It is difficult to identify all the sources of this inner family confidence,
but one or two are relevant. My father—and in this he expressed
the dominant view within our extended family—was keen that we
should learn everything that institutions like schools, universities, the
BBC, and the British Museum could teach us. In this sense he was
thoroughly and unashamedly assimilationist, where assimilation was
not so much into one's immediate environs—and certainly not into
working-class sensibilities—but into the best that Britain had to offer,
into its elite, world-class institutions. This, after all, was part of the
reason for having come to Britain and the justification for staying and
enduring difficulties and reversals. Yet at the same time, there was
an expectation that we would eschew the emergent 1960s morality
of "swinging London" that bewildered my father: not just because it
went against his sense of civilized behavior, but because elite Britain
seemed to be welcoming, even leading it. This eroded his admiration
for what he understood Britain to stand for.[2] Independently of this but
reinforced by it, he insisted that we should never forget "who we are."
We should never deny that we are Pakistanis (later this became Asian,
and then Muslim) in order to join a social circle, to get a job, or even
to avoid a skinhead's taunts. This identity—composite and shifting
but ultimately settling on Muslim—should be accepted with pride. As
a lone parent of teenage children and working long, exhausting hours
outside the home, he was not able to tie this identity down to many
behavioral requirements, but we acquired the notion that the limit of
assimilation was shame of one's origins and that sometimes our origins would be a burden to us, but it was better to defend our ethnic
identity than let it and our community be rubbished.

I have gone into some detail here at the risk of nostalgic self-
indulgence. I believe that some of the themes of this book are rooted
in these descriptions from childhood, for example, not seeing ethnic
minority formations as taking place only in working-class locations
or enjoying any special, symbiotic relationship with the white working class. I could say the same in relation to the failure of becoming
socialized to see Britain in terms of white and black: a view that is said
to be projected on to the world by racists but which certainly was not
shared by my skinhead tormentors, who practiced differential racism
decades before analysts noted the phenomenon. My understanding
and highlighting of the aspirations of the migrant generation, in par-

ticular the work ethic and the drive for educational qualifications, as well as their anxieties, also is rooted in that childhood, so too my emphasis on ethnic pride and an ethnic diversity in which Muslim identity has become prominent and my sense of the importance of recognition to minorities' sense of inclusion and well-being and the damage that misrecognition does.

Bearings

With the disciplinary and biographical background I have described, I began reflecting and debating about issues of racism and equality based on my own experience and knowledge and through that drawing attention to the lived experience of neglected victims and voices. A key example for me was how Asians were not heard in the rush to theoretically and politically see Britain in terms of a black-white dualism (Modood 1988, 1994c; see also Sudbury 2001, 34–35; Glynn 2002). I was suspicious of theories that claim to know what people really mean and don't take seriously what people say. I have continued to eschew approaches in which analysis consists of some kind of ideological or political opposing of the social meanings and practices one is analyzing. I am not against a normative stance, as will be apparent from all aspects of this book. I use normative ideas such as racial equality to guide and structure empirical inquiry or offer a normative position as a direct critique of another normative position or as a positive position in its own right. In each case, what is intended is a contribution to a debate, not a one-sided deconstruction that epistemologically and normatively privileges the point of view of the analyst. Another way of making the point is that I see myself as seeking to achieve an understanding of society that is anchored in the comprehension of agents themselves—i.e., of ourselves as agents. This does not mean that the inquiry is merely descriptive, uncritically accepts the confusion, contradiction, and obfuscation of social life, and ignores the motives behind certain discourses and practices. But the inquiry is not a different order of understanding as suggested in Michael Banton's contrast between ordinary language and science (Banton 2001). Social inquiry must seek a degree of system, evaluation of evidence, conceptualization, and so on that are more thorough than that of practical action, but all this intellectual activity only makes sense if it illuminates the perceptions of actors: this includes social structure, for there is no social structure independent of the understanding of agents (Winch 1958).

The approach that I follow is eclectic and syncretic, with no one privileged methodology or theory that singularly explains what is important. For me, a theory is not something you have to be for or against; it's a question of whether it helps me see something that I am otherwise missing. My starting point has been (using terms from Miles 1982) less "science" than "common sense," particularly in the areas of law and policy. My thinking on race[3] began with voluntary and professional equality work rather than through academia. Hence the way I have pursued the subject has been informed by the initial and continuing political purpose: how to achieve a society in Britain that is not racially stratified and in which recent non-white migrants and their progeny can come to have a genuine sense of belonging to Britain without having to disavow their ethnic identities.

Racism and Culturalism: Blacks, Asians, Muslims, and Jews

To highlight the British Asian experience within the context of British race relations, what kinds of things should one focus on? One of the things I have argued is that conceptualizations of race and racism, and hence also of antiracism and racial equality, have been too narrowly defined. They are too dependent on the black-white relationship—not just the contemporary relationship but the whole Atlantic slavery triangle of Western Europe–West Africa–America. This Atlantocentric perspective was dominant when I entered this field in the late 1980s. Intellectually and politically it was shaped by the assumption that the key issue was color racism, understood as white domination of non-whites. This meant a racial dualism rather than a rainbow diversity. As racial dualism has been the U.S. experience, it was assumed Britain had to learn from the United States and that where the United States was today, Britain would be tomorrow. It was also assumed that people of African descent in particular suffered from racism or were paradigmatic of what it meant to be non-white in Britain and elsewhere. My very first argument was that Britain could not be understood in terms of a racial-dualist framework (Modood 1988, 1992).

In this Atlantocentric version of racism, which is certainly one of the most classical and enduring versions, phenotype explains the existence of certain cultural traits (Miles 1989, 71–72). These traits are mainly negative in the case of blacks, people of African descent.

As a result, racism or racial discrimination comes to be thought of as unfavorable treatment on the grounds of color. I refer to this as color racism. While the stereotypical physical characteristics of blacks are taken to be enough to fill out the image of them as a group, as a race—for example, strong, sensual, rhythmical, and unintelligent— the racialized image of Asians is not so extensively linked to physical appearance. It very soon appeals to cultural motifs such as language, religion, family structures, exotic dress, cuisine, and art forms. These are taken to be part of the meaning of "Asian" and of why Asians— which in Britain means South Asians—are alien, backward, and un- desirable. Such motifs are appealed to in excluding, harassing, or dis- criminating against Asians—both in constituting them as a group and in justifying negative treatment of them.

South Asians, then, are clearly visible as a non-white group: they are a principal object of racist victimization, of negative treatment by whites on the grounds that they are an undesirable "Other." They suffer, therefore, from color racism. But they also suffer from cultural racism: a certain culture is attributed to them, is vilified, and is even the ground for discrimination. Of course, black people too can be culturally vilified, and so the color racism/cultural racism distinction is not simply a black/Asian distinction (CMEB 2000). Nevertheless, I contend that the putative defects or strengths of black culture are at- tributed to aspects of their physicality—such as low IQ or rhythm— or to what whites have done to them, such as deprive them of certain heritages. The perception of Asians, whether it be in some hard-core racist discourses, such as those of the British National Party, or im- plicit in the wider British society, is that their defects lie deep in their culture rather than in a biology that produces their culture. This means that Asians, more than blacks, suffer a double racism. This does not mean that Asians suffer more racism—such as harassment, discrimina- tion, and institutional exclusion—than do blacks in Britain. That is a complex empirical question, and one would have to be sensitive to the fact that the answer may vary by class, age, gender, geography, social arena, and so on. I think that systematic research of this sort would indeed show that the racism against Asians has been underestimated since at least the 1960s. My point is that research of this kind requires a conceptualization of racism that includes cultural racism as well as color racism and an understanding that Asians suffer a double or a compound racism.

In crafting the term "cultural racism" I am not arguing that there is some *necessary* connection between race and culture within racist discourse and practice. For quite contingent reasons, racism can become historically connected to slavery or underclass; so similarly with racism and culture. Racism and sexism are conceptually quite distinct but can come together in distinctive stereotyping and treatment of black women or black men; similarly, the cultural racism against Asians is a distinctive construct, not reducible to its constituent parts. Again, one can have racism without nationalism, and nationalism without racism, but their combination can be lethal.

Cultural racism, as I argue in chapter 1, is a two-step racism (or alternatively, is a second step, with color racism being the first step). The interesting question arises whether it could be a one-step racism: could color racism decline and fade away and yet cultural racism remain and perhaps even grow? One can certainly imagine a future in which a group such as Asians could continue to have their culture vilified while color racism simultaneously declined. This might mean that assimilated or hybrid Asians, those not strongly identified with Asian culture, might not experience exclusion by whites. If that were to happen, there might be a basis for not wanting to describe the anti-Asian perceptions as racism. This distinction between what might be called racism proper and culturalism is commonly held and continues to be argued for (Blum 2002; Fredrickson 2002). It seems to me that to discriminate only against those people who are perceived to be culturally different, i.e., to make an absolute distinction between cultural Asians and physical Asians, might be borderline racial discrimination. Cultural essentialism and inferiorization may be involved, and it would certainly share some of the qualities of racist stereotyping and practice today, but it may be that it would be better to regard it as cultural prejudice and cultural exclusionism rather than racism per se. Certainly one can see the difference between the scenario just described and one where color racism declines but Asians continue to be viewed as a racial group. In this case the prejudice would still be motivated by a characterization of Asian culture, but discrimination would be exercised against all people of Asian ancestry, regardless of their fit against the image of Asian culture. This would certainly be cultural racism, even if color racism had receded, because all or nearly all of a group, identified by color and descent, are being judged by an essentialized image of a group. In the previous scenario a target group is being negatively constructed, and negative treatment follows from this construction; but if persons are targeted only on the basis of their behavior and not on the basis of their ancestry, then might we have something that we should call culturalism rather than racism? I am torn, however, as this case seems to go against what we would expect from community and social dynamics.

Since cultures and cultural practices are usually internally diverse, containing and omitting various "authentic" elements and adaptations and mixes, the culturalized targeting of Asians may be expansive rather than purist and so in one way or another will catch most if not all Asians. Some children will grow up in communities that are culturally very Asian. Most of these children will develop feelings of family, neighborhood, community, and discourses to counter anti-Asian discourses. If as adults they move away from the culture of their childhood, they may still retain communal feelings of loyalty, solidarity, and self-defense. Anti-Asians are therefore likely to target them in some ways, just as atheists in Northern Ireland can be asked if they are Protestant or Catholic atheists—their repudiation of religious doctrine is not seen as enough to distance them from a targeted community. In my hypothetical scenario, a nonreligious Muslim might still be targeted as a cultural Muslim/Asian, and a noncultural Asian might still be targeted as an Asian by community, which means Asian by background, which means birth and ancestry. So it is not clear that culturalism, where it is associated with distinct communities, can be really distinguished from racism in practice, even if it can be in theory.

If a movement from cultural racism to cultural exclusion without racism seems difficult to envisage in the near or medium-term future, a sense of historical perspective, of what is possible in the long run, may be helpful. Consider the movement the other way round, as in the case of anti-Semitism. Jews have been blamed by Christians for the death of Jesus since early in the Christian era, centuries before those modern ideas we have come to call "racism." The move from religious antipathy to racism may perhaps first be witnessed in post-Reconquista Spain when Jews and Muslims were forced to convert to Christianity or be expelled. At this stage, the oppression can perhaps be characterized as religious (Fredrickson 2002). Soon afterward, converted Jews and Muslims and their offspring began to be suspected of not being true Christian believers, and a doctrine developed among some Spaniards that this was because their old religion was in their blood. In short, because of their biology, conversion was impossible. Centuries later, these views about blood became quite detached from religion and in Nazi and related doctrines were given a thoroughly scientific-biologic cast and constitute a paradigmatic and extreme version of modern racism. What was once a form of religious persecution became, over a long, complicated, evolving but contingent history, not just a form of cultural racism but one with highly systematic biological foundations.

Because of that legacy, throughout the West today anti-Semitism is without question regarded as a form of racism ("Semitic" is taken to mean only Jews, not other Semites like the Arabs). In Britain, as in most of Western Europe, discrimination against Jews is unlawful racial discrimination. While few cases are brought to the law, and Jews seem to be disproportionately overrepresented in most elite occupations, many Jews will argue that anti-Semitism is still present. By this they mean not just the existence of some neo-Nazi fringe extremists, but mainly an insidious if latent prejudice. Yet virtually no one except for the neo-Nazis believes that what prejudice there is against Jews— often linked to snobbery from "old money" and envy from below—is derived from any biological discourse, latent or otherwise.

In anti-Semitism in Britain today, we have an example of a racism that has slipped back into being a mild culturalism or communalism. While some people dispute whether contemporary anti-Muslim prejudice can properly be called cultural racism as opposed to religious intolerance, no one, as far as I know, asks if anti-Semitism is racism. Indeed, started off by some Jewish organizations and taken up by the National Union of Students in Britain, it is now commonplace for it to be asserted that some of the views of contemporary militant Muslims, or fundamentalists, about Jews are racist. Political Muslims reply that they are opposed not to Jews but to Zionism and the colonial militarism of Israel. My purpose is not to resolve this controversy but to point out the politically selective ways in which the terms "racism" and "racist" are applied. If an exclusionary "-ism" without biology is not racism, then militant Muslim venom against the Jews is not racism. It is true that there are some aggressive passages about the Jews in the Qur'an (though they require far more careful interpretation than is often given them), but none of them make any reference to biological difference. Moreover, Muslims welcome converts from all faiths and ethnic groups, including Jews, and the possibility of conversion is a condition that some scholars believe rules out belief in the biological determinism that is a necessary condition of racism as a doctrine (Fredrickson 2002). So it seems that militant Muslim discourse about Jews is more like medieval Christian vilification than racism.

Regardless of what one thinks about contemporary anti-Semitism/anti-Zionism, the important historical point is religion can be the basis of racialization as long as the religion of a group can be linked to physical ancestry and descent. So race is not just about color, and definitely not just about white and non-white (though it can be predominantly that in some contexts). Racialization has to pick on some features of a people related to physical appearance and ancestry, otherwise racism cannot be distinguished from other forms of groupism. Physical appearance is central to race, but, as in the case of cultural racism, it can be a marker only and not necessarily denote a form of determinism.

Distinguishing Cultural Racism

I have, then, very flexible sociological concepts of race and racism. As I understand it, the term "cultural racism" or "new racism" has come to have a certain currency in the United States, where it is taken to mean a characterization of a racial group, typically African-Americans, such that the problems and disadvantages of that group are attributed to culture and not to biology. This is similar to my meaning, though in the European context cultural racism or culturalism directed to a racialized or racially marked group may involve an antipathy to the group because it is perceived to be an alien culture rather than merely an inferior one. In short, in Europe when the target group is Muslim or "Eastern," the focus of cultural racism is not primarily about attributing causes for social pathologies or economic disadvantage (or even that the target group is perceived as disadvantaged).

There is an understanding of cultural racism, or new racism, that appreciates the last point. It is found in the works of certain British authors who believe this racism emerged as a distinct ideology in England in the 1970s (Barker 1981; Gilroy 1987; Solomos 1991). They argue that such a culturalist discourse is common color racism dressed up in culturalist garb in order to avoid the charge of racism, that it is "coded" racism (see also Miles 1989, 84–87). My view is that cultural racism is not a proxy for racism but a form of racism.

Stuart Hall recognizes that cultural racism has a distinct "logic," different from but related to biological racism (Hall 2000). He argues, however, that I fail to see that "these two 'logics' are always present" in any actual case and as a result I draw too sharp an opposition between the two and treat them as rivals in a zero-sum game (224, 239). I do believe they are connected: for example, in chapter 1 I describe color racism as the ground floor on which cultural racism is built in contemporary Britain, but I remain unpersuaded that they must both be present in every practice or set of attitudes that we might wish to call racism. The connection is contingent, not a priori. My view is that racism involves some reference to physical appearance or ancestry but does not require any form of biological determinism, only a physical identification on a group basis, attributable to descent. Moreover, it is possible to have color racism, namely, the explanation of cultural traits by reference to biology, without cultural racism, even if the two are typically combined to some degree or other. My belief that on the whole color racism is declining in Britain except where anti-Asian cultural racism is present is an empirical claim, which Hall recognizes. Others have disputed the claim because they say it creates a hierarchy of oppression in which some groups experience more hostility and exclusion than others (Cohen 1996, 19–20; Gillborn 1996, 25; Anthias 1998, 19; cf. Song 2004, 870–71). I cite some evidence in support of my view in chapter 1, to which I would like to add two recent examples. First, for some years it has been clear that the racist and anti-immigrant British National Party (BNP) has been disproportionately targeting South Asians. This is clear from their literature and where they choose to be politically active. Looking at their electoral results over a number of years shows that they calculate rightly as to where they can hope to stoke up racist support; their best results tend to be in towns where the principal non-whites are Asians. With the disturbances of 2001 and then with post–9/11, the BNP has increasingly begun to distinguish between Asian Muslims and other Asians, arguing that the former are violent, criminal, and disloyal, fail to integrate, and so on (evidence of all remarks relating to the BNP can be found on their Web site at www.bnp.org.uk).

My second example is the BBC TV documentary, *The Secret Policeman*. Broadcast in October 2003, it consisted of recordings, using hidden cameras, of some policemen on a residential training course over some months by a journalist pretending to be a policeman and a friend. While there are a few recorded remarks about blacks as muggers and drug dealers and so needing "discriminatory" policing, these are balanced by other remarks, often by the same individual, such as, "To be honest, I don't mind blacks, proper blacks" and "My best mate is black." The overwhelming bulk of bile and violence is directed at "Pakis," who are said to be taking over the country and should all be thrown out; as Hitler did to the Jews, so should Asians have done to them in Britain; and at least one officer said he would certainly kill an innocent Asian if he was sure he would not be found out. This is only a small selection of the remarks about Asians from this documentary, and there are no friendly remarks to balance them. This documentary, together with the case of the BNP, demonstrates that most hostility is directed toward Asians/Muslims. It may be that evidence that runs the other way has also to be taken into account. But that is to recognize that the issue is an empirical inquiry, open to different answers at different times and places, and so a hierarchy of racisms cannot be ruled out simply because it does not sound nice. It is sometimes said that prejudice against one group usually goes with prejudice against other groups. If so, how does one make sense of the policeman who says, "I don't mind black people. Asians? No."? Other examples of such selective racism can be found in chapter 1.

It is widely claimed that cultural racism naturalizes culture, that it treats culture in a quasi-natural or biological way, as if culture inheres in a group so that it is automatically reproduced, it does not change over time, and the relevant cultural traits are found in all members of the group. Lawrence Blum, for example, argues that the distinctive feature of racism is "inherentism": that certain qualities are inherent to a group, and it is a secondary issue whether these qualities are perceived to be hereditary or cultural, racial or ethnic (Blum 2002; cf. Miles 1982, 157; and Miles 1989, 74). Avtar Brah argues that "a characteristic feature of . . . racism has been its focus on cultural difference as the primary signifier of a supposed immutable boundary; a view of the Asian as the 'alien' *par excellence;* the ultimate 'Other'" (1996, 168). We have already noted that for Fredrickson the distinctive feature of racism is that ethnocultural differences are regarded as "innate, indelible and unchangeable" (2002, 5). This is, of course, related to the distinction between racism and a prejudice directed only at those members of a racial group who practice a certain culture/religion, which I discussed earlier. While I think that there is something right in this characterization and that most racisms are inherentist, I would caution against taking the analogy with nature too far. If we look at, for example, the racial stereotypes that operate to exclude some people from certain kinds of employment, for example, that blacks are less intelligent than whites, it is clear that they are not applied in a uniform way. Discriminators may be biased but are open to the possibility that certain black individuals are exceptions to the rule. If there is an inherentism, it affects the generality rather than each individual; it is to be measured in averages rather than deterministic laws of nature (see chapter 1). Moreover, stereotypes are capable of accommodating change; sometimes stereotypes can change radically. Until *The Satanic Verses* affair, Asian men were stereotyped as unassertive, overdeferential, and docile, not able to stand up for themselves. Within a few years, the prevalent stereotype of Muslim men (in Britain, the majority are Asian) included the idea that they were inflexible, always demanding something, fanatical, and aggressive.

Cultural Racism and Assimilation

Robert Miles very usefully deploys a concept of articulation to explain how different ideologies can connect and work together, such as racism and nationalism, and it may be that cultural racism is best seen as an articulation of racism and culturalism (1989, 87–90). For him, this has the advantage of preserving the analytical clarity of "racism" while recognizing that in practice it can sometimes be mixed up with another kind of exclusionary "-ism." But if we accept that racism does not necessarily involve inherentism, then we do not have to rule out cultural racism as an example of racism. Moreover, we can allow ourselves to be much more sensitive to contemporary meanings and new meanings if we allow that concepts can often drift from their original meanings. Fredrickson acknowledges that "culture can be reified and essentialised to the point where it becomes the functional equivalent of race" (2002, 7) but insists that cultural intolerance and religious intolerance are not racism because they allow assimilation, and so at worst are forms of culturalism. In deciding whether a particular case is racism and what is culturalism, we are not determining the degree of oppression. Fredrickson, for instance, is clear that we are determining the grounds of oppression, not the scale of it. For example, he argues that in Reconquista Spain, when Muslims and Jews were forced to become Christians or be expelled, the *moriscos* (the Muslim converts) were treated worse than the Jewish *converses,* but since the former were more likely to live in separate communities, in their case it is difficult to distinguish between racism and culturalism (Fredrickson 2002, 34). The racism may be less clear yet the oppression may be greater. He also endorses the view that North African Muslims in France and Muslims in Bosnia, Palestine, India, and other places where they seem to be oppressed in ethnicized ways are not victims of racism (144).

George Fredrickson takes two ambiguous positions on assimilation. The first is that even where a dominant group demands total assimilation, including something as deeply humiliating as *coerced* religious conversion, as the Spanish demanded of conquered Muslims in the fifteenth and sixteenth centuries, this is not racism because it assumes that the dominated group can be changed and so can be assimilated into the dominant culture (2002, 40, 146). I think my view of cultural racism deals with this, namely, that a culture of a group that is already racialized can be the basis of a more elaborate racism.

Fredrickson's second position is that "racism is not operative if members of stigmatized groups can *voluntarily* change their identities and advance to positions of prominence and prestige within the dominant group" (2002, 7; my italics). I think that even here some cultural racism is possible: for example, there can be some anti-Semitism even while assimilated Jews are allowed to and able to rise to top positions. While voluntary assimilation is clearly better than coercion, and indeed is desirable in some ways, the issue is why assimilation is necessary. If the reason is antipathy to the culture of a racialized group, then cultural racism is present. Hence in contemporary discussions of racial and ethnic equality, assimilationism is seen as part of the problem, not part of the solution.

Against suggestions of articulation and functional equivalence, I reiterate that a group that is already racialized can suffer from cultural vilification, and in this compound prejudice it is very difficult to distinguish racism from culturalism. Crucially, the latter can *interact* with a preexisting racism to form a new "-ism" called cultural racism, which may have a worse effect than the sum of racial discrimination and, say, religious discrimination, let alone separately. Yet either can be a trigger for the other, and when both are present and interact there is cultural racism. In these circumstances, cultural vilification can be part of an exacerbated racism or an additional dimension of racism, not merely an adjunct to it.

The idea that religions and cultures are capable of change while racial groups, as understood by racists, are not is quite misleading. This can be illustrated by my point that a discriminator at, say, a job interview may be open to the suggestion that some members of a phenotypical group are counterexamples to the stereotype associated with a racial phenotype without feeling that the stereotype is unsound. That is, racist stereotypes are more like probabilistic generalizations (i.e., they survive exceptional counterexamples). If so, this narrows the gap between racism and culturalism, for both are susceptible to exceptions and new learned behaviors. If I am told that this probabilistic stereotyping is not racism, my reply is the Wittgensteinian one that "meaning lies in use" (Wittgenstein 1968). Whatever historians say about classical racism, I am interested in what is racism today, and I am partly guided by what is called racism in social life today. While there is limited research that one can point to, it does seem that a person using the vocabulary of race today, and even engaging in acts of racial discrimination, does not have to hold any strictly deterministic biological ideas in order to give meaning to their discourse and practice. While Miles in his concept of institutional racism (1989, 83–87) is concerned about when the discourse of race fades, I am concerned about when the discourse of race continues but the meaning changes. The point in relation to Fredrickson is that space for voluntary assimilation of so-called racial groups is compatible with racism. Indeed, the history of the descendants of forcibly transported and enslaved Africans has involved selective assimilation, the degree and kind determined by whites.

Conversely, the idea that religion is about belief that can be voluntarily renounced, but race is about one's immutable biology, is also too simplistic. As in Northern Ireland, the South Asia I am from is contoured by communal religious identities. It has nothing to do with belief. If you assert "I am an atheist," people will still think it is meaningful to ask, "Yes, but are you a Muslim, a Hindu?" Talk of giving up one's religion is likely to be seen as a form of selling out. In such a context, religion can be less a matter of individual choice than when some "in-between"-skinned people in the United States assert their blackness rather than "pass." The question of choice has to do with social structure, not religion qua religion. It is clear that in some

European or Western societies the group that is deemed to be most unassimilable is Muslims. In Britain and France, for example, black people are generally regarded as much more assimilable than Asian and North African Muslims. The political party in France most associated with racism, Le Front National, explicitly campaigns on the proposition that Arab Muslims are unassimilable, not because it has given up racist ideology but because it is able to racialize Arabs without appeals to biological immutability.

Racism, then, can be involved in diverse and contradictory views about assimilation, including that a group cannot assimilate because of its religion, that coercive assimilation is necessary, and even in the subtle pressures to assimilate that may coexist with a policy of voluntary assimilation but may betoken a racialized attitude toward a group and its cultural "otherness." This latter helps to explain why in the late twentieth century several societies, such as Canada, the United States, and Britain, were influenced by the idea that to require minorities and migrants to assimilate as a condition of citizenship, or of inclusion more generally, is a form of inequality. These societies assume that the culture of the majority is superior to that of the minorities and is the norm, and that deviations from the norm are a sign of inferiority and not something from which the majority might learn something of value. Aspects of a culture can be so important that they are integral to a sense of self; to require that civic equality or social acceptance depends on erasing this identity is to treat people with disrespect and not allow them to be themselves in the way that other citizens are allowed (Young 1990). Where these identities are connected with race and ethnicity, the disrespect can be a form of racial inequality and racism. This can be done without a conscious policy but is nevertheless oppressive for it consists of treating people as other than they are and making them into something they are not and do not want to be. It is to fail to recognize them, and Charles Taylor (1994) has brought out well the importance of recognition to personal and collective self-respect and equality. Misrecognition (like invisibility in other literatures on equality) can be a major social harm. In many ways, the experience of British Asians has been a struggle against misrecognition, as they have tried to slough off the imposed identity of political blackness (see chapter 1). This has been most dramatic in the case of Asian Muslims, especially Pakistanis, who in less than a decade transformed themselves from a relatively passive element of the "black" constituency into a highly energized, vociferous, and mobilized group asserting a religious—not a color-based or even an ethnic—identity, a theme of the second half of this book. There I also endorse the view that the politics of recognition can be developed further to emphasize that there is an emergent ideal of equality that repudiates the need to privatize all difference in the name of a formal or civic-republican equality. Equality is interpreted as balancing the ever-present power of hegemonic identities, usually disguised as universal, with the public recognition, even celebration, of marginal or suppressed identities. This opens the space for moving beyond mere toleration toward the creation of civic/public/national/ state identities that incorporate minority ethnic and religious identities, guided by the ideal that all citizens should be able to see something of themselves in the overarching, yet internally plural, public identities. In short, they should be able to feel they belong to the country or countries of which they are citizens.

Multiculturalism and Secularism

The above implies, I argue in the second half of the book, an active state policy of multiculturalism, i.e., recognizing the country or polity as a legitimate and irreducible plurality, as a "community of communities" (CMEB 2000) and not just as a liberal association of autonomous individuals. It means reimagining or re-forming our national identity, our Britishness, so that all can be part of it without having to deny or privatize other identities that are important to different Britons. However, in talking about the multicultural, it is important to bear in mind that we are talking about at least two different kinds of development. On the one hand, there is hybridity and multiple identities, the mixing of different heritages, and the refusal to be defined by any one or even a limited number of core identities. This is particularly identified with popular youth culture and with some African-Caribbeans but increasingly also with some second-generation Asians, especially Indians. On the other hand, there is the development of communities, especially ethnoreligious groups, who are keen to emphasize one or at least a limited number of core identities and are mobilizing as political actors and seeking quasi-corporate representation at local, national, and perhaps even transnational levels. Asian Muslims are a prime example of this. I argue that it is important that political multiculturalism recognizes the legitimacy of both developments, particularly in the context of an inevitable liberal, secularist bias in the intellectual, political, and recreational culture in favor of the first against the second.

The bias I have in mind can be found once again in Fredrickson. Indeed, one of the reasons I have argued at length against his definition of racism is because of its secularist bias. Fredrickson's race/religion dichotomy makes it plausible to argue that policy remedies against racism and religious intolerance should be quite different from each other. Hence with little argument, Fredrickson is able to conclude that while "persisting racial prejudices and inequalities make the complete separation of race and state counterproductive, the first line of defence against militant sectarianism would seem to be a total separation of church and state" and that this separation should be modeled on that in the United States (147–48). The ideas of a church-state separation and that religion and religious groups should not play a role in politics and democratic contests are, of course, in one form or another, extremely popular, almost universally supported by intellectuals not just in the United States but also in Western Europe and many other places in the world. It is seen by liberal democrats, socialists, and republicans as one of the central tenets of their politics, to such an extent that it is simply taken for granted and thought not to need discussion. A rare but influential example of an argument for secularism in political theory is Rawls's *Theory of Justice* (1971). Rawls argues that for a state to favor any religion or worldview is to impose beliefs on its citizens, which infringes on freedoms that no person should rationally give up, and so the just state should protect religious freedoms but be neutral between religions. Rawls's theory, however, while designed with religious diversity in mind, favors neutrality on all cultural matters, not just religion, and so may not be entirely supportive of Fredrickson's position as quoted. In fact, the dominant multiculturalism in liberal theory departs from Rawls by separating the realm of cultural identities into religion and the rest, and favors explicit recognition in relation to, say, minority languages and customs, but nonrecognition in relation to minority religions. For example, Will Kymlicka argues that the strict separation of state and ethnicity, "the religion model," is incoherent but is content with the separation model as long as it is applied only to religion (1995, 107–8; 2001, 24).

I believe that this secularism is less liberal than it seems and is

part of the political culture and policy assumptions that make it difficult for Western societies to be just to Muslims. It is an obstacle
to seeing the problems of Muslims and sympathizing with them, to
seeing aspects of the oppression of Muslims, to recognizing Muslims,
and to offering solutions to them similar to those given to other oppressed and disadvantaged groups. This is elaborated in chapters 6
to 8. In chapter 6, I show that it is contradictory to legislate against
incitement to racial hatred and anti-Holocaust denial but to respond
with uncompromising declarations about freedom of speech to the offense that the book *The Satanic Verses* gave to Muslims. In chapter 7,
I argue that there is an incompatibility between multiculturalism
and radical secularism. The politics of recognition and related feminist positions have successfully shown the limits of the public-private
separation necessary for a state to be culturally neutral. Relatedly
and controversially, it follows that secularism cannot be neutral between religions. This is discussed by reference to ideal types of state
and the conceptions of individual and community that inform them,
specifically in relation to Islam, Western European secularism, and
the church-state connection in England. The presence of new religious
minorities means the existing constitutional compromises, a moderate
secularism, need to be reformed in the spirit of inclusiveness rather
than neutrality. That is to say, one needs to constructively consider
how existing arrangements can be made more plural. Conversely, a
move from the status quo of moderate secularism toward radical secularism creates, intentionally or otherwise, political obstacles in the
path of the accommodation of Muslims. In chapter 8, I argue that at
least some of the current Muslim assertiveness is a politics of catching up with racial equality and feminist achievements.

Here I will add a pragmatic point that I have brought with me
from my policy background to my theoretical work. In Britain, there
is a political discourse and policy framework around eliminating racial discrimination—laws, policies, agencies, a political movement.
Therefore, in addition to the analytical merits of the case, there is an
argument for integrating anti-Asian culturalism and Islamophobia
within the discourse of racial equality and multiculturalism rather
than risk having it marginalized as simply a religious or cultural issue.
Racial equality began with color, but by the 1980s had gone ethnic
(decisively through the judgment of the House of Lords on *Mandla v.
Lee* in 1982, which gave legal protection against discrimination to

Sikhs; Jews, though white, were already covered). And I extended the analysis to cover Muslims a few years before others had thought about it as an issue.

Ethnicity

To conclude this introduction I ought to say something about ethnicity. There are real differences between groups of people such as Pakistanis and the white British (and whatever other groupings may be contained within these), and that these differences are usefully conceptualized as those of ethnicity is implicit in the work presented in this book. However, just as with racist conceptions of ethnic minorities, so these groups and their self-understandings are not static and monolithic, and I have always tried to draw attention to this. I have also emphasized that there can be strong lines of continuity, that change is not always welcomed by minority groups, and that not everything changes at the same pace, for example, as a study of the contrasts among British Asian groups shows (see "Conclusion"). Moreover, groups can be distinctive, even in all this change, even if the idea of ethnicity as discrete, bounded populations is simplistic and false. Despite this explicit emphasis on changing ethnic identities (the title of one of my books [Modood, Beishon, and Virdee 1994]), it is a mystery to me that a number of authors have found an essentialized, reified, static conception of an ethnic group as a discrete, bounded population of cultural absolutes in my work (Anthias 1998, 7, 16; Alexander 2002, 508). However, no page numbers, much less quotations, are presented, so no means to penetrate the mystery are offered.

One of the reasons I use a discourse of ethnicity is that it allows us to capture the historical, the element of agency, and meaning "from below." But this is to see that some relationships, some distinctive ways of thinking and living, and some senses of group identity exist. These may be ambivalent and subject to change, including an intensifying of group consciousness in the face of external contact or domination and a projection of a (re)imagined past in order to account for a certain groupness. Nevertheless, while these group identities may be subject to racialization, they cannot be reduced to racialization, as I contend in chapter 2. Ethnic groups, in their subjectivity as well as in socioeconomic circumstances, are creations within political and ideological processes. These formations are not simply "imposed" but are the outcome of power relations, struggles, negotiations, and shifts in circumstances and meaning, in which subordinate groups are not passive. Hence much of this book is about assertiveness, an example of which are the debates about group labels discussed in chapter 2. One of the arguments of the concluding chapter is that antiracism and ethnic assertiveness have been key processes of social integration. Nor is the element of collective agency confined to the political or oppositional.

Given the same economic situation, different groups may react in different ways. Some respond to high levels of unemployment by becoming demoralized, others by seeking extra qualifications or starting up businesses or getting involved in crime. These differences between groups are not primordial and atemporal; they are contingent, historic, and subject to change. They are nevertheless real. They are part of the ways in which one group of people is different from another in terms of its history, norms, community structure, relation to other groups, and so on, and so is part of what I understand by ethnicity.

"Ethnicity" here refers to subjective and objective features of a group, and of membership in a group, defined by descent. While I am unable to offer a comprehensive definition or theory, let me list at least five dimensions of ethnic difference so as to give ethnicity in Britain some content:

- *Cultural distinctiveness:* Norms and practices such as arranged marriage, existence of specific gender roles, or a religion.
- *Disproportionality:* A group may be marked by a disproportional distribution of a characteristic that is not distinctive (e.g., high unemployment); while the distribution may be a structural product of opportunities and obstacles within the wider society, it can shape attitudes within the group as well as toward the group, a sense that they are not typical but different (e.g., poor, intelligent, athletic, and so on).
- *Strategy:* Responses to a common set of circumstances (e.g., high unemployment) may lead some groups to become demotivated or politically militant or self-employed; where differential strategies persist they can come to contribute to group consciousness and to distinguish groups.
- *Creativity:* Some groups are identified with some innovations (e.g., longer shop hours or a clothing style) even though the innovations are taken up by the mainstream.
- *Identity:* Membership of a group may carry affective meanings that may motivate or demotivate (e.g., black pride in a history of resistance to oppression; as Muslims we must aid fellow Muslims in a time of need).

These dimensions are not wholly distinctive from each other but mutually form each other, and all are shaped and changed through interaction with other groups and especially with the dominant groups and existing socioeconomic structures. The dimensions involve perceptions of meaning, attitudes, and agency; they are not merely internal to a group. They are not confined to a particular sphere, such that they are appropriate to the private rather than to the public, nor are they manifest in only specific social or policy contexts. As can be seen from these brief examples, ethnicity can be found in economic and political as well as personal relations. In chapters 3 and 4, I offer an analysis of the differential educational and economic progress that the main non-white groups in Britain have made. Some of this progress is quite surprising, especially for those who analyze these groups primarily by reference to racism and/or class, and I argue that these differential rates of progress, indeed, differential trajectories, cannot be understood without some acknowledgment of ethnic difference.

The essays that follow are interventions in British debates and the course of events in Britain. Hopefully, other places in the world, not least the United States, can learn something from these studies of what is happening in Britain, just as British political and societal actors have certainly borrowed and benefited from the racial equality struggles in the United States. A hundred years ago, the African-American theorist W. E. B. Du Bois predicted that the twentieth century would be the century of the color line (1995); today, we seem to be set for a century of the Islam-West line. If this is the case, it may well be instructive for Americans and others to inquire into how a racial equality politics produced multicultural assertiveness, which in turn has given rise to, and is attempting to address, unforeseen Muslim claims making. This might assist in understanding some of the protests and agitation among Muslims in the United States and other Muslim populations, engagement with whom is so central to American foreign policy and security.

Part I

Racisms, Disadvantage, and Upward Mobility

One

"Difference," Cultural Racism, and Antiracism

A New Racism?

During the 1980s, several sociologists and antiracists discerned the growing presence of a British "new *racism*" (Barker 1981; Gordon and Klug 1986; Gilroy 1987). It was argued that, following the Holocaust and the comprehensive discrediting of nineteenth-century scientific racism, racism based on biological theories of superior and inferior races was no longer intellectually and politically viable as a public discourse. Instead, what had emerged was a racism based on cultural differences, on the "natural" preference of human beings for their own cultural group, and on the incompatibility between different cultures—the mixing or coexistence of which in one country, it was alleged, was bound to lead to violent social conflict and the dissolution of social bonds. It was a racism said to have been first articulated in the speeches of Enoch Powell in the late 1960s, nurtured in the New Right intellectual circles of the 1970s, burst into prominence in the early 1980s with the publicity accorded to the polemical output of writers associated with the radical right-wing journal the *Salisbury Review,* and then disseminated by many newspaper columnists and lead writers in both the broadsheets and the tabloids.

Several commentators have seen that this "new racism" is not peculiar to the English New Right but part of a much larger intellectual

27

and political movement. Etienne Balibar, for example, has argued that it is part of "a racism in the era of 'decolonisation,' of the reversal of population movements between the old colonies and the old metropolises" (1991, 21). It has developed in a way that gives expression to the perceived problem of assimilating or integrating culturally primitive and backward peoples into modern civilizations, for example, into the France of the "land of the Rights of Man" (24). He sees its prototype in modern anti-Semitism, of which he writes:

> Admittedly, bodily stigmata play a great role in its phantasmatics, but they do so more as signs of a deep psychology, as signs of a spiritual inheritance rather than a biological heredity. (24)

Such an interpretation of racism, Balibar points out, is particularly helpful in explaining the French colonial oppression of Muslims and of contemporary Muslimophobia, and he borrows a term from P. A. Taguieff to identify it as "differentialist racism." David Goldberg, too, is surely right in his judgment that "since World War II, and especially in the past fifteen or twenty years, the cultural conception of race has tended to eclipse all others. It has become paradigmatic" (1993, 71).

A culturalist racism, then, should not be supposed to have originated with the British New Right. It has a much greater international and historical depth. It could be said that in the long history of racism it is nineteenth-century biologism that is the exception, and certainly Europe's oldest racisms, anti-Semitism and Islamophobia, are culturalist (Ballard 1996). Even the contemporary version of culturalist racism identified as "new racism" certainly predates the speeches and writings of New Right politicians and intellectuals, who in fact gave an ideological expression to an extreme version of a commonsense or folk racism that has been around for some time. It is surely as old as the New Commonwealth immigration and settlement in Britain against which it was directed and that gave rise to its development, although it has become more explicit as the presence of these settlements, and the multicultural challenge they pose, has become more evident. I shall call this folk sentiment, as well as the culturally grounded differential treatment, practices, policies, and ideologies that it has given rise to or is part of, cultural racism, to distinguish it from biological racism, which it presupposes. While biological racism is the antipathy, exclusion, and unequal treatment of people on the basis of their physical appearance or other imputed physical differences, saliently in Britain their non-whiteness, cultural racism builds on biological racism a further discourse that evokes cultural differences from an alleged British, civilized norm to vilify, marginalize, or demand cultural assimilation from groups who also suffer from biological racism. Postwar racism in Britain has been simultaneously culturalist and biological, and while the latter is essential to the racism in question, it is, in fact, the less explanatory aspect of a complex phenomenon. Biological interpretations have not governed what white British people, including racists, have thought or done; how they have stereotyped, treated, and related to non-whites; and biological ideas have had increasingly less force both in the context of personal relationships and in the conceptualization of groups. As white people's interactions with non-white individuals increased, they did not become necessarily less conscious of group differences, but they were far more likely to ascribe group differences to upbringing, customs, forms of socialization, and self-identity than to biological heredity.

A central feature of this combined racism was that the non-white presence in Britain was conceived of in terms of a double contrast. The first, a contrast between white/European/British and "colored"/black/non-European, was a distinction based on skin color. A further subdivision, of the "colored" group into Asians and West Indians, was also essential to the identification and definition of racial groups and constituted the second dualism. As I shall shortly show, these dualisms exist in commonsense or folk typologies as well as in the New Right discourse. But before we explore these contrasts, let us briefly consider what kind of antiracist response was made to them.

Antiracisms and Asian Identities

There have, in fact, been two different antiracisms. The early response, exemplified by the Campaign Against Racial Discrimination (CARD) in the 1960s, and influenced by the American civil rights movement under the leadership of Martin Luther King Jr., was to repudiate biological racism by arguing that all human beings are equal, irrespective of color, and are entitled to the same civic rights within the nation-state. This color-blind humanism gave way—first in the United States and more gradually in Britain, where it became prominent in the 1980s—to two forms of color-conscious antiracisms. One form consisted of the recognition of the essential need to monitor the socioeconomic disadvantages of non-whites, and the structural bias against them, in all the public institutions of a white society in order to identify discrimination and measure both inequality and the extent of progress made toward its elimination.

The second form of antiracism consisted of raising black consciousness, in getting black people to emphasize their blackness and take pride in their roots, to express their solidarity with other black people and their struggles, and to organize as black people in mutual self-help and collective empowerment (Malcolm X 1966; Cleaver 1968; Blauner 1972). This movement was, in effect, to create a new black identity or black political ethnicity. The result was that the racists' first contrast, the black-white opposition, was accepted, even sharpened, by awareness of racism, but reinterpreted. When this American antiracist movement was pursued in Britain, it highlighted a problem. In Britain there was a second cleavage, the West Indian/ Asian dualism. Despite the different political and cultural histories that this cleavage represented, British antiracism, having accepted the first opposition between black and white, continued to deny any political or antiracist strategic significance to this internal division (e.g., Gordon and Klug 1986, 23). I have argued in a series of articles that this denial has been a sociological falsification, politically naive, and has had a deleterious effect on the ability of Asians to mobilize for antiracist struggles (Modood 1992, 1994c). Since the source of my feeling that British antiracism has not taken sufficiently seriously the existence and nature of cultural racism is not merely sociological but a matter of personal experience as an Asian living in Britain, it may be helpful to say a little about that starting point.

The effect of these antiracisms on Asians (to be told—or to argue—that there were no real black-white differences, and later that "color" was the basis of ethnic pride and political solidarity) was to create a schizophrenic contradiction in many Asians' sense of identity. During the period in which these were the dominant public antiracist views, young British Asians were being brought up by their families and communities to feel that we *were* different qua Asians and qua specificities of religion, language, caste, national/regional origins, and so forth. We came to notice over time that it was our continued cultural differences that were resented by many of the British as alien and that made us a target of harassment and attack. Initially, the migrant generation were unsure of how long they expected to be in Britain—many expected and wished to return to their homelands in due course, and few sought any public policy of multiculturalism. The general feeling was that even if our modes of living were to be modified through a process of settling in and adapting to life in Britain, some essential core of continuity had to be maintained. This was not, it must be stressed, a crudely conservative view; Asian parents knew, even if they did not always relish the prospect, that changes would occur if their children and grandchildren were to be accepted, as indeed they wished them to be, by white British people and to succeed in the new society. Different parents, different Asian communities, had different views on the pace of change and what should and must not be changed. In my family, national origins (Pakistan) and language (Urdu) were considered to be of lesser importance and hence detachable from the core value, which was defined as Islam (for an account of my father's Islam, see M. S. Modood 1990). This did not mean a rigid "fundamentalist," anti-Western, antimodernist religiosity (it particularly did not mean this in the 1960s and 1970s), but it did mean that the new ways of living, gradually becoming a part of British society, had to be ultimately justified in terms of compatibility with the Muslim faith and the welfare of Muslim people. The ultimate form of selling out, of self-abnegation, I was taught, was to be a traitor to Islam and to be indifferent to the fate of Muslims.

Only about half of the South Asians in Britain are Muslim, and not all Muslims are equally committed to a Muslim identity (which is certainly open to a number of interpretations). Some Pakistanis see their cultural heritage and Pakistani identity as inseparable from, and hence of greater value, than their Muslim lifestyle. Some valorize only their Punjabi or North Indian cultural identity, and others their common past struggle against British imperialism. My point is not to reduce the complexity and range of identities and commitments in the South Asian communities to the religious, though I do believe that religion is much more central to British Asian ethnicity than many antiracists would like to acknowledge. Rather, I argue that South Asian immigrants to Britain believed, and taught their children to believe, in the uniqueness of their culturally distinct beliefs and practices and felt that this cultural heritage was of value and under threat (Modood, Beishon, and Virdee 1994). The threat came not just from racism; it also arose from the fact of migration and settlement in a society very different from the original one—in which, for example, religion played a very different role in structuring collective identities. Yet the antiracisms of both the earlier and the later periods ignored these issues, and with them the significance of Asian ethnicities. This meant that there was no language in which to debate cultural difference and the extent to which Asian cultural differences were increasingly being racialized, no language in which to give expression to ethnicity while seeking, at the same time, to oppose racist stereotyping and public expressions of contempt, as well as right-wing culturalist constructions of identity; there was no form of words to express loyalty to one's own minority community within a public discourse of equality and civic integration.

The second form of antiracism was an advance on the first in that it brought issues of representation as well as policy under critical political scrutiny; it was a less defensive antiracism in that it did not assume that cultural homogeneity was a prerequisite of a common citizenship. It highlighted the crucial issue of identity. Yet from an Asian point of view, the black-consciousness movement was in other ways less preferable to the earlier civic antiracism because the assertive identity it promoted to unite the victims of racism focused on color. Ironically, this was at a time when cultural racism was on the increase, eclipsing other forms of racism, and when Asians were asking themselves what were the core identities they felt were under threat and most worth preserving, and hence were least interested in defining themselves in terms of a global color identity.

The second antiracism therefore excluded Asians and other victims of racism who did not see their primary identity and incorporation into British society in terms of color, or at least it was an antiracism that was insensitive to the concerns and vulnerabilities of such groups. Yet the secondary status of Asians in antiracism went further. As I have suggested, there was one ethnic identity that this second antiracism was compatible with and usually went hand in hand with: black consciousness, or a black pride movement, where "black" meant African roots and origins in the enslavement of African peoples in the New World. Hence, the 1980s antiracism consisted of (in the case of white people, a solidarity with) an oppositional blackness based on an inversion of the racist white-black/colored divide, together with a celebration of the positive elements of black diasporic African heritage of struggle and of the achievements of the contemporary bearers of that heritage. There was tension between these two versions of blackness—political solidarity of all non-whites and a black diasporic African ethnicity—but no real antiracist criticism of what was perceived as a natural and benign conflation. Yet my experience in racial equality work is that the assertion of any other non-white minority identity—Asian, Indian, or Muslim—was condemned as culturalism, as racism (!), or as divisive of the antiracist effort and minority unity (Modood 1994c). This created an antiracism that failed to acknowledge the existence of cultural racism and therefore to contend with the specificities of anti-Asian racism. An absurd situation had emerged in which antiracists were encouraging self-pride and assertiveness in the racially subordinated, but were intolerant of Asians defining themselves, their circumstances, frustrations, and aspirations except in approved ways.

This opposition to Asian ethnicity has been anomalous within the broader left-wing politics of the last two decades, in which the solidarities of class or social citizenship have been superseded by an ideal of equality based on the view that "a positive self-definition of group difference is in fact more liberatory" (Young 1990, 157). It is a politics that has informed not just black power antiracism, but the gay pride movement and, above all, radical feminism. Those elements of the old left that found such politics divisive have found themselves having to accommodate it or risk irrelevance. Nevertheless, the intolerance of Asian self-definition came not just or even primarily from the old left; the charge that Asian self-definition is divisive is heard as frequently from advocates of the politics of difference (Gilroy 1987).

The Complexities of Racism

More recently, not unrelated to a hypothesizing of the existence of a new racism and partly following the lead of some in the field of cultural studies (e.g., Gilroy 1987, 1990), a reappraisal of antiracism as a strategy and mode of discursive representation has been initiated. One of the arguments for a reappraisal is that contemporary racism was, but no longer is, a unitary phenomenon, that Britain has become multiracist. Support of this diversity is evidenced by the fact that white people who are racists toward some ethnic groups can admire other ethnic groups because of, for example, aspects of their subcultural styles:

> Most typically, of course, many White working-class boys discrimi-
> nate positively in favour of Afro-Caribbean subcultures as exhibit-
> ing a macho, proletarian style, and against Asian cultures as being
> "effeminate" and "middle-class." Such boys experience no sense
> of contradiction in wearing dreadlocks, smoking ganja and going
> to reggae concerts whilst continuing to assert that "Pakis Stink."
> (Cohen 1988, 83)

Les Back found these insights confirmed in his ethnographic study
of a large South London council estate in 1985–87 (Back 1993). He
observed among the young whites on the estate a "neighbourhood
nationalism," side by side and in tension with a British nationalism.
While the latter was understood as a preserve of whites, the former
was based on racially mixed groups of friends and the prestigious
position of black youth cultures and styles in the area and embraced
blacks as well as whites. The Vietnamese on the estate were excluded
from both these local patriotisms and therefore incurred "the full
wrath of the new racism which defines 'outsiders' in terms of 'cultural'
difference" (228). Back believes that this situation is interestingly new.
Indeed, it is relatively new in terms of British sociology and antiracist
discussions. I would suggest, however, that, like the "new racism" itself, these inconsistent and differential racisms are as old as the immigration and settlement they are attempting to make sense of and live
with. British race relations policies and antiracisms are premised on
the assumption that the problem is of an exclusionism typified by the
notice that some landladies in the 1950s put in their front windows:
"No Coloreds," the fuller version being "No Irish, No Coloreds, No
Dogs" (Cohen 1988, 14); notices evoking memories for those newly
arrived immigrants, like my father, of signs outside the clubs of the
British in India: "No Indians, No Dogs." The imagined solution to
this exclusionary tendency is symbolized by the black and white hand-
shake that serves as the logo of the Commission for Racial Equality.
But neither the problem nor the solution was ever quite so simple. The
"No-Coloreds" racism was not unitary: racists always distinguished
between the groups they rejected, and while the likelihood that someone who discriminated against one group also discriminated against
other groups probably was high, the culturally constructed grounds of
rejection varied depending on the immigrant group.

Alastair Bonnett cites a BBC interview with some teddy boys just
after the 1958 racist attacks in Notting Hill (Bonnett 1993, 19–20,

using an interview transcript in Glass 1961). He observes that while there is a reductionist, homogenizing racialism—"they're all spades"—it is constantly qualified as particular groups (notably Jamaicans and Maltese) are identified and "extricated from the 'racial'/color based logic involved in drawing a clear line between 'spades' and 'us'" (20). My own memories of my working-class secondary modern school in North-West London in the second half of the 1960s are very much in line with Back's South London observations, making doubtful the suggestion that he has discovered a new phenomenon. While there was indiscriminate racist name-calling, the black and white boys had interracial friendships and a natural respect for each other, focused, above all, on soccer, which was greater than either had for Asian boys. The school roll included many skinheads and other adherents of the cult of Paki-bashing who appeared to me at the time to have a very clear perception of an elemental difference between Pakis (aka Indians and Asians) and non-Pakis. The contrast that Cohen referred to, cited above, between "pushover" Asians and "hard" West Indians was certainly in place, though the more recent contrast between academic, obedient Asians and disruptive, dull (male, but not female) African-Caribbeans was, with Asians still struggling with the English language, as yet in its infancy. Mairtin Mac an Ghaill (1988), on the basis of observation in a Midlands working-class secondary school in the 1980s, has argued that this pair of stereotypes is fostered by (racist) teachers. I do not remember it either being limited to the teachers or actively led by them (see also Gillborn 1990; Willis 1977).

This perception of "colored immigrants" as coming in two kinds, black/Jamaican/West Indian/African-Caribbean and Paki/Indian/Asian, is not confined to schools, youth, or the working class. Despite the way in which antiracists represent racist discourse, the actual speeches and literature of, say, Enoch Powell, the National Front, the Conservative New Right, or the British National Party constantly make this distinction, and this is evident even in the quotes that some antiracists use (e.g., Gordon and Klug 1986, 17–19; Gilroy 1987, 45–46). In the only in-depth research of how racial stereotypes work in job selection, Richard Jenkins (1986) undertook a study of middle managers across a range of public and private sector organizations. Through interviews, he identified eight stereotypes in what the managers said (the percentage figure records the proportion of managers who gave expression to a stereotype):

1. West Indians are lazy, happy-go-lucky, or slow.   43%
2. Asians are hard workers.   34%
3. Asians are more ambitious and academic.   14%
4. West Indians are aggressive and excitable.   12%
5. West Indians mix better with whites.   13%
6. Asians are clannish and don't mix.   13%
7. West Indians have a chip on their shoulders.   11%
8. Asians are lazy, less willing.   11%

None of the stereotypes is about—to use the managers' favored term—"colored people" as such. What emerge are once again two groups and, interestingly, only one stereotype, "laziness," that applies to both (cf. 1 and 8), and even there, the percentages suggest a contrast rather than a similarity. In this respect, racism, especially British racism, is quite different from sexism. Of course, there are stereotypes about different kinds of women, for example, the bossy, the demure, and the man hater. But, unlike the case with non-whites, there are some fundamental stereotypes about women *as such*: they are less rational, more emotional; physically weak and lacking in toughness; more caring; and so on. While the managers' categories could only exist in the context of a society in which racism was present, it would be quite wrong to suppose that stereotypes such as those are confined to a special group of people, racists, or white people. A Runnymede Trust survey found that about the same number (nearly 50 percent) of African-Caribbeans as whites assented to the proposition "Asian people work harder than White people" (the Asian figure was nearly 70 percent); similarly, about 15 percent of whites and nearly the same number of Asians agreed to "White people are more intelligent than black people" (Amin and Richardson 1992, 44).

These fundamentally contrasting images and generalizations about Asians and West Indians are not hidden away in private conversations, to be teased out through subtle research. They are commonly found in the mass media, especially in the tabloid press. Bonnett has interestingly brought out how, in the 1980s, even among opponents of non-white immigration such as the *Sun* newspaper, there is a softening of a blanket rejectionism as worthwhile qualities are found in one or another minority group (1993, 25–29). Usually such positive qualities are attributed to one but not the other group, so that the two groups are not just distinguished but implicitly contrasted. From the examples that Bonnett offers, two sets of contrasts can be identified, one favoring African-Caribbeans, the other Asians:

1. Asians are law-abiding, hard-working, resourceful, and respectful of traditional family values; blacks lack the discipline and structures to resist an inner-city underclass culture of drugs, vice, crime, and violence.
2. Asians have a profoundly alien culture; they do not share and do not want to share the Judeo-Christian outlook and/or a democratic individualism; black people, typified by the celebration of the boxer Frank Bruno as a "Great Briton," are patriotic Britons who enrich a shared popular culture and bring honor to national sporting teams.

Bonnett goes on to point out that while these sweet-sour contrasts are based on very old, long-standing stereotypes and cultural relationships, they nevertheless more than hint at a new right-wing redefinition of Britishness by de-emphasizing whiteness in favor of characteristics such as law-abiding, family loving, individualism, and so on, which minorities may already have or can learn (or be taught) to emulate. It is a vision that claims to be color-blind, while propagating a culturally intolerant British nationalism, suggesting that contemporary racist sentiment is capable not just of the kind of neighborhood nationalism of a working-class council estate, but of effacing color racism while reinforcing cultural racism at a macro level (not that cultural intolerance is confined to the right; see Weldon 1989). Moreover, as Bonnett also notes, in the late 1980s and early 1990s a third racialized grouping emerged in public discourse as a target for racist graffiti and attacks, a group apparently particularly suited to focus the unease evoked by alien cultures and their seeming lack of respect for, and incompatibility with, the British way of life. I refer here, of course, to Muslims, for one of the purposes of this book is to highlight that Muslimophobia is at the heart of contemporary British and European cultural racism (Modood 1990, 1992).

The Rise of Cultural Racism

The implications of the development of a seemingly color-blind nationalism, which appears to be gaining support, need to be spelled out. While it is just possible that it will give us a post-biological racist cultural intolerance, it is much more likely that the hostility against perceived cultural difference will be directed primarily against non-whites rather than against white minorities. That is to say, even if it should be the case that color racism may come to be negligible in its own right, it is still possible for it to operate in conjunction with cultural racism. What we would have is a situation in which color racism is triggered by, and only becomes potent in combination with, cultural antagonisms and prejudices. It is by no means an impossible development for color prejudice to decline while discourses attacking the collective cultures of minority groups rise. At this point, cultural racism would have come into its own—not without color racism but as the dominant factor. It is quite possible that we shall witness in the next few decades an increasing de-racialization of, say, culturally assimilated African-Caribbeans and Asians along with, *simultaneously,* a racialization of other culturally different Asians, Arabs, and non-white Muslims.

Having anything but a European physical appearance may be enough in contemporary European societies to make one a possible object of racist treatment (not that only European societies can be racist, see, for example, Dikötter 1990). But such phenotypical racism can also be the foundation of a more complex form of racism. I am not, however, arguing that wherever there is biological racism there must be cultural racism too, or that cultural exclusionism occurs only in the context of racism or should be relabeled as "racism." Ethnic hierarchies and religious discrimination, for example, can and do exist in all-white or all-black societies—in societies where groups are not differentiated by physical appearance. My argument is that racialized groups that have distinctive cultural identities or a community life defined as "alien," will suffer an additional dimension of discrimination and prejudice. The hostility against the non-white minority is likely to be particularly sharp if the minority is sufficiently numerous to reproduce itself as a community and has a distinctive and cohesive value system that can be perceived as an alternative, and a possible challenge, to the norm. It is particularly important to recognize that racism constitutes opposition to, discrimination against, not just individuals but, above all, communities or groups. Racism normally makes a linkage between a difference in physical appearance and a (perceived) difference in group attitudes and behavior. In contemporary settings the linkage is not usually crudely genetic or biological but is likely to rest on history, social structure, group norms, values, and cultures. The causal linkage is unlikely to be perceived as scientific or determining but as probabilistic and therefore allowing of exceptions. Thus, European people can have good personal relations with certain non-white persons and yet have stereotypes about the groups those persons are from, believing that the groups in question have major adjustment problems (chips on their shoulders, and so on). These whites are likely to deny that they are racists ("my best friend is black"). Indeed, this denial can be genuine, for it is possible not to be a racist in individual relationships or in the context of shared cultural assumptions and yet be a racist in one's attitudes toward groups. Such collective racism can be overridden in the course of interracial friendships and shared lifestyles where a non-white friend, for example, can demonstrate that he or she is the exception to the stereotype; on the other hand, it is also clear that, despite such one-to-one relationships, stereotypes may continue to be held by the white friend (and, of course, not only by whites) to apply to the group as a whole.

Cultural racism is likely to be particularly aggressive against those minority communities that want to maintain, and not just defensively, some of the basic elements of their culture or religion and if, far from denying their difference (beyond the color of their skin), they want to assert this difference in public and demand that they be respected just as they are. Some of the early researchers on racial discrimination in England were quite clear about the existence of color and cultural components in racial discrimination, and yet thought the former much more important. A leading study by W. W. Daniel, for example, concluded:

> The experiences of white immigrants, such as Hungarians and Cypriots, compared to black or brown immigrants, such as West Indians and Asians, leaves no doubt that the major component in the discrimination is color. (1968, 209)

This was further confirmed for Daniel by the finding that West Indians experienced more discrimination than Asians, and he takes the view that people who physically differ most from the white population were discriminated against most, and therefore, he argues, "prejudice against Negroes is most deep-rooted and widespread" (209). In contrast, he thought that lighter-skinned Asians suffered from some discrimination for cultural reasons, but that this would tend to decrease for British-educated second-generation Asians. While his prediction appears, on the surface, reasonable, it overlooked the increasing significance that cultural racism was to play in determining attitudes to ethnic minorities.

The annual Social Attitudes Survey, which began in 1982, has consistently recorded, as have other surveys, that the English think there is more extreme prejudice against Asians than against African-Caribbeans. They show that while between 45 to 62 percent think there is a lot of prejudice, in every year an increasing number of people thought there was more prejudice against Asians than against blacks. Between 1983 and 1987 the difference was between 3 to 7 percent, and between 1989 (year of the Rushdie affair and the emergence of a public discourse about Muslims) and 1998 it went up to between 8 to 12 percent, an average of nearly 10 percent. This marks more than a fifth in excess of the figure for blacks. The more detailed breakdown, available in the 1986 survey report, shows that the difference is mainly accounted for by those under the age of thirty-five and those in social classes III (manual), IV, V, and other (Airey and Brook 1986, 163). In other words, anti-Asian racism appears to be on the increase. Perhaps an even better measure of the difference between attitudes to these two major ethnic groups can be found among the white respondents who admitted to being prejudiced themselves: 14 percent said they were prejudiced against Asians compared to only 5 percent against black people; the figures for the under-thirty-five-years-old group were 20 percent and 5 percent respectively, and the factorial difference was even greater in the North and Midlands (164). The Fourth National Survey, conducted in 1994, found that all ethnic groups, except the Chinese but including the Caribbeans, believe that prejudice against Asians is much the highest of all ethnic, racial, or religious prejudices; and it is believed by Asian people themselves that the prejudice against Asians is primarily a prejudice against Muslims (Modood et al. 1997, 133–34).

These survey findings are confirmed by several qualitative or personal accounts, for example, by Dervla Murphy (1987) in her documentation of racism in Bradford and Birmingham, and by the Scottish-Nigerian writer, Adewale Maja-Pearce (1990), in his travels around Britain. Both found that white people expressed more hostility toward Asians, especially Pakistanis, than any other group (e.g., Murphy 1987, 214). Maja-Pearce was moved to write, "This obsessive hatred of people from the Indian subcontinent is paralleled in recent (pre-Bosnia) history by a well-known event in central Europe" (72). Part of the explanation for the failure of Daniel's prediction may be found in Michael Banton's observation, made just a decade later, that the English seemed to display more hostility towards the West Indians because they sought a greater degree of acceptance than the English wished to accord; in more recent times there seemed to have been more hostility towards Asians because they are insufficiently inclined to adopt English ways. (1979, 242)

Indirect Discrimination

My attempt thus far to establish that there is such a thing as cultural racism has focused on stereotypes, prejudices, and discourse, on perceptions and attitudes that not only are part of a climate of opinion but that lead to direct acts and practices of racial discrimination in areas of social life such as employment, housing, schools, social services, electoral politics, and so on. There is, however, also a dimension of indirect discrimination involved in this racism. I take my idea of indirect discrimination from the British Race Relations Act (1976). A practice or policy may make no reference to race or ethnic groups but may nevertheless disproportionately disadvantage some groups more than others. For example, a company policy that gives preference in filling jobs to local people is formally nonracist (and even may date from the time when Britain was not multiracial), but if the local population happens to be predominantly white, the policy disadvantages minority groups. If there are no countervailing justifiable reasons in favor of the policy, related, for example, to the efficiency of the business, then this constitutes indirect discrimination.

It should be clear that many kinds of nonracist forms of socioeconomic inequalities, especially forms of class exclusivity—for example, a bias in favor of Oxbridge graduates for certain kinds of elite jobs—are prima facie cases of indirect racial discrimination (see, for instance, CRE 1987). Cultural differences, too, can be the basis for unintended discrimination. Every society has ways of doing things—customs, norms, cultural preferences, and rewards—that reflect a majority view or that of a particularly prized cultural group. Membership in a nondominant cultural group can deprive one of, say, excellence in the dominant language and its modes of representation, or access to certain useful social networks. A member of any group that has failed to master or accept the established norms may find it systematically and cumulatively more difficult to meet the target those norms underwrite. Such norms may vary from the unwillingness to engage in the social drinking of alcohol to what counts as acceptable, professional, and appropriate clothing, accent, or manner of speech. To be disadvantaged because of one's religion or culture is to suffer discrimination. The English custom that requires staff to work on Fridays, the day of collective worship for Muslims, and does not demand work on Sundays, may have no justifiable grounds other than local custom. What is taught in schools, the character and delivery of medical and social services, the program schedules of television and radio, the preference for certain forms of entertainment and culture— can all be sites of culture-blind indirect discrimination.

I cannot possibly pursue here the different kinds of issues that have arisen in these different fields and that, together, give substance to what I might call the outer, indirect, part of the concept of cultural racism. A very good example of a debate about the kind of ethnocentrism I have in mind has been raging in American academia and elsewhere, regarding the demands by feminists and ethnic minority activists that university curricula and intellectual canons reflect a multiculturalism appropriate to the country as a whole, encompassing groups that have been historically marginalized and culturally denuded, "written out" as agents (as opposed to objects) of intellectual inquiry (for an attempt to moderate the debate see Barber 1992). My own focus has been on how South Asians and especially South Asian Muslims have been marginalized and written out of equality debates and antiracist perspectives, the theme of Part II of this book.

A More Plural Antiracism

I am aware that the concept of cultural racism as elaborated here will seem perverse to some. It will seem yet another example of what Miles (1989) calls an "inflation of the meaning of racism" created by bringing together two things, racism proper and cultural prejudice or ethnocentrism, that are apparently quite distinct, thereby obscuring the real nature of racist thinking and practices. Against that I would argue that while it is true that there is no logical connection between cultural prejudice and color racism, by the same token there is no logical connection between racial discrimination and class inequalities, and yet when the two do come together, the concept of racial disadvantage is a good one to describe the situation. Or again, there is no necessary connection between racism and sexism (for the opposite view, see Balibar 1991, 49), but we know they can be connected, and when they are, a distinctive phenomenon is created in the form of stereotypes about submissive Asian women or the strong black woman who cannot keep her man (Anthias and Yuval-Davis 1992, 125). Similarly, there may be only a contingent, matter-of-fact connection between color prejudice and cultural prejudice, true for only certain times and places; nevertheless, when the two kinds of exclusionism and oppression come together, we have a distinctive phenomenon worthy of its own name and conceptualization. In this conceptualization, far from obscuring racism we learn something about it: contrary to just about everybody who writes about racism, including those who emphasize the specificities of different kinds of racisms and their articulations with nation, gender, class, and so on (Miles 1989; Anthias and Yuval-Davis 1992), contemporary British racism is not dependent on any (even unstated) form of biological determinism. True, there is always some reference to differences in physical appearances and/or a legacy of the racism of earlier centuries, but the reference is not necessarily to a deep biology; minor phenotypical differences are all that is required to mark out racial groups, to stereotype them, and to treat them accordingly. Being able to pick out individuals on the basis of their physical appearance and to assign them to a racial group may be an essential aspect of the definition of racism, but physical appearance stands only as a marker of race, not the explanation of a group's behavior. Racists impute inferiority, undesirability, distinctive behavioral traits, and so on to a group distinguished by their appearance, but this does not imply an assumption on their part that the behavioral qualities are produced by biology rather than by history, culture, upbringing, or by certain norms or their absence. In the extreme case, cultural racism, as I have argued, does not necessarily hinge on color racism, merely a color racism *at the point of* cultural racism. Ironically, then, it is not the contemporary racists that make biology the cause of culture, but those antiracists who define the "new racism" as the view exposed by some antiracists "that there are biologically-determined differences between groups of people which are so fundamental as to lead to unbridgeable gaps in culture and lifestyle" (Gordon and Klug 1986, 22). Perhaps the tactic of understating the cultural dimensions of racism is intended to have a simpler thesis to refute, and to focus energy and debate merely on color racism. But if so, it fails to oppose racism and to create the basis of a movement that all racially victimized groups can identify with.

If the New Right's "new racism" of Enoch Powell and the *Salisbury*

Review did anything, it was to make explicit and to elaborate a *cultural* determinism, without apparent biological claims, the purpose being to raise doubts about the possibility of assimilating cohesive "alien" minorities into the nation and to challenge the feasibility of the reformist goal of a pluralist, multicultural British nationality. To interpret a thesis of cultural determinism directed at phenotypically identified groups as a disguised form of biological determinism, as some antiracists have done, is to understate its persuasiveness for those who are unmoved by a crude biologism. An antiracism narrowly focused on color racism is therefore at best a partial, at worst a misdirected, riposte to the New Right and the complex and damaging racism in contemporary Britain. It is an antiracism that, by failing to meet discourse with counterdiscourse, fails also to connect with many British South Asians' anxieties and energies.

The growing calls to revise and update antiracism by pluralizing the concept of political blackness are to be welcomed (e.g., Hall 1992a, 255; Parekh 1994, 102). An element of this project depends on the argument that a black political identity does not compete with or replace other identities, for example, Asian, for, it is argued, different identities refer to different aspects of a person's subjectivity or are emphasized in different situations, say, one in politics, the other to do with culture. As no one has yet given this idea any content, I am unsure as to what is being proposed. Who, for example, is to decide what is a political situation and what is a cultural one? As a matter of fact, most of the minority of Asians who think of themselves as black do not think this in relation to specific contexts but to what they perceive as a pervading fact of social existence (Modood et al. 1997). Moreover, is "blackness" really available to Asians when some of the most thoughtful and acclaimed contributions to the development of "blackness" are not about downgrading the cultural content but increasing the reference to African roots and the Atlantic experience (e.g., Gilroy 1987, 1993)? Can political blackness really hope to replace, emotionally and intellectually, an ethnic blackness, with all its powerful resonances and appeals to self-pride, with a notion that is supposed to unite in certain limited contexts for pragmatic purposes? It is because I think that "blackness" contains so much of the history, sorrow, hopes, and energy of descendants of African enslavement in the Atlantic world that I do not think that it can be turned into a politics that is neutral between different non-white groups. It cannot have the same meaning or equally give strength to those who can identify with that history and those who cannot.

There is in racial discrimination and color racism quite clearly a commonality of circumstance among people who are not white. It is partly what gives sense to the term "ethnic minorities" and to suggestions for a "rainbow coalition" (Modood 1988, 402). The question is not whether coalitional antiracism is desirable, but of what kind. My personal preference and commitment is for a plural politics that does not privilege color identities. We must accept what is important to people, and *we must be evenhanded between the different identity formations*. Political blackness is an important constituent of this pluralism, but it can't be the overarching basis of unity. The end of its hegemony is not without its problems and dangers, but it is not to be regretted. A precondition of creating/re-creating a coalitional pluralism is the giving up of the corrupting ideal of a solidaristic monism.

A new public philosophy of racial equality and pluralism must aspire to bring into harmony the pluralism and hybridity that exists on the ground, not to pit it against itself by insisting that some modes of collectivity trump all others. That was the error of the British antiracism of the 1980s.

Two

If Races Do Not Exist, Then What Does? Racial Categorization and Ethnic Realities

Antiracist Categorization

Some years ago Michael Banton wrote, "In my view the lack of an agreed nomenclature is one of the most revealing features of racial and ethnic relations in Britain today" (1987, 175). That he could write this in 1987 must have meant that he felt that his arguments over many years resisting the inclusion of Asians under the category "black" (e.g., Banton 1976) had not been in vain. In fact, they had been far from successful; it would be fair to say that in 1987 there was an agreed nomenclature in the public discourse of race. Those who believe that, for reasons of tidiness as well as effective antiracism, the way forward lay in establishing the hegemony of the term "black" seemed by that point to have won the day. The term was not so securely established that academic or policy document writers felt no need to justify the use of "black" to mean all non-white minorities, but this justification, even in the case of writers who were not wholly sympathetic to such reduction, usually consisted of a footnote simply explaining that the usage of the all-inclusive "black" was now an established fact (e.g., Nanton 1989, note 1; Mullings 1992, note 1; Saggar 1992, xii; S. J. Smith 1993, note 1).

One can get some appreciation of the path toward this linguistic and media consensus by looking briefly at British parliamentary language. In 1969 the favored term was "coloured," with "non-European" and "non-white" considered patronizing and "black" being "offensive and inaccurate" (House of Commons 1969, 7); the White Paper introducing the 1976 legislation speaks of "black and brown." When the matter of terminology was raised by the Home Affairs subcommittee in 1982, the then chairman of the Commission for Racial Equality (CRE) informed it that despite the fact that the majority of Asians would not self-classify themselves as "black," this is "the conventional way now of regarding all those who suffer from the particular disadvantage related to colour" (House of Commons 1982, para. 391).[1] This understanding grew through the mid- to late 1980s, as is reflected in virtually all CRE publications, local authorities' race discourse, academic texts, the "quality" press, radio and television, as well as in documents of most central government departments and many large employers. As Stuart Hall has written, "In this moment, politically speaking, 'The Black experience,' as a singular and unifying framework based on the building up of identity across ethnic and cultural difference between the different communities, became 'hegemonic' over other ethnic/racial identities" (1992a, 242; cf. Y. Ali 1991, 195, and Sudbury 2001, 34–35).

And yet, by the early 1990s, Banton's words ring true. An incisive analysis of this contrast has been offered by Alastair Bonnett. He argues that the significant extent to which the inclusive political concept of Black has entered "non-political" discourse marks quite a significant victory for antiracism. Yet the increasing evidence of its inability to maintain this victory is ultimately a result of the political failure, central to the practice of antiracism, to root itself in the non-white, especially Asian, communities (Bonnett 1989, 8–9; see also Bonnet 1993). I have on a number of occasions argued that the concept of Black was rightly not accepted by Asian communities because it was incompatible with their sense of themselves and harmful to their interests (e.g., Modood 1988, 1994c). I shall not return to that here but would like to explore the sources of Banton's objections to the race terminology that became hegemonic in the 1980s during the period of its rise.

What Lies beyond Racial Categorization?

Banton's explicit discussion of the suitability of the new terminology of "black" (where others thought the issue was not worth more than a prefatory footnote) and his unfashionable stand against it reflect a long-standing interest in what groups are called and what they call themselves. He has taken issues of nomenclature and political vocabulary to be not just trivial arguments about words but a fundamental indicator of social and political change and of how a particular race relations situation is developing—hence his historical and comparative interest in what language, fineness of distinction, and mixing of different categories of status and of ideology have been in use in different times and places in the Atlantic world and beyond. He has had a recurring interest in the classifications used in various censuses and the options that they allow or rule out (e.g., Banton 1983, 55–57) and in U.S. debates among those of Latin American origins on whether they should be categorized by national origins (Cubans, Mexican Americans) or by language (Spanish-speaking) or prefer to be called Latinos, Chicanos, or Hispanics, debates full of passion and politics that some commentators have dubbed the "Battle of the Name" (Banton 1988, 116). While some radicals have claimed (usually without consistency since they themselves police all language for political correctness) that focusing on group labels and self-definition is a distraction from the elimination of material inequalities, this was certainly not the view of the late 1960s U.S. black power radicals and other allied new left movements. Their view has been given a new retrospective importance in Omi and Winant's claim that "the forging of the new collective racial identities during the 1950s and 1960s has been the enduring legacy of the racial minority movements" (1986, 91).

Although Banton places an emphasis on labels and identity options that is not characteristic of British sociology of race, he places an entirely different evaluation than Omi and Winant on the movements they refer to. Banton's interest in formal and informal classifications and how they change is informed by a concern to avoid the emergence or persistence of situations with hard group boundaries, where each individual must be in one or another group, and where in most or all social contexts status and life chances are determined by reference to the group into which one has been classified. The most severe case is where all individuals in a society are classified in one of two discrete groups, white and black, and where one group is absolutely subordinate to the other, usually by ongoing coercion and use of state power. In both historical and contemporary terms Banton has repeatedly identified the American Deep South as the worst case of this racial dualism (1983, 28–29). He seems to have two main objections to hard group boundaries, whether as legacies of domination or as strategies for equality. The first is that they lead, even if motivated by worthy goals, to social divisions, where individuals have few opportunities for social mobility and relate to each other not as individuals but as members of groups, and political reform takes the form of polarized confrontation and (avoidable) conflict. The second is that soft boundaries, overlapping, movement of individuals between groups or identification with one group in some contexts and with another in other contexts, increase options for individuals, especially those individuals who do not neatly fall into one group or another; it is therefore more compatible with the promotion of individual freedom and self-expression (Banton 1983, 396–97). It is interesting here to see a before-its-time "postmodernist" emphasis on multiple identities and boundary-crossing hybridity of the kind evoked by those such as Stuart Hall, who came to speak lyrically of "new ethnicities" and against "ethnic absolutism" and yet a few years earlier had embraced an absolutist racial dualism (cf. CCCS 1982 with Hall 1992a).

The historical case used to illustrate the opposite of the Deep South is Brazil. In the former a person's status depended first and foremost on whether they were deemed white or black, so that regardless of intelligence, education, occupation, income, social behavior, personal rectitude, and so on a black must always be inferior in status to a white and liable to certain disabilities and exclusion. In Brazil a dark skin color and non-European ancestry did and does count against an individual's status, but only as one of a number of factors of the kind listed in the previous sentence, such that a black lawyer can enjoy a higher social status than a white clerk (Banton 1988, 32–38). As a result, while many British sociologists and political reformers have looked to the race relations scene in America as an explanatory and normative guide, indeed as a source of prediction for British race relations ("What happens in American inner cities today, will happen in English inner cities in X years' time"), Banton has argued that Britain, which is probably an intermediate case between Latin America and the United States, can be guided also by the experience of the former (1988, 132). In particular, he claims that we should take advantage of the softening and overcoming of racial divisions by not encouraging the formation of polarized racial groups; the prejudice against a dark skin should be mixed with other measures of individual status in order to avoid the formation of racially exclusive classes and underclasses, of color as caste. He challenges American arrogance on the subject, suggesting that Americans can learn from others, including Britain, and argues that the views of eminent American social scientists, such as Talcott Parsons and Carl N. Degler, who suggest that racial dualism is a precondition of antiracism, are a form of American ethnocentrism (Banton 1983, 67–71). He could also have added that the malign effects of the hegemony of the dualistic approach are felt not just in its influence outside the United States but also within it. Clara Rodriguez's argument about the difficulties that Puerto Ricans have faced in America because they find it difficult to locate themselves in the American black-white, "race-over-culture racial classification system," predominantly defining themselves as "other" in the census and in response to survey questionnaires, applies no less to other communities from the Spanish-speaking world and to those from the Pacific and Asia. (While it is possible that a length of continuous residence in the United States makes Puerto Ricans more likely to try to fit into a black-white classification, there is an ambiguity as to which of these colors they are: the overwhelming majority of those who choose either, choose white, even though most of them are aware that others, especially whites, may classify them as black). Rodriguez's claim that through the Puerto Ricans "we are witnessing the strongest challenge ever to the U.S. bifurcation of race" (1991, 108) makes much more sense when one considers the new large presence in that country of people whose point of departure was neither Europe nor Africa, and the political emphasis on "diversity" that the new demography has given rise to.

Banton's perspective therefore leads to an entirely different evaluation of what Omi and Winant celebrate, namely, the emergence of black consciousness in America. While Omi and Winant identify with the formation of a black political ethnicity that followed the civil rights movement, Banton is at one with the thinking that gave rise to the civil rights movement. He describes this thinking as

> The political movement for racial equality in the first half of the twentieth century organised around an attack on mistaken racial beliefs and their use to justify racial inequalities. The idea that people could be meaningfully divided into racial categories and that they should be treated according to their category membership rather than their individual merits, was vigorously denied. The categories should be dissolved. (1988, 85)

He then goes on to begin a new paragraph on the later movement of black consciousness with *"all this was soon to change"* (my italics). Why should black consciousness *not* involve an attack on mistaken racial beliefs and the dissolving of categories? Only, I suggest, if we hold, as I believe Banton does, that the reality that racial categorization obscures is that of individuals.What really exists are individuals; hence if we were to stop treating people according to mistaken racial beliefs, we would treat people on their merits as individuals. In a number of places Banton suggests that voluntary ethnicity is the ideal of race relations (e.g., Banton 1983, 397), and he is well aware of the fact of group competition in the absence of racism; he therefore has some notion of relevant collectivities whose existence does not depend on false racial beliefs. Yet the equating of antiracism with individualism and of collectivities with coercion is, as stated earlier, a feature of his perspective even if it is not always consistently applied. I think, however, the fact of ethnicity (and the limitations of individualism) needs to be given far greater prominence. Underneath or beyond a case of racist categorization may be not just individuals but real collectivities, common and distinctive forms of thinking and behavior, language, custom, religion, and so on; not just modes of oppression but modes of being (Modood 1990b, 159). These may partly be a matter of continuities with pre-racism, partly a matter of absorption of racist categorization or of a molding by the forces of racism, partly a response to and struggle with those forces, partly new creative identities and hybridities and reaching out for new post-racism unities, including nonrace relations forms of solidarities, e.g., those of gender. The presence, absence, or contribution of these and other dimensions will vary from case to case. The only a priori point I am making is that ethnic groups can predate racism, can be shaped by it, but can also survive it; as the Omi and Winant case strikingly shows, they can use the challenge of racism to create new forms of solidarity and consciousness by invoking, among other things, ancestral legacies. Moreover, these suppressed collectivities may not be a matter of free choice, such that anyone can choose to be a member or cease to be a member at will. They may involve complex networks of obligations, solidarities, power hierarchies, communal sanctions, conformist pressures, and so on. They may not even be desirable collectivities, especially from the point of view of liberal individualism and other political philosophies.[2] These collectivities are what racism suppresses, and so antiracism entails a freeing of these collectivities from racist categorization and domination.

The collectivities in question are not primordial or permanent or ahistorical or isolated from other collectivities and social movements. Nevertheless, they are, at any one time, capable of some degree of historical and contemporary *description*. I believe this has an important implication for antiracism and for the study of race relations: we cannot identify, challenge, or oppose racist categorizations, stereotypes, and ideology without knowledge of these descriptions. An analysis of racism and a strategy of antiracism that is not informed by appropriate ethnic histories is seriously inadequate. Yet British race sociology and its Marxist alternatives are ahistorical in just this way, though it has to be said that Banton has consistently wanted to place the study of race within historical inquiry. Yet even then the emphasis has been on the history of racism, not on identifying what racists distorted. I am, admittedly, defining antiracism narrowly. Let us say that in a context such as contemporary Britain, beyond antiracism as opposition to the theorizing and practice of racist categorization, there is a further political goal: the well-being of ethnic minorities. My argument extends to this wider goal, for that too requires knowledge of ethnic minorities, of what collectivities exist. The inquiry into real collectivities (as opposed to racist representations) is, therefore, a precondition not just of defeating racism but also of allowing the victim groups to recover, to negotiate social space, and to flourish.

Race Relations and Class Relations

The criticism I have offered of Banton's perspective identifies an important shortcoming of his individualism: its tendency to ignore the existence of nonracial or only partially racial, yet nonvoluntary, collectivities. My argument is not simply between individualism and collectivism, nor between what Banton describes as anascopic (looking up from the "micro") approaches such as his own and catascopic (looking down from the "macro") approaches such as Robert Miles's (Banton 1991, 117). I would like to show this by a brief consideration of the relevant aspects of Miles's work.

On first sight the differences between Banton and Miles seem great. Miles's approach is avowedly Marxist; Banton's conclusions derive from a study of the Atlantic rim and of central Africa while Miles's intellectual and historical framework is a European one. Yet the two share many views in common. Certainly I find that many things with which I find myself in agreement in Banton's work are also found in Miles's, such as arguments that race and racism cannot be reduced to the historical experience of the "black-white" encounter; that racialization of Muslims, Jews, the Irish, Gypsies, Slavs, and so on is important to understanding the complexity and variety of racism (Miles 1989, 51–61); that "black" is not an adequate concept to capture the sociology of non-white people in contemporary Britain (Miles 1982); that the new non-white immigrants and their descendants do not form a separate socioeconomic class, nor are they distinctively located in one class (Miles 1987). Moreover, Miles uses a broad concept of racism, so that it is not necessarily linked to a biological division of humankind and can be linked to ethnicism and nationalism, yet he understands racism to be not social relations or practices per se but a set of false beliefs. Racism is a form of signifying "the other" (and hence "the we"), using phenotype as a criterion to explain cultural traits and to effect exclusionary practices with structural inequality as a result (1989, 71–72). Racism is an ideology, and like all ideologies, false, though it is not just a "false doctrine," for as an ideology it helps people to make practical sense of and order their world (80). With such a view of racism, Miles is clearly able to recognize that the objects of racism, racialized beings, have a reality of their own, and he is able to insist that a study of ethnic minorities in Britain cannot begin with them as merely "objects of racism and discrimination who only become subjects in their reaction to these ideological and practical constraints" (1982, 4).

Miles is in a position to replace false collectivities with true ones, in a position to overcome what I have identified as a deficiency in Banton. On his view we overcome the false ideology of race and race relations by linking it to a theory of material causes, not a narrow economistic theory but something broadly Marxist, in that the core idea is that of "modes" or "structures" of production that give rise to wider social systems in some causal systematic way (Miles 1982). This is all too familiar a view in Western social theory. Against it, I insist that the material explanation (though ideal-material is a far from happy distinction) is dependent on a case-by-case historical or contemporary study, not on the truth of a theory. Such case studies may seem like a truncated or superficial form of inquiry, what Miles calls mere "cataloguing" or "documenting" of "phenomenal relations," mere empiricism (62–64), but it is in fact historical understanding. By this I do not mean to imply that the agent's understanding of causes, of the wider picture, of long-term developments, and so on is the correct explanation of any events in question (cf. Modood 1989, 116). Rather, it is an expression of skepticism about a metaphysics of history, about theories of progress (e.g., Whig or Hegelian or Marxist) or any general theory of social change. It is skepticism about a theory of essential relations, i.e., of a conceptual framework stating what is essential and what is merely phenomenal, what is merely social consciousness and what is "the underlying historical and structural processes" (Miles 1982, 62–63)—skepticism about whether such theories are possible, and whether they are necessary for historical and social explanation. Of course, there are always issues of how to evaluate agents' self-understanding and of how to weigh up the different contributory causes that form part of the total picture, but, I repeat, we do not need a general theory in order to resolve those questions as they arise on a case-by-case basis. The illusion that we need a theory (and that it is possible) is born of the categorical division that Miles makes between description and explanation, between phenomenon and essence, between appearance and reality. Appearance and reality, I suggest, are usually closely intertwined and located in the same phenomenon; they are more like understanding and misunderstanding, a correct calculation and a mistaken one, seeing a picture clearly and under a shadow; it is most unhelpful to think of them as occupying different chunks or sites of social life or to suggest that the reality of a dimension of society (e.g., religion) lies in something outside itself (e.g., economics). It is, incidentally, because I do not accept the philosophical basis for such absolute distinctions that I find it a waste of ink to put "race" in scare quotes (as if class, nation, gender, inflation, justice, university, and so on are more natural than race and so less worthy of sociological scare quotes).

Even if we accept that studies of ethnicity fail to identify the material causes of racism—because they are studying something else— I fall back on my earlier and main point, which, as I understand it, Miles accepts: that just as racism (or its effects) has a reality, evidenced in differential treatment and statistical inequalities, that cannot be reduced to ethnicity, so, similarly, ethnicity has a reality that cannot be reduced to inquiries into the causes of racism. The objects of racism, ethnic groups, are then human subjects with pre-racialized historical and cultural collective identities that cannot be defined by race or racism, or by structures of production. This still leaves open the possibility that the facts of ethnicity (which of course will have economic and political dimensions and consequences) can sometimes explain, perhaps even in some loose sense predict, outcomes, if and to the extent that we can correctly identify groups and patterns of distinctive behavior, and that ethnography, broadly conceived, may form substantive explanatory inquiries.

The Role of Ethnicity

Besides Banton and Miles, John Rex has been of considerable influence in shaping the sociology of race in Britain and is another example of a theoretical approach without a central use for the concept of ethnicity. He looks on ethnicity as no more a form of group self-understanding than are physical characteristics. While he shares the view that race is an externally imposed identity on a group of people who may not have thought of themselves as being a group, he holds that ethnicity is also in this category. In the way that the categorizations of a dominant group can create a quasi-group out of those who share similar physical appearance, so an ethnic group is a quasi-group based on what are perceived by nonmembers to be distinctive cultural characteristics of a given population. Rex makes an explicit analogy with Marx's distinction between a "class-in-itself" and a "class-for-itself." The existence of a racial or ethnic quasi-group depends on its treatment by a dominant group or its socioeconomic location. The quasi-group becomes a group in the full sense when it uses its racial and/or cultural—and/or whatever other resources are available—to develop forms of organization to defend or promote its interests against the other group(s) (Rex 1986, 81). An ethnic population is no more a group than a population sharing merely physical characteristics, yet either could become a group if its members developed a sense of group identity and developed the means to pursue their collective interests.

Rex is clear that the study of what is called race relations is simply a variant of the sociology of group conflict or social stratification (1986, 17). Moreover, when it comes to understanding postwar Britain, he is in no doubt that "immigrant workers relate to their society of settlement primarily through the terms of their employment and through the industrial class struggles in which they engage" (1981, 18). Not that he believes that ordinary color-blind Marxian analysis is adequate to this situation. One of his important strictures against that approach is that the relevant historical context for British race relations is not just capitalism but the social structure of the British Empire taken as a whole. Another difference with the Marxian model is the identification of class other than by reference to the mode of production or to the economy in a strict sense. He is well known for having developed the application of the concept of housing classes, where significant life chances are determined by access to housing rather than by the division of labor or ownership of production (Rex and Moore 1967). He was thus able to demonstrate that, even where non-white immigrants might be integrated in the workplace, they were not necessarily accorded the same rights as their white peers in matters of residence and education. From our point of view, what is of importance is the implication that it is natural that ethnic quasi-groups will develop forms of class action that in some contexts may be based on the unity of labor, but in other contexts may be based on their special situation as recipients of racial discrimination. When ethnic community organization emerges in response to this situation, it cannot be dismissed as a form of false consciousness for it is genuinely related to differential rights and status (Rex 1981, 21).

While Rex could not be accused of a view of race relations in which ethnicity is squeezed out, nevertheless the insistence that some form of class or conflict analysis is primary and all else, including ethnicity, merely serves to flesh out this form of analysis results in a highly ambivalent view of the role of immigrant cultures and forms of life. He recognizes not only racism and how it affects the behavior of quasi-groups, but also how they will utilize their culture and sense of groupness to serve their interests; he goes so far as to say:

> transported and migrating workers will not be simply so much dust to be blown around by capitalism either in other colonies or in the metropolis itself, but rather men, constituted by their own social and cultural systems and acting accordingly. (1981, 8)

Nevertheless, he gives little indication of how ethnographic studies of ethnic quasi-groups, their internal structure and evolution, theoretically relate to his race relations paradigm. While he has no time for the grand theories of ethnicity, such as Barth's, which he believes to be sociologically naive, he welcomes piecemeal studies of (quasi-)ethnic groups (Rex 1986, ch. 5). He allows, for example, that there is "often a considerable disparity between the way a quasi-group saw it-self and the way in which others saw it," and that this is of interest to the sociologist of race relations, yet he does not offer the theoretical means of relating such discrepancies to what he sees as race relations (29). An issue such as this one—and there could be many others to do with differing perceptions on personal relationships, work, religion, and so on—cannot simply be a matter of "fine-grain." We do not have to accept semi-metaphysical theories of ethnicity to believe that issues about group identity, religion and secularity, gender roles, and so on have to be accommodated in a general perspective on race rela-tions, on what kinds of conflict are likely and when, or what kind of group consciousness and development is likely in a given social mix, and so on. Rex is clearly not against ethnographic studies and seems to believe that they are crucial to trying to understand what is likely to be the future of South Asian Muslims in Britain (1988, 1989). My point is that his paradigm of race relations as class conflict does not give any theoretical guidance on the interrelationship between the modes of being of an ethnic (quasi-) group and social domination and racial inequality.

Where there is an explicitly theoretical guidance on the inter-relating between the mode of being and the mode of oppression of a group, the two modes are likely to be seen as inhabiting different social worlds. An example of where this separation is theoretically embraced is Susan J. Smith. She holds that a group's racial identity is constructed by racist ideology and that this identity, whether it be true or false to the group's mode of being, is the only relevant identity when the subject of study is racial inequality (1989, 12). Oppressed groups will have cultural and religious contours, but these are not relevant to the study of race relations, say, of Bangladeshis in East London. Issues of culture are of significance only when the oppressed group develops a culture of resistance to structured subordination.

Thus, the only forms of culture relevant to race relations are those that directly contribute to imposing or resisting racial inequality. Consequently, Smith argues that this allows her to dispense with the notion of "ethnicity" (1989, 13). But this means that racial minority groups become shadows, for by becoming all race and no ethnicity, their very existence as a group depends on their perception by white people. This leads not only to inadequate explanations, and some-times nonexplanations, of events, but also to suppression of group identities, and it undermines a vital ingredient in antiracist strategies, group pride.

Challenging Stereotypes through Ethnic Self-Expression

How then are we to identify the groups that exist under or beyond or at least semi-independently of racist categorization? We cannot assume that behind every racial category is an ethnic group; an analysis in terms of individual merit or socioeconomic classes or interest groups may be appropriate in some contexts, as ethnicity may in others, and these different forms of analysis are not mutually exclusive. Nor can we expect that for each racial category there must be one ethnic group, for it is just as likely that a category groups people together who have nothing special in common (and quite possibly, histories of enmity and their own racial hierarchies) other than what the racist imputes. Racial categories may be like the artificial boundaries of some postcolonial independent states, reflecting colonial administrative divisions and great powers' geopolitics, forcing together those who do not belong together and separating those who do. I do not have anything like a theory of groups, and I doubt if we need one (though we may need one for specific purposes, e.g., to define ethnic group in law, as in the *Mandla v. Lee* case). Our inquiries must begin from a number of different starting points (including the approaches discussed here), but it is important to let groups speak for themselves. This will mean picking out groups that already feature on the landscape as well as those who, obscured by more familiar categories, claim to be groups, sometimes drawing on ancient, other times novel, emergent distinctions. Yet we will inevitably, as a starting point, have to be guided by racial categories, for they offer a negative pole of a dialectical encounter that can generate positive self-identities. We learn about groups as they actually exist, about their values and circumstances, about how they perceive themselves and their struggles and opportunities by allowing stereotyped groups to challenge, reinterpret, or falsify stereotypes about themselves. This is, of course, linked to the earlier discussion about the importance of self-definition and correct group labels in antiracism, in placing self-generated group identities at the center of racial equality. It also offers a means of converting ignorance, half-truth, and prejudice into knowledge, and I take that to be an important goal of any field of study.

I am aware that stereotypes are rarely entirely false; they are more a form of systematic vilification, deliberately focusing on unfavorable aspects or ignoring disadvantaged and oppressive circumstances. Stereotypes have the power to create perceptions and expectations, and behavior in accordance with those expectations, so that the stereotypes become self-fulfilling (e.g., if the police and magistrates think that young blacks are muggers, then disproportionate numbers of young blacks will be investigated, arrested, charged, prosecuted, and sentenced for such crimes, reinforcing the original stereotype and its vicious effects). Finally, stereotypes have as much to do with power and material interests as with ignorance and cannot be challenged without power. What Edward Said calls "Orientalism" is a very good, if somewhat sophisticated, example (1985). Nevertheless, despite the pull in other directions that these remarks legitimately suggest, I think they leave me able to continue to assert the central argument of this chapter: racialized groups represent forms of life that have a reality of their own that goes well beyond racialization, and, therefore, antiracism includes creating intellectual and practical space for that reality and for it to change, develop, adapt, borrow, synthesize, and so on under nonoppressive or nonracialized conditions.

Three

Ethnic Diversity and Racial Disadvantage in Employment

The postwar migration to Britain from the Caribbean and the Asian subcontinent, while based on imperial ties, was very much driven by economic imperatives. The rebuilding of the war-shattered economy created a demand for labor that could not be satisfied by the British population alone. The demand was particularly acute in the National Health Service, in public transport, and in many sectors of manufacturing; qualified and unqualified labor from the Caribbean and the subcontinent, especially young single men, were invited to fill the vacancies. Early studies of these migrants in the British economy show that, regardless of their social origins and qualification levels, Caribbean and Asian people were very largely confined to low-paid manual work and racial discrimination in recruitment was widespread, even after being outlawed (Daniel 1968; D. J. Smith 1977). The Policy Studies Institute (PSI) Third National Survey, undertaken in 1982, found that while some progress in relative job levels and earnings among these non-white groups had occurred, they were disproportionately suffering from high levels of unemployment despite the burgeoning number of self-employed in some groups (C. Brown 1984). Moreover, racial discrimination in the labor market seemed as prevalent if not as overt as before (C. Brown and Gay 1985). The Labour Force surveys of the late 1980s (T. Jones 1993) and the 1991 census

(Ballard and Kalra 1994) confirmed the trends of the early 1980s: the minorities were upwardly mobile, expanding in self-employment, but with much higher levels of unemployment than whites. It was abundantly clear, however, that each of these conditions applied to some rather than all Caribbean and Asian ethnic groups (Modood 1991). Increasingly, economic differences between migrants have become much more pronounced and much better substantiated by statistical data.

In the 1970s and 1980s theorists sought to explain racial inequality; the PSI Fourth Survey made clear that racial inequality *and* ethnic diversity needed to be explained. Insofar as there is a fundamental divide in employment by ethnicity, it is not a black-white divide but a divide between white, Chinese, African Asian,[1] and Indian men on the one hand, and Bangladeshi, Pakistani, and Caribbean men on the other. There are difficulties in creating a single measure that encompasses both sexes, but if both sexes are taken into account, there seems to be a tripartite division. The Chinese and African Asians are in broad parity with whites, the Indians and Caribbeans are somewhat disadvantaged, and the Bangladeshis and Pakistanis are extremely disadvantaged.

Upward Mobility and Racial Disadvantage

The findings of the Fourth Survey[2] depict a pattern of inequality but also of a divergence in the circumstances of the main minorities. Many aspects of this diversity are not new and, especially the radically differing economic-educational profiles of African Asians and Indians on the one hand, and Pakistanis and Bangladeshis on the other, were apparent in the 1970s (D. J. Smith 1977). They were somewhat obscured in the 1980s when attention came to be focused on the disproportionate impact of unemployment on the ethnic minorities. This, combined with a tendency to overgeneralize from the condition of the worst-off groups to the minorities *as such*, led sociologists to continue to assert that the ethnic minorities were "at the bottom of the occupational and income scale" (Anthias and Yuval-Davis 1992, 62). This chapter will present the findings of the Fourth Survey on job levels and earnings and examine whether the differences between minorities are consistent over time and, if not, whether they are narrowing or widening. For example, are some groups experiencing more mobility across job levels than others?

Job Levels

Table 1 presents male job levels as found in the 1982 and 1994 PSI surveys. For the sake of comparison with 1982, the self-employed are not included, even though the 1994 survey found that self-employment disproportionately contributed to the presence of South Asians and Chinese in the higher job categories. The table shows that the period 1982–94 was one of structural change and that all groups, though in differing degrees, participated in the change. The main change is a movement from manual to nonmanual work. In 1982 a fifth of white and African Asian male employees who had jobs were in the top employment category; in 1994 it was over a quarter, though with whites overtaking the African Asians. The Caribbeans and Indians, starting from a much lower base, have roughly doubled their representation in the top category of employees, but the mobility of Pakistani employees has been more modest and may even have been proportionately downward for Bangladeshis. There is no 1982 data for the Chinese, but the 1994 survey confirms the census records, that of these groups the Chinese are most represented in the top nonmanual category.

For white men it seems that this upward movement has come from contraction in skilled manual and foremen work, whereas junior and intermediate nonmanual work have grown for the minorities, and the proportions engaged in semiskilled and unskilled manual work has declined. With the exception of the African Asians, in 1982 about four-fifths of employed South Asian and Caribbean men were in manual work; in 1994 it was about two-thirds. For the Caribbeans the loss is evenly spread across the manual categories; for the South Asians, especially the Indians, their presence in semiskilled jobs has declined. The employment profile of Indian men has shifted most substantially during this period. At the start of the 1980s they were preponderantly in manual work, like the Caribbeans, Pakistanis, and Bangladeshis; however, while these three groups are still largely in manual work, the Indian profile has become much closer to that of the whites, African Asians, and Chinese. The Caribbeans, Pakistanis, and Bangladeshis have experienced some movement up the occupational hierarchy, but their overall position continues to be a disadvantaged one compared to the other groups.

A good way of capturing this lessening of racial disadvantage among male employees is by scoring the job levels on a common scale.

Table 1. Job levels of male employees in 1982 and 1994 (percent).

Job levels	White		Caribbean		Indian		African Asian		Pakistani		Bangladeshi		Chinese	
	1982	1994	1982	1994	1982	1994	1982	1994	1982	1994	1982	1994	1982	1994
Professional/managerial/employers	19	30	5	11	11	19	22	26	10	14	10	7	41
Other nonmanual	23	21	10	20	13	28	21	31	8	18	7	22	26
Skilled manual and foremen	42	31	48	37	34	23	31	22	39	36	13	2	5
Semiskilled manual	13	14	26	26	36	22	22	17	35	28	57	65	20
Unskilled manual	3	4	9	6	5	7	3	3	8	4	12	4	8
Nonmanual total	42	51	15	29	24	47	43	57	18	32	17	29	67
Manual total	58	49	85	69	76	53	57	43	82	68	83	71	33

Source: Modood et al. 1997.

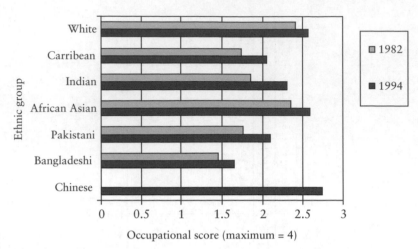

Figure 1. Relative improvement in male employees' job levels, 1982–94.
Source: *Modood et al. 1997.*

One can then derive an average for each ethnic group for 1982 and 1994 and measure the degree of movement.[3] In Figure 1 it can be seen that all the minority groups made relatively more improvement during this period than whites, though only African Asians have achieved parity with whites (the Chinese are best off in 1994, but there is no 1982 data for comparison).

It is important to bear in mind that during this period there was a growth in self-employment that benefited ethnic minority men. In fact, it makes much more difference to the ethnic minority than white men's job levels; within both the nonmanual and manual job levels self-employment marks an upward movement for ethnic minority men. This is particularly important because of the importance of self-employment in the economic profile of certain groups: a third of all Chinese, Indian, African Asian, and Pakistani men in paid work rely on self-employment (Modood et al. 1997; Modood, Metcalf, and Virdee 1998).

Job Levels: Women

The pattern of women's movement across job levels has some parallels with that of the men, especially in the growth of nonmanual work, which has been greater for women than men, and for some minorities more than white women (Table 2). While women continue to be fewer than men in the professional/managerial/employer category, there has been a significant increase among white women in these jobs; the position of African Asian women seems to be slightly better than in 1982, but the other minority women are much more poorly represented in this category, and Indians possibly worse so than a decade earlier. The exception is the Chinese, who were not included in the 1982 survey, but were very much concentrated at the top end of the job levels in 1994. Intermediate and junior nonmanual work has grown substantially since 1982 for all minority groups for whom data allows a comparative analysis, and Caribbeans, Indians, and African Asians are now disproportionately in this category. Pakistani and Indian women in full-time jobs are still, however, disproportionately manual workers, especially at the semiskilled level.[4]

If we measure the movements in women's occupational levels through scoring the job levels on a common scale, as we did for the men, we get the results displayed in Figure 2. This shows that Caribbean women have made the most progress, closely followed by white and African Asian women. The result is that white and African Asian women maintain the relatively advantaged position they had in 1982,

Table 2. Job levels of full-time female employees in 1982 and 1994 (percent).

	White		Caribbean		Indian		African Asian		Paki- stani	Chi- nese
	1982	1994	1982	1994	1982	1994	1982	1994	1994	1994
Professional/ managerial/ employers	7	21	1	4	5	3	7	14	7	38
Intermediate and junior nonmanual	55	58	52	76	35	61	52	66	60	55
Skilled manual and foremen	5	3	4	2	8	2	3	3	3	–
Semiskilled manual	21	17	36	18	50	32	36	17	29	7
Unskilled manual	11	1	7	1	1	3	3	–	–	–
Nonmanual total	62	78	53	78	40	64	59	81	66	93
Manual total	37	21	47	21	59	37	42	19	33	7

Source: Modood et al. 1997.

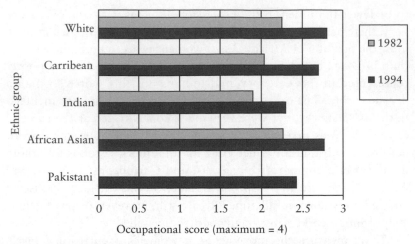

Figure 2. Relative improvement in female employees' job levels, 1982–94.
Source: *Modood et al. 1997.*

but Caribbean women had almost caught up with them in 1994. Indian women had made less progress and were on the whole in a similar position to Pakistani women (the latter are much less likely to be in employment, and in fact were too few in 1982 for comparison with 1994). The position of Chinese women is by far the best of all women.

These findings about job levels are consistent with the general trends of upward mobility and from manual into nonmanual work identified in successive Labour Force Surveys (T. Jones 1993) as well as in the 1991 census, though they are not as sanguine about the presence of Pakistani and Bangladeshi men, and ethnic minority women in general, in the top jobs category.[5] By comparing Labour Force Survey data for 1966 with 1991, Iganski and Payne (1996) are able to show that there has been a substantial decline in the differentials between whites and each of the main ethnic minority groups.

Earnings: Men
Earnings data can be a useful alternative way of looking at equality in employment, especially as job-level analysis uses some very broad categories so that any inequalities within a category may be missed. Earnings data offer a more precise comparative measure, but suffer from their own limitations. People have a reluctance to state their earn-

ings to researchers and may not give accurate answers. There was a high refusal rate for the earnings questions in the Fourth Survey among South Asians. Nevertheless, given the survey's large sample sizes, it offers one of the best, if not the best, sources of data on comparative earnings.[6] Table 3 compares the mean weekly earnings of full-time male employees of the different ethnic and religious groups. The average for ethnic minority men was below that for white men, but there was parity between whites, African Asians, and Chinese, with the Caribbean men a bit behind, Indians even more so, and the Pakistanis and Bangladeshis a third or more below whites. The inclusion of religious groups in Table 3 allows one to see that the addition of Indian and African Asian Muslims to Pakistanis and Bangladeshis raises the Muslim mean weekly earnings from what it might otherwise be.

This comparison of African Asians and Hindus to other South Asians is a striking new development that has not been properly recorded before. At the time of the PSI Second Survey of Racial Minorities in 1974, it was clear that the African Asians, who at the time were recent refugees from East Africa, were much better qualified, had a better facility in English, and were more likely to be in nonmanual work than Indians; correspondingly, Indians were in a much better position than the Pakistanis (D. J. Smith 1977). On the other hand, perhaps partly because of their recent arrival in Britain and perhaps because of their larger numbers in white-collar work in which overtime and shift-work premiums were not available, their median gross male weekly earnings were 15 percent below that of whites, 10 percent below Indians, and were in fact the lowest for all groups (83). The PSI Third Survey in 1982 found that while average earnings for Asian men were nearly 15 percent below those of white, there was little difference between Indians and African Asians, or between Hindus and Sikh, both these pairs of Asian groups being much better off than Pakistanis and, especially, Bangladeshis (C. Brown 1984, Tables 109 and 114). By 1994, the tripartite earnings differential between whites, Indians, and Pakistanis is still in place, as it had been in the previous two decades, but African Asian men have moved from the bottom to the top of these relativities. In the 1970s they were averaging less than the Pakistanis, in the 1980s they were equaling the Indians, and in the 1990s they seem to have caught up with the whites. Similarly, in the 1980s Hindu and Sikh men averaged the same earnings,

Table 3. Male full-time employees' earnings.

	White	Caribbean	Indian	African Asian	Paki-stani	Bangla-deshi	Chinese	Hindu	Sikh	Muslim	All ethnic minorities
Mean weekly earnings*	£336	£306	£287	£335	£227	£191	£336**	£338	£249	£223	£296
Comparison to earnings of whites		-9%	-15%	same	-32%	-43%	same	same	-26%	-34%	-12%
Weighted count	541	255	154	152	76	42	72	162	84	140	751
Unweighted count	493	179	169	144	113	78	43	154	84	233	726

Source: Modood et al. 1997.

*Means calculated from midpoints of 16 earnings bands.

**Cell size less than 50.

but in the 1990s Hindus earn over a quarter more than Sikhs. The earnings position of African Asians found here is consistent with earlier findings about their job levels. As a group they were always highly qualified and were largely in the professions, administration, and business in East Africa. After becoming political refugees, rebuilding their livelihoods, and establishing themselves in Britain, they seem to have made considerable progress in re-creating their prosperity.

Earnings: Women

The position of full-time women employees was very different from that of men's. Female weekly earnings were considerably lower than men's in all ethnic groups, but the biggest gender gap was among whites (Table 4). As a matter of fact, the average earnings of ethnic minority women was better than for white women, though it is unlikely that this extends to Pakistani or Bangladeshi women (the cell size is too small for certainty). This is an important finding that shows the limits of the idea of "double discrimination," the view that besides the general disadvantage of women, non-white women suffer an additional inequality (Bhavnani 1994).[7] Caribbean women had the highest average earnings (or possibly Chinese women: the Chinese sample was rather small). The differential between groups of women, however, was less than for men. Interestingly, there was no difference in the averages for Indians and African Asians, and yet the earnings for Sikh women were significantly less than for Hindus.

Finally, as with job levels, so too with earnings, it is important to bear in mind that some minority groups are disproportionately involved in self-employment, a category that has not been included in the analysis. In fact, the survey found that while white male employees earned more than their self-employed counterparts, the reverse was true of ethnic minorities except African Asian men (Modood et al. 1997, 121). The mean earnings for self-employed Indians and Chinese were over a fifth higher than those of whites, while for Pakistanis they were a fifth lower. Yet as Pakistani self-employed males earned more than those employed by others, in general self-employment contributed to narrowing the earnings gap. Ethnic minority women who were self-employed on average earned more than their white peers (though the sample sizes are relatively small).

Table 4. Female full-time employees' earnings.

	White	Caribbean	Indian	African Asian	Pakistani/ Bangladeshi	Chinese	Hindu	Sikh	Muslim	All ethnic minorities
Mean weekly earnings*	£244	£267	£252	£254	£181**	£287**	£258	£223	£221**	£259
Comparison to earnings of whites		+10%	+3%	+4%	-26%	+26%	+5%	-9%	-9%	+6%
Weighted count	345	278	103	90	34	48	93	65	46	552
Unweighted count	337	206	94	72	36	28	81	50	47	436

Source: Modood et al. 1997.

*Means calculated from midpoints of 16 earnings bands.

**Cell size less than 50.

Economic Mobility and Racial Disadvantage

There is an overall trend of progress in the job levels and earnings of ethnic minorities and a narrowing of the differentials between the ethnic majority and the minorities. As all the ethnic minorities have higher, sometimes much higher, levels of participation in postcompulsory education (see chapter 4), and increasing levels of admission into higher education (eighteen- to twenty-seven-year-old Asians, excluding Bangladeshis, are more than twice as likely to be in higher education than their white peers), it is most likely that the minorities will continue to improve their relative position in the economy. The differentials between minorities may become more pronounced as some groups consolidate the advantaged profile they have begun to develop.

If today the ethnic minorities cannot be collectively described as being disproportionately confined to low-skill, low-paid work, it may be because they are returning to their premigration occupational levels. It is sometimes asserted that migrants "have tended to be from the poorest and most underprivileged groups of their countries of origin" (Anthias and Yuval-Davis 1992, 77). This is almost certainly not the case. An analysis of 1972 data from the Nuffield Social Mobility Survey found that nearly a quarter of the non-white migrants had professional class origins, predominantly higher professional class, which was twice the proportion of the native English; and over half had social origins in either the petty bourgeoisie or the farming classes (the figure for the English was 16 percent) (Heath and Ridge 1983). The analysis shows that there was, however, a serious downward social mobility as people of professional origins failed to secure professional posts, and the petty bourgeoisie was "proletarianized": children of self-employed traders, artisans, and farmers met the demand for labor in British factories (ibid.). An earlier PSI study also found that the initial effect of migration was downward social mobility as the overwhelming majority of migrants could get only manual work, including persons with academic qualifications, even degrees, who may have been in white-collar work before migration (D. J. Smith 1977). The Fourth Survey suggests that among the first generation, Indian men were among the most qualified and, one might conjecture, suffered particularly from racial bias that made it difficult for them to get nonmanual work. The initial downward mobility was accepted because it still offered much higher earnings than available in the countries of origin, but it is not surprising that those individuals who have been able to resist the proletarian character ascribed to migrant labor and their families should have endeavored to do so. It is therefore not inappropriate to see the above-average upward social mobility among some minorities as a reversal of the initial downward social mobility produced by migration and racial discrimination in the early years of settlement in Britain.

This certainly has not developed to a point where there is an ethnic parity or where the concept of racial disadvantage is redundant. Table 5 sets out the extent of the employment disadvantages of ethnic minority men compared to white men. Six key indicators of advantage/disadvantage have been chosen, and for this analysis employees and self-employed are combined. The figures in Table 5 are derived from treating the position of whites as a baseline against which the minorities are given a score. Where the positions are the same, this is represented by a 1; where a minority group is under- or overrepresented relative to whites, a figure is given showing the scale of the under- or overrepresentation. Table 5 shows that most, but not all, of the groups are still disadvantaged, but not evenly so. However, all minorities are substantially underrepresented in the most elite jobs, employers and managers in large establishments. This could be said to be a glass ceiling that affects all non-white men equally.

Beyond that, the differences between the minorities are as important as their position relative to whites. By the rest of the measures, the Chinese are more advantaged than whites, and the African Asians are broadly similar to whites. The Indians are somewhat disadvantaged, but are closer to whites than to the remaining three minority groups who despite any progress they may have made continue to be significantly disadvantaged. Caribbean men at some points are in a similar position or more advantaged than Indians but are significantly more disadvantaged in relation to job levels and unemployment. The Pakistanis are in all respects more disadvantaged than the Caribbeans except that due to their much higher level of self-employment, which yields on average low incomes, they score slightly higher for presence in the professional, managers, and employers category. Finally, the Bangladeshis are as a group the most disadvantaged. Ethnic minority men fall therefore into two broad groups: those who are close to parity with whites (the Chinese, African Asians, Indians), and the others who are significantly disadvantaged.

Table 6 offers a similar analysis of employment disadvantages for

Table 5. Employment disadvantage of ethnic minority men.

Advantage/Disadvantage	Chinese	African Asian	Indian	Caribbean	Pakistani	Bangladeshi
1. Employers and managers in large establishments	0.5	0.3	0.5	0.5	0.3	0.01
2. Professionals, managers, and employers	1.5	1.0	0.8	0.5	0.6	0.6
3. Supervisors	0.9	0.8	0.6	0.7	0.4	0.4
4. Earnings	1.0	1.0	0.9	0.9	0.7	0.6
5. Unemployment rates	0.6	0.9	1.3	2.1	2.5	2.8
6. Long-term unemployed*	–	(1.6)	3.1	5.9	7.7	7.7

Source: Modood et al. 1997.

Note: Disadvantage is expressed as a relation to whites, who are taken to represent 1. A figure below 1 gives the degree of underrepresentation in that category compared with whites of the same sex. The figures include the self-employed.

*Those unemployed for more than two years as a proportion of those economically active in their ethnic group, relative to white men.

Table 6. Employment disadvantage of ethnic minority women.

Advantage/Disadvantage	Chinese	Caribbean	African Asian	Indian	Pakistani	Bangladeshi
1. In paid work*	1.1	1.0	1.0	0.9	0.3	0.1
2. Professionals, managers, and employers	1.9	0.3	0.8	0.7	0.8	–
3. Higher and intermediate nonmanual	1.4	0.9	0.7	0.8	1.1	–
4. Supervisors	1.1	1.1	0.8	0.6	0.6	–
5. Earnings	–	1.1	1.0	1.0	–	–
6. Unemployed	0.7	2	1.3	1.3	4.3	4.4

Source: Modood et al. 1997.

Note: Disadvantage is expressed as a relation to whites, who are taken to represent 1. A figure below 1 gives the degree of underrepresentation in that category compared with whites of the same sex. The figures include the self-employed.

*Based on all women aged sixteen to sixty not in retirement, full-time education, or long-term illness.

women. The key measures used in Table 6 are not the same as those used for men but reflect the fact that the low participation rate of some groups of women is an indicator and source of disadvantage. Moreover, too few women are managers and employers in large establishments to generate large enough sample sizes for analysis. Table 6 shows that the scale of differentials between women of different ethnic groups is much smaller than is the case for men, but otherwise the ethnic groups are stacked up in a similar order as men. There are, however, two distinctive features in the comparative circumstances of women. First, the low economic activity rates for Pakistani and Bangladeshi women creates a division between these groups of women and all others that does not exist for men. It could be said to have some parallel with the high levels of Pakistani and Bangladeshi male unemployment, which also exists among women from these groups, for both Pakistani and Bangladeshi men and women have in common very low levels of paid work, especially as employees. The second difference in employment disadvantage between men and women is that the position of Caribbean women relative to white and other women is much better than Caribbean men's. While Caribbean women are grossly underrepresented in the top jobs category and have a high rate of unemployment, they are strongly represented in intermediate nonmanual work and as a result have an above-average share of supervisory posts and above-average earnings.

If we combine the sexes, the position of the minorities in employment relative to whites seems to fall into three bands:

1. Disadvantage confined to top jobs in large organizations: Chinese and African Asians
2. Relative disadvantage: Indians and Caribbeans
3. Severe disadvantage: Pakistanis and Bangladeshis

Explaining Diversity

Racial disadvantage, then, continues to be a fact even if it does not apply to all ethnic minority groups. Moreover, this disadvantage is partly attributable to discrimination in employment. Controlled tests, whereby white and ethnic minority persons respond to advertised vacancies for which they are equally suitable, have been conducted since the 1960s and tend to reproduce the result that at least one-third of private employers discriminate against Caribbean applicants, Asian applicants, or both (Daniel 1968; D. J. Smith 1977; C. Brown and Gay 1985; Simpson and Stevenson 1994). Discrimination is found not just in face-to-face encounters or telephone calls but has also been found in tests using written applications where it is clear from the applicant's name or biographical details that they are not white (Noon 1993; Esmail and Everington 1993). BBC Radio 5 sent almost identical curriculum vitae from six fictitious candidates to fifty firms in 2004 and found that while the two candidates with "white" names were invited to interview on 23 percent of the applications, the results for those with "African" and "Muslim" names were 13 percent and 9 percent respectively (http://news.bbc.co.uk/go/pr/fr/-/hi/business/ 3885213.stm). The Commission for Racial Equality continues every year to publish findings of direct or indirect discrimination in the practices of specific employers and sometimes whole professions or industries such as accountancy (CRE 1987) or hotels (CRE 1991b). The number of complaints of racial discrimination made by individuals to the CRE and to industrial tribunals rises most years. The Fourth Survey found that 90 percent of white people and three-quarters of minority ethnic persons believe that some employers discriminate. One in five of the minority ethnic respondents said they had been refused a job on racial grounds; nearly half had had this experience at least once in the previous five years (Modood et al. 1997, 131).

The structure of inequality cannot be explained simply by reference to differences in qualification levels or to racial bias. Vaughan Robinson suggests three possible lines of inquiry to "explain the disparity between groups which share similar skin colour" (1990, 284). One approach "stresses the differential incorporation or marginalisation of the groups and the impact that this might have upon the desire for social mobility in a society which is perceived as alien" (284). Malcolm Cross, for example, has distinguished between class exclusion and class segmentation as two different socially structured forms of racial inequality. While high levels of representation among the unemployed and low-paid is a symptom of class exclusion, class segmentation takes place when a group is allowed to enter the higher occupational classes but is confined to a subset of the higher occupations (1994, 232). Cross believes that the Caribbeans are subject to class exclusion, while the racism against Asians within British employment practices has the effect of incorporation through segmentation of the existing class structure.

The distinction between class segmentation and class exclusion may be an important one, but Cross's application of it through an Asian-Caribbean dichotomy is unfeasible. Pakistanis and Bangladeshis fit Cross's definition of the excluded much better, especially as the high levels of Pakistani unemployment predate those of the Caribbeans and consisted of actual job losses as the textile and related industries collapsed during the 1970s and early 1980s. In contrast, for the Caribbeans unemployment rose more gradually as successive cohorts of those leaving or graduating from school found that the supply of jobs, especially for those without qualifications, had dried up. Robinson found that while 5 percent of all workers who had a job in 1971 did not have one in 1981, 8 percent of Caribbeans did not, and 19 percent of Pakistanis did not (1990, 280). Cross thinks that the longer-term prospects of the Pakistanis and Bangladeshis are of class segmentation rather than exclusion because, in contrast to the Caribbeans, economic marginalization has not led to a sociopolitical alienation. The Pakistanis and Bangladeshis are still committed to economic advancement; the young will acquire, he believes, qualifications that will enable them to compete for the kind of jobs that will be available. The impact of racism and economic disadvantage seems, however, to have blunted the motivation of a sizable proportion of younger Caribbeans (Cross 1994, ch. 8, 10). While there is some truth in this contrast, the prediction that Pakistanis and Bangladeshis will develop a similar class profile to other South Asians grossly understates the current scale of the disadvantage of Pakistanis and Bangladeshis and takes no account of the cultural differences among South Asians (Modood, Beishon, and Virdee 1994); of a political alienation, sometimes expressed in terms of a political Muslim identity, which is itself a product of and further stimulates anti-Muslim prejudice (Modood 1990a); or of anxiety about a possible trend of criminalization among young Pakistanis and Bangladeshis, which in some ways parallels the experience of Caribbean male youth (Nahdi 1994).

In any case, the position of young Caribbean men (and to some extent women) is itself paradoxical: some of the highest rates of unqualified and unemployed and also some of the highest average earnings (Modood et al. 1997). It is possible that the high earnings averages are a product of the high unemployment, for by taking more potentially lower earners out of the earnings sample, the sample is biased in favor of higher earners, especially among manual workers. Yet it does not have this effect on Pakistanis and Bangladeshis, who also have high rates of unemployment among those sixteen to thirty-five years old. It is more likely that the paradoxical findings are pointing to an economic polarization among young Caribbean men who are to be disproportionately found among both the long-term unemployed and the middle band of earners. In this respect the Caribbeans may be becoming more like the Pakistanis and Bangladeshis rather than vice versa. The aspect of these latter groups that probably suggests to Cross that they will progress like the other South Asians is the presence within them of a highly qualified professional and business class. Yet this class is not new among Pakistanis and Bangladeshis: it was picked up in the PSI surveys of the 1970s and 1980s (D. J. Smith 1977; C. Brown 1984). What is remarkable is that it has hardly grown between 1982 and 1994 (see Table 1). Indeed, if the unemployed are added back into the figures on which the analysis is based, there is no growth at all among Pakistanis and Bangladeshis in the proportion of men in the top jobs category, in contrast to other groups. At a time of general upward mobility for men, this would in fact be a relative decline. The Fourth Survey suggests that in relation to qualifications of migrants, the internal polarity among those from the subcontinent, with a disproportionate number having degrees and a disproportionate number having no qualifications and many speaking little English, was in strong contrast to the relative homogeneity of the Caribbeans (Modood et al. 1997). This tendency among Caribbeans of disproportionate grouping around the middle is also found in Robinson's (1990) longitudinal study of social mobility between 1971 and 1981, as also in the findings about earnings in this chapter. The paradoxical statistics about young Caribbean men may be pointing to a postmigration, a relatively recent internal polarization among Caribbeans, while the class divisions among Pakistanis and Bangladeshis, and the divisions between these two and the other South Asian groups, have deepened by the collapse of those industries that provided jobs to the Pakistanis in the 1970s, but in fact stretch back to premigration origins.

While Cross is right not to want to conflate the disadvantaged profiles of Caribbeans with those of Pakistanis and Bangladeshis, the differences in question cannot be captured by his differential use of exclusion and segmentation and give no grounds for his Caribbean-Asian dichotomy or for projecting an optimistic view of upward social mobility for Pakistanis and Bangladeshis. If one wanted to explore these questions further, one could perhaps proceed by asking how differently postindustrial long-term unemployment would impact on excluded groups if one was composed of tightly knit, hierarchically organized families and communities and ongoing connections with the country of origin, and the other was not. Such a reformulation would not be a basis for reliable predictions (for there are too many other variables to take into account, especially in relation to changes in the economy), but it would bring one closer to raising some of the issues that lie behind Cross's discussion. It also leads us to a form of explanation identified by Robinson.

Robinson's second possible explanation for the disparity between minorities "stresses the groups' histories prior to migration, and the traditions and resources they can therefore mobilise to gain mobility" (1990, 284). This approach has been most developed to explain the phenomenon of immigrant self-employment as found in many countries, especially in North America, and which is often critical in facilitating upward social mobility (Waldinger, Aldrich, and Ward 1990) and connects with a sociological tradition that arose through studies of European migration to the large American cities in the early part of this century (Lal 1990). While the resources in question are of a complex sort and relate to culture, religion, and gender, one simple measure is qualifications. There does seem to be a strong correlation between the qualifications of the first generation and the extent of current disadvantage depicted in Tables 5 and 6 (Modood et al. 1997). This lends particular support to the general view that the post-migration social mobility of groups consists of the re-creation of a comparable class profile the group had in the country of origin before migration. We have, of course, seen that similar qualifications do not yield similar occupational advantages for all groups, and it is likely that some of the differences are explained by forms of direct and indirect discrimination.

This leads to the third possible explanation of disparities posed by Robinson: that different groups are stereotyped differently, perhaps influenced by the roles allotted to groups during British colonial rule (1990, 285). In chapter 2 details were given of research on middle managers' perceptions of minority workers and their ethnicity in the early 1980s that found that stereotypes (not always negative) related to two groupings, Caribbeans and South Asians, and that radically different stereotypes were held of the two groups. The most common view expressed of Caribbean workers was that they were lazy, happy-go-lucky, or slow, while the most common view of Asians was that they were hard workers (see chapter 2 and Jenkins 1986). It has been argued that similar antithetical images of the main non-white groups are in fact pervasive in commonsense and media representations (Bonnett 1993). In the last decade or so, it has increasingly been argued that contemporary racism cannot be understood only in terms of an undifferentiated color racism, but that groups are racialized, and praised or condemned, on the basis of alleged cultural traits rather than any kind of biology (Barker 1981; Gilroy 1987; Cohen 1988), and that groups such as South Asian Muslims suffer a distinctive and complex kind of racism (Modood 1992, 1996a). The Fourth Survey found that nearly half of South Asians who complained of racial discrimination in recruitment believed that their religion was a factor in the discrimination, and so did a quarter of Caribbeans, further suggesting the complex nature of discrimination as perceived by those who believe they have direct experience of it (Modood et al. 1997, 132–33). The survey also found that all groups believed that the most prejudice is directed at Asians and/or Muslims (133–34).

It has to be said that it would be wrong to expect racial disadvantage, both its decline and its persistence, to be only or even primarily explained in terms of race, discrimination, or ethnic differences. There is a general agreement that the most important fact is of economic restructuring. The changes in job levels for the minorities, no less than for the majority population, are above all a consequence of the continuing loss of jobs in manufacturing, especially those that require low levels of skills, in favor of the service sector, which has seen a continuous growth in higher-level jobs and lower-level part-time work. It is this fundamental and continuing shift, together with the demographic shortages that have increased job opportunities for women and some minorities, that is the cause of the differential advantage and disadvantage experienced by the different minority groups and is the context in which the more specific factors that have been discussed are played out.

Conclusion

Ethnic minorities in Britain can no longer be said "to be at the bottom of the occupational and income scale." While this description is true of some minorities, others are less likely to be at the bottom than white people. The commonality between the ethnic minorities is that they are less likely than white people to be at the top, but some minorities are now well represented near the top and in the middle. In general, the ethnic minorities are reversing the initial downward mobility produced by migration and racial discrimination in the early years of settlement in Britain. This is happening despite the persistence of racial discrimination and the emergence of new forms of prejudice, such as that against Muslims. Nevertheless, while some groups are reestablishing their premigration middle-class profile, some minority groups or subgroups are among the most marginal and disadvantaged people in Britain. The confluence of the continuing severe disadvantage of Pakistanis and Bangladeshis with the rise of an anti-Muslim prejudice marks one of the biggest challenges to racial egalitarians in Britain today. While the disadvantage of Pakistanis and Bangladeshis actually predates the rise of anti-Muslim prejudice, the latter threatens to exacerbate the former and to prevent the formation of goodwill required to act against the chronic disadvantage of Pakistanis and Bangladeshis.

Postscript

The Fourth Survey and in particular Modood et al. (1997), on which this chapter draws, was one of the first systematic demonstrations that non-white groups had very different employment positions and trajectories and that Asian Muslims, particularly Bangladeshis and Pakistanis, had a position that was much worse than that of other groups, though the position of young Caribbean men was worrying, too. This analysis has been confirmed by all subsequent surveys and the 2001 census and has been incorporated into government policy, which began to formulate group-differentiated policies targeted at the most disadvantaged groups in the late 1990s, especially with the objective of improving the qualifications and skill levels of recent and prospective entrants to the labor market.

The Cabinet Office (2003) report, drawing on a number of sources from the mid- to late 1990s and in particular on the Labour Force Survey for 2000, confirmed the patterns discussed in this chapter, not least the differential earnings, while pointing out that all minorities suffer an earnings "ethnic penalty" in relation to their qualifications (Heath and McMahon 1997; Berthoud 2000; for first signs that this penalty might not be persisting for British-born graduates, see Heath and McMahon 2005). Moreover, drawing on secondary analysis of the Fourth Survey, especially M. Brown (2000), it elaborated the differences between Hindus, Sikhs, and Asian Muslims, confirming the severely deprived position of the latter. Accordingly, it reinforced the argument for targeted interventions with a special focus on disadvantaged Muslims.

The 2001 census also confirmed the pattern in relation to levels of economic activity, unemployment, self-employment, and job levels. For example, it found that while 11 percent of employed white people were in professional occupations, for Indians and Chinese it was respectively 18 and 19 percent, and for Bangladeshis and black Caribbeans it was 8 percent. It also brought out some aspects of what this implies for occupational segregation: "one in six Pakistani men in employment were cab drivers or chauffeurs, compared with one in 100 White British men. Two in five Bangladeshi men were either cooks or waiters, compared with one in 100 White British men. The proportion of Indian men working as doctors, at 5 per cent, was almost 12 times higher than the rate for all White British men" (National Statistics Online 2004).

The 2001 census included—for the first time in 150 years—a question on religion, allowing analysis by religious groups. The results are, again, in line with the Fourth Survey. For example, while the national unemployment rate was 5 percent, it was 7 percent for Hindus and 14 percent for Muslims (and, interestingly, it was less than 4 percent for Jews). Or again, while 16 percent of the economically active were in higher management and professional occupations, the figures for Jews, Hindus, and Muslims were 26 percent, 20 percent, and 12 percent respectively.

It is clear, then, that there is no simple black-white divide, nor a black-white-Asian divide; some non-white groups are catching up or overtaking whites, while others are severely disadvantaged. The inclusion of categories such as Jewish (and Irish) in the census suggests that the position of whites also may be ethnically and religiously varied.

Four

Ethnic Differentials in Educational Performance

In Britain the groups commonly referred to as ethnic minorities did not just happen to have recently migrated and settled in Britain, nor do they just happen to suffer racism in Britain. Rather, they are groups whose identity in British society is shaped by migration and race as well as distinctive ethnicities. They are "racialised ethnicities" (Modood, Berthoud, and Nazroo 2002; see also CMEB 2000). Ethnicity, race, and migration must shape the choice of groups under discussion here and frame the presentation offered. These groups have many features in common with the rest of British society, such as the determining character of social class, but the concern here is with what distinguishes them from the rest of society and the interaction of the *differentia* and the commonalities.

From Diverse Beginnings

The educational profiles of the non-white minority groups, at the time of migration and now, are quite diverse. Some minority groups are proportionally less qualified than their white peers, and some much more so. This is true if we look at the population as a whole or at those who have recently finished their education. Broadly speaking, the ethnic minority population can be divided into two: the Caribbeans, Pakistanis, and Bangladeshis have lower average levels than whites; the Indians, African Asians, Chinese, and Africans are more likely than whites to have higher qualifications.

Among the critical factors in explaining the educational levels of these groups today is the qualification profile at the time of migration. This can be seen in Figures 3 and 4. Figure 3 shows the proportion among the minority groups without qualifications divided into three "generations"[1] and also shows the qualification levels of whites for the most recent two generations. The source of the data is the PSI Fourth Survey, conducted in 1994.[2] Beginning with the migrant generation, we see that the six minority groups covered by the Fourth Survey fall into two groupings. The Caribbeans, the Pakistanis, and the Bangladeshis had high proportions without GCSE or equivalent qualifications,[3] between 60 and 75 percent. On the other hand, only about 45–50 percent of Indian, African Asians, and Chinese migrants were without this level of qualification. All six groups, however, have made educational progress across the generations, though among Bangladeshis it is only among the young that the proportion without qualifications has declined. The Caribbeans (taking men and women together) initially made the most progress. This meant that the second-generation Caribbeans were no longer included in the same group as Pakistanis and Bangladeshis; they had caught up with the other minorities and, in fact, their white peers. As native English speakers with qualifications from British examination boards, they were the migrant group one would expect to make most initial progress, though note that we are discussing not the acquisition of a high-level qualification but the possession of any qualification at all. Caribbean women were more likely than other women to have a qualification, which certainly contributed to the good overall average achieved by the second-generation Caribbeans. With today's twenty-somethings, the gender gap has widened to the point that while exactly the same proportion of whites and Caribbeans have no qualifications (a quarter), with white women a little more likely than men not to, among Caribbeans nearly a third of men have no qualifications compared to a sixth of the women.

The Pakistanis and the Bangladeshis have made the least progress in reducing the proportion within the group with no qualifications. Among all other groups about a fifth to a quarter had no GCSEs, but the proportions in these two groups was about double this. Figure 3 shows, in terms of having no qualifications, that some of the ethnic

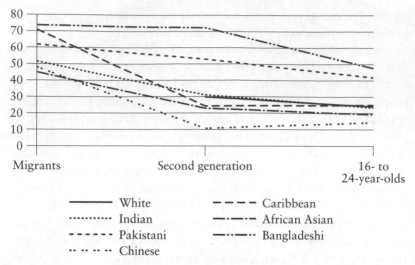

Figure 3. Percentage within ethnic groups with no GCSE or equivalent qualifications, by generation.

minority groups were similarly or better placed than their white peers and some much worse, and that this has not been achieved recently but has been true for some time and partly reflects migrants' starting points. The groups who are worse placed than whites are the Bangladeshis, the Pakistanis, and Caribbean males.

Figure 3 is only part of the story. It is perhaps more important to look not at those who have a qualification but at those who have higher qualifications. Figure 4 presents the original profile and generational progress in relation to those who have an A-level or higher qualification.[4] Once again three migrant groups stand out as well qualified: the Chinese, African Asians, and Indians. Three groups were much less well qualified, the Bangladeshis especially but also the Pakistanis and the Caribbeans. Again, all groups except the Bangladeshis made progress in the second generation, though the progress of the Pakistanis was quite minor. Once again the Caribbeans made the most dramatic progress, though the African Asians were the best qualified at this level, considerably ahead of whites. Figure 4 does not show this, but while all other groups, even the Bangladeshis, were well represented at degree level, very few Caribbeans with higher-level qualifications had degrees (just 2 percent of the migrants and 7 percent of the second generation). Many of their higher qualifications were vocational qualifications like HNCs or in nursing. In contrast, nearly 10 percent of Pakistani and Bangladeshi migrants and a quarter of Indian, African Asian, and Chinese migrants had degrees. This meant that some groups like the Pakistanis and Bangladeshis were very internally polarized, with disproportionate numbers of highly qualified and unqualified. But it meant that all these groups had significant proportions of university-educated persons. It is therefore not surprising, as we shall see, that these groups have gone on to be well represented in higher education in their second and third generations. That they have not all made equal progress in this regard can partly be correlated to the extent that they had British or overseas qualifications. Thus the relatively limited progress of second-generation Indians may be a reflection of the fact that the migrants disproportionately had Indian degrees, compared to the Chinese and African Asians, whose qualifications in the main were from British examination boards and institutions.

Two other important factors need to be noted. First, in terms of gender, male migrants were better qualified than women, especially among the Bangladeshis, Indians, and Pakistanis. In all groups men were much more likely to have degrees; Caribbean women, however, were and remain much more likely than the men to have higher qualifications. Second, a further factor accounting for the divergent profiles is that in the pursuit of qualifications some groups are more

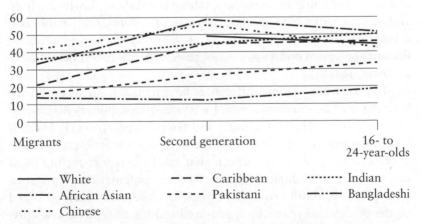

Figure 4. Percentage within ethnic groups with A-level or higher qualifications, by generation.

vocationally than academically qualified, and so the qualified among them are less likely to have degrees. This is particularly the case with the Caribbeans and whites, who are much more likely to have a higher vocational qualification than the South Asian groups, who have a stronger academic orientation.

Schools and Young People

In most ethnic minority groups, the second and third generations have made significant progress, as have their white peers. Among sixteen- to twenty-four-year-olds, far fewer are without a qualification than the older generations. The position of Indians, African Asians, Chinese, and Africans is comparable with that of whites, except at degree level where the position of these minorities is distinctly better. Ethnic minority women have made particular progress. By 1995, girls were more likely than boys to achieve five higher-grade GCSEs in each of the principal minority groups. Pakistanis and Bangladeshis, however, continue to have the largest proportions without qualifications, and the positions of young Caribbean men is not better than that of their elders.

Data from local education authorities suggest that at the beginning of schooling, and at the time of the first national tests at age seven, the difference between Caribbeans and whites are relatively slight and sometimes in favor of the Caribbeans. South Asian children, often coming from homes in which English, if spoken at home, is a second or third language, begin their school careers with low averages. But while in secondary school the Asians slowly catch up and, in the case of some groups, overtake the whites, the Caribbeans' average steadily drops below the national average (Owen et al. 2000; Richardson and Wood 1999; Gillborn and Mirza 2000; Berthoud et al. 2000, 10).

Explanations of these differences have tended to focus on Caribbean males, who experience very high rates of disciplinary action and exclusion from school (Gillborn and Gipps 1996, 50–53). There is general agreement that they have the most confrontational relations with teachers and are the group that teachers report feeling most threatened and frightened by. One type of explanation emphasizes teacher racism (Gillborn 1998; Connolly 1998). This can be based on the perceptions of teachers, acquired and fostered through a staff-room culture and through disciplinary problems with previous pupils, that lead to low expectations about the behavior and work of Caribbean boys and can lead teachers to interpret certain behavior more negatively than the same behavior exhibited by white or Asian males and perhaps lead to preemptive disciplining (Gillborn 1990, 1998). There can also be forms of indirect discrimination at play, whereby procedures and organizational arrangements, which may have nothing to do with race and ethnicity directly, may nevertheless have disproportionately negative impacts on Caribbean boys. Caribbean boys are disproportionately placed in lower sets and thereby less likely to be prepared for certain exams (Gillborn and Youdell 2000). (Of course, it is quite possible for an arrangement that negatively impacts on one minority group to have positive impacts on another.)

An alternative type of explanation emphasizes that the high levels of confrontations with and disciplining of Caribbean boys are at least partly due to what the boys bring into school with them (Sewell 1997; Mac an Ghaill 1988). It is argued that they draw on a youth/street culture, specifically "on a Black collectivist anti-school ideology, on a pro-consumerism and phallocentrism" (Sewell 1997, 108). This culture gives black boys strength to resist racism, but it undervalues academic achievement; indeed, academic aspirations are disparaged as a form of "acting white," and the living out of this black masculinity inevitably leads to failing to meet the norms of school behavior. "In this way, a vicious cycle can develop in which what is perceived as a lack of respect from teachers is met by an aggressive response from pupils who in turn are punished for the behavior" (Pilkington 1999, 415). Among the black community the development of a "gangsta" culture and the absence of good male role models at home, as well as in schools, are mentioned as causes of concern (Abbot 2002; T. Phillips 2002; Clunis 2002; Bright 2004), but these matters continue to be a matter of controversy (Jasper and Sewell 2003).

Both explanations may be true, but the former raises an unnoticed paradox: if racism leads to victims being turned off school and dropping out, why do Asians have such high staying-on rates and make academic progress? While recognizing that there are significant differences between the racism experienced by Caribbeans and Asians, as captured in the plural idea of *racisms* as discussed in chapter 1 (see also CMEB 2000, ch. 5), ethnographic research suggests, in ways consistent with surveys, that Asians experience more frequent and more violent racial harassment from other pupils than the Caribbeans (Gillborn 1998; Virdee, Modood, and Newburn 2000). As far as I know, no one has tried to research why this high level of peer racism and bullying does not keep Asians from having high levels of motivation and persisting to achieve performance.

Suffice to say that, as far as I know, no convincing explanations exist to fully account for the above differentials. I suggest, first, that the research and policy focus for the last three decades has been on why Caribbean males do not make progress in British schools and not on why some Asian groups do make progress; some focus on the latter must surely help us to understand better some of the processes in relation to ethnicity, racism, schooling, and attainment. Second, it seems to me that what happens in schools is probably only a small part of the story. I return to this issue later when I offer some speculation about causal processes.

What cannot be denied is that ethnic minorities in general manifest a strong drive for qualifications, and once they begin to acquire qualifications, they seek more. For example, when we look at those with a GCSE or higher qualification who were continuing in (or had returned to) full-time education, we see a degree of minority commitment quite different from that of whites. While among the qualified sixteen- to twenty-four-year-old whites about a quarter were likely to be in full-time education (slightly more for women, slightly less for men), nearly half of the ethnic minority women and well over half of the men were. The commitment to education is manifest in groups that were not particularly well qualified at the time of migration: qualified Caribbeans of both sexes in this cohort were considerably more likely to be in full-time education than their white peers, and the qualified Pakistanis/Bangladeshis had the highest participation rate in the Fourth Survey for each sex (Table 7).[5]

Some of the high level of minority participation in noncompulsory full-time education is likely to be a reflection of the fact that ethnic minorities used to take longer to achieve their qualifications, but this has declined. Moreover, whites, especially white men, are more likely to be employed and to be pursuing their further education and training on the job or in training that is linked to their job (Drew, Gray, and Sime 1992; Drew 1995; Hagell and Shaw 1996). Furthermore, the presence of high rates of youth unemployment, especially among those without qualifications, and the knowledge that ethnic minorities suffer much higher rates of unemployment may all be thought to add to the explanation of why the ethnic minorities have high staying-on rates.

The evidence is, however, that the ethnic minority youngsters who stay on do so for positive reasons. A study of sixteen-year-olds in six inner-city areas also found that minority ethnic individuals were more likely to stay on than whites; of those that stayed on, half wanted to go to university eventually, while less than a fifth gave as one of their reasons that it was better than being unemployed (Hagell and Shaw 1996, 88). Further analysis of that survey shows that Asians were no more likely than whites, and Caribbeans little more likely, to say that they stayed on in education because it was better than being unemployed. On the other hand, ethnic minorities were much more likely than whites to say that they wanted to improve their educational qualifications or go to university. The knowledge that qualifications are necessary for getting a (desirable) job may well motivate ethnic minorities more than whites, but it seems to do so positively rather than negatively (see also Basit 1997; Wrench and Qureshi 1996). There may be features about schools that ethnic minorities wish to avoid, for they disproportionately transfer from school to Further Education Colleges (FE) to study subjects and for exams that are available at school. Moreover, some minority groups, especially the Caribbeans, drop out of school at the age of sixteen and pick up their studies at FE at a later date (Owen et al. 2000).

Higher Education

Given what we have seen of the higher participation rates among the ethnic minorities, it will come as no surprise to learn that, contrary

Table 7. Proportion of qualified sixteen- to twenty-four-year-olds who are full-time students (percent).

Has O-level or higher and is a full-time student	White	Caribbean	Indian/ African Asian	Pakistani/ Bangladeshi	All ethnic minorities
Men	21	34	63	71	58
Women	28	40	47	48	46
Weighted count					
Men	163	105	166	105	413
Women	145	137	187	101	471
Unweighted count					
Men	116	48	110	119	293
Women	119	73	124	119	334

Source: Modood et al. 1997.

to the claims of most commentators at the time, the monitoring of admissions to higher education (beginning in 1990) did not reveal an underrepresentation of ethnic minorities (Modood 1993b). Moreover, all minority groups, with the possible exception of the Caribbeans, have increased their share of admissions since then. Ethnic minorities as a whole are about 50 percent more successful in achieving university entry than white applicants, but not evenly so. More than twice the proportion of eighteen- to twenty-four-year-old Africans, Chinese, "Asian-Others," and Indians enter university than do whites, and no minority group is underrepresented, as can be seen in Table 8. Some gender differences persist—Caribbean men and Bangladeshi women are underrepresented, but in the latter case there is a trend toward equal or even overrepresentation. Otherwise, only the whites are underrepresented in both genders. So the minority groups, with the exception of Caribbean men, are on different points of an escalator, all moving upward relative to whites, and in fact some groups exceeded the government's target of 50 percent participation by age thirty some years ago.

While some minorities are very well represented in competitive subjects, they are, except the Chinese, still generally more likely to be in the less prestigious, less well-resourced post-1992 universities.

Table 8. Domiciled first-year full-time and part-time students, 1997–98 (percent).

Group	In higher education	18–24s in higher education	18–24s in Great Britain	18–24s gender balance in higher education (M–F)
White	84.9	85.2	92.0	48*–52*
Indian	4.1	4.7	2.0	51–49
Pakistani	2.5	2.7	1.8	56–44
Bangladeshi	0.7	0.7	0.7	58–42*
Chinese	0.9	1.0	0.4	50–50
Asian-Other	1.2	1.2	0.4	52–48
African	2.1	1.4	0.6	48–52
Caribbean	1.3	1.0	0.9	40*–60
Black-Other	0.6	0.5	0.7	38*–62

Source: Higher Education Statistics Agency, 1991 census, and Labour Force Survey, 1999–2000.
*Denotes underrepresentation.

This is especially true of Caribbeans (Modood and Acland 1998), who are also more likely to be mature students (more than half of Caribbean women students are over twenty-five years old) and part-time students (Pathak 2000; Owen et al. 2000). A-level scores, subject preferences, preference for local institutions, and type of school or college attended are all factors that explain the concentration of ethnic minority groups, except the Chinese, in the new universities and that have implications for career prospects. Returning to the topic of school racism, analysis shows that lower A-level predictions by schools on university applications do not seem to be a factor. In fact, schools make more generous predictions for ethnic minority candidates, with the most optimistic forecasts made about black African and Caribbean students, contrary to what one might expect on the basis of the teacher racism we considered earlier (Shiner and Modood 2002, 217). Moreover, a separate analysis of several years' data and controlling for A-level scores and other factors failed to show that higher education taken as a whole displays any bias against ethnic minority candidates (Leslie, Abbott, and Blackaby 2002). That analysis, however, suffers from two limitations. First, it is an analysis of admissions and so cannot isolate institutional offers from candidates' decisions. Second, it does not distinguish between different types of institutions. These two limitations are overcome in Shiner and Modood 2002. This study found that, after accounting for all the factors mentioned above and several others, there was a clear institutional effect. Table 9 presents the results of a multivariate analysis that shows that, comparing similarly qualified candidates and controlling for factors such as private schools, gender, and so on, new (post-1992) universities respond more positively than old universities to non-white applicants, and within this sector Chinese, Bangladeshi, and Indian candidates appear to be favored over whites. White candidates have a 73 percent chance of eliciting an offer from a new university, which is lower than that of their ethnic minority peers. When applying to old universities, however, there is strong evidence that minority candidates face an ethnic penalty. Institutions within this sector are most likely to select white and, to a lesser extent, Chinese candidates from among a group of similarly qualified applicants. Given the much larger proportion of applications from ethnic minority groups, although ethnic minority applicants may be admitted to old universities in reasonable numbers, they generally have to perform

Table 9. Rates of acceptance based on ethnic background.

Old universities	New universities
Most preferred:	*Most preferred:*
Whites (0.75)*	Indians (0.85)
	Chinese (0.83)
	Bangladeshis (0.82)
Less preferred:	*Less preferred:*
Chinese (0.68)	Pakistanis (0.77)
Black Caribbeans (0.65)	Black Africans (0.76)
	Black Caribbeans (0.75)
	Whites (0.73)
Least preferred:	
Indians (0.58)	
Bangladeshis (0.57)	
Black Africans (0.57)	
Pakistanis (0.57)	

Source: Shiner and Modood 2002.
*Probability of initial offer to identical candidates for equivalent courses.

better than their white peers in order to secure a place. As the type of institution from which you graduate can make a big difference to your career prospects, this bias can have serious, long-term implications for ethnic stratification (Shiner and Modood 2002). It ought to be borne in mind, however, that some ethnic minority groups have a disproportionately large number of their eighteen- to twenty-four-year-olds in higher education, and therefore are digging deeper into the talent available in that age group. Hence, it is not surprising that a larger proportion of their applicants enter institutions that require lower A-level entry scores. If we were to compare like with like, the peers of some who enter these universities are whites who are absent from higher education. This does not negate the generalization that ethnic minorities have to do better than whites to get into older universities, which, therefore, are complicit in an institutional discrimination that is hindering and slowing down the dismantling of an ethnic stratification.

Some Speculation about Causes
Other than the factors mentioned above, social class is probably the most powerful one in explaining the educational outcomes discussed

here. But its effect is heavily qualified, for example, by gender norms and expectations in different communities, as we see in the contrasting effects among the Bangladeshis and the Caribbeans, though we must not assume that cultural identities governing gender or other kinds of norms are static. There is both quantitative and qualitative data that cultures, which until recently might have been portrayed as opposed to the education of and employment of women, seem to be producing growing cohorts of highly motivated young women (Ahmad, Modood, and Lissenburgh 2003). Caribbean ethnicity, however, other than through a distinctive gender effect, has a lesser effect than the others on class and sometimes diminishes the class-based likelihood of success (Penn and Scattergood 1992; P. Taylor 1992; Gillborn and Gipps 1996). The class position of Pakistanis and Bangladeshis is, as we saw in the previous chapter, lowest of all groups. Moreover, it is made worse by the fact that on the whole they have larger households and that married women are unlikely to be in paid employment outside the home, resulting in fewer earners and more dependents in a household. South Asians and the Chinese, however, seem to do better than they should do, given their parental class. This can be seen from Table 10, which shows university entrants in 1998 by ethnicity, gender, and parental social class. It shows an absence of gender difference but, unsurprisingly, class is a major factor: in nearly every group, the offspring from parents with non-manual jobs exceed, sometimes by a large margin, those from parents with manual jobs. This is particularly the case among whites but is also of considerable magnitude among Africans and Caribbeans. It has much less significance for Indians and Chinese, groups in which entrants are almost equally likely to come from nonmanual as from other backgrounds, including unemployment. And the conventional class analysis does not hold at all for Pakistanis and Bangladeshis, among whom households headed by a manual or unemployed worker supply nearly two-thirds of the entrants.

To some extent, it can be countered, this was because the South Asian and Chinese entrants' parental social class and educational capital was better than that suggested by their parents' occupations, for their occupational levels were depressed by migration effects and discrimination in the labor market. Due to this racial discrimination migrants often suffered a downward social mobility on entry into Britain, as discussed in the previous chapter. The only jobs open to them were often below their qualification levels and below the social class level

Table 10. University entrants by ethnicity, gender, and parental social class, 1998.

	White		Chinese		Indian		Pakistani		Bangladeshi		Black-Caribbean*		Black African	
	M	F	M	F	M	F	M	F	M	F	M	F	M	F
Nonmanual	67.1	67.4	52.5	52.7	48.5	48.4	36.5	36.1	36.3	35.8	52.1	56.4	51.5	54.8
Manual	25.2	24.6	33.7	33.7	39.5	39.7	39.7	38.2	39.2	38.9	26.9	24.4	20.5	19.3
Unknown**	7.7	8.0	13.8	13.6	12.1	12.0	23.8	25.8	24.5	25.3	21.0	19.2	28.1	25.9

Source: Ballard 1999.

*Includes Black Caribbeans and Black Others.

** The vast majority of parents whose social class was classified as unknown by the Universities and Colleges Admissions Services (UCAS) appear to have been unemployed.

they enjoyed before migration. This meant that many not only valued education more than their white workmates but saw it as part of the process of reversing the initial downward mobility, especially in the lives of their children. If we recall the qualification levels of the migrants as presented in Figures 3 and 4, this argument that migrants' occupational class in Britain is not reflective of their true class or of their attitudes to education seems to have some plausibility, particularly in the case of the African Asians and perhaps also the Indians, but less so with other groups. In any case, class analysis by itself, even after taking initial downward mobility into account, is incomplete without acknowledging the economic motivation of migrants and the desire to better themselves and especially the prospects for their children. The belief in the value of education in achieving upward mobility and respectability is related to this, as is the strong academic orientation of groups such as the South Asians and the Chinese. The same factors are likely to be operative in the case of Africans, who were not included in the Fourth Survey but emerged in the 1991 and the 2001 censuses as the group with the highest proportion of persons with higher qualifications (Owen, Mortimore, and Phoenix 1997; Frean 2003).

It is worth noting here the general sociological claim that there is such a thing as an Asian trajectory or an Asian future, which includes social mobility by education, self-employment, and progression into the professions (Cross 1994; Peach 1996). The implication is that it is wrong to divide South Asian groups into the successful and the disadvantaged, for the latter are likely only to have less longevity of residence in Britain (measuring families and communities, not just individuals) or to have suffered temporary setbacks (perhaps due to economic restructuring). Today's successful Asians (like the Indians) are yesterday's disadvantaged Asians; today's disadvantaged Asians are tomorrow's successes. This view probably overhomogenizes South Asians, ignoring the differential educational and employment backgrounds at the time of migration of different South Asian groups and differential degrees of segregation and factors peculiar to Muslims, as mentioned in the previous chapter. Nevertheless, there may still be something in it, and it does have the merit of consistency with some perceivable trends. It is, for example, supported by the fact, visible in Table 10, that South Asian university entrants are less likely than other groups to come from nonmanual backgrounds. In particular, when we compare the three disadvantaged groups, the Pakistanis, the Bangladeshis, and the Caribbeans, the latter are much more likely to come from nonmanual backgrounds than the former, even though they have a similar manual/nonmanual profile in the workforce, at least with regard to male workers (see Tables 1 and 2 in chapter 3). This does lend some weight to the idea that there is an ambition among South Asians to be university educated, which is not constrained by class, but on the contrary is seen as integral to social mobility ambitions.

I suggest that ethnic minority parents, especially the South Asians and Chinese, are probably less knowledgeable of the school system and participate less in school activities than their white peers. I doubt that they spend more time on helping with or discussing schoolwork with their children at home, the content of which will be less familiar to them than to white parents. Yet I believe they foster high expectations (even to the point of pressuring the children), give encouragement, maintain discipline (e.g., ensuring that homework is done), send children to and help with supplementary classes, and so on. In short, what they give is not a transfer of knowledge and skills but a sense that education is important, that teachers should be obeyed, and that academic success takes priority over other pursuits, especially recreational youth culture. So if we want to know what is driving these groups onward through large-scale, sociologically corroborated disadvantages, I suggest we give serious attention to the possible following causal sequence:

- Parents, other significant relatives, and community members share some general but durable ambitions to achieve upward mobility for themselves and especially for their children and believe that higher education is important in achieving those ambitions and so prioritize the acquisition of higher education.
- They are successfully able to convey this view to the children who to a large degree internalize it, and even where they may not fully share it they develop ambitions and priorities that are consistent with those of their parents.
- The parents have enough authority and power over their children, suitably reinforced by significant relatives and other community members, to ensure that the ambition is not ephemeral or fantastic and that the children do whatever is necessary at a particular stage for its progressive realization.

This possible causal triad connects with other and wider social dimensions, for example, identity. People act (or try to act or fail to act) the way they do because it seems to them to be the living of an identity that they believe they have or aspire to have; certain behaviors make sense or don't make sense, become possible or "impossible," easy or difficult, worth making sacrifices for, and so on if certain identities—like ethnic or minority identities—are strongly held. The above triad may cluster with other beliefs and behaviors that give some Asians a sense of who they are, their location in the world, and what is expected of them. This can be a fruitful inquiry even if we reject ethnic essentialism (and are careful not to impose too restricted a purview of *which* adult-children relationships are important). The self-concept that "we as a group are striving and struggling to achieve higher status and prosperity, respectability, in this land where the dice are loaded against us but success is achievable, and you have to play your part" can be bound up with, say, being Indian in Britain, even if only contingently and not essentially so. The transmission of a normative identity will, I believe, be more important than, for example, parent-child "quality time," talking together about schoolwork or friendships, or any specific skills and knowledge transfer. Indeed, Asian migrant parents may have little relevant economic-human capital to transmit, but subsequent human capital acquistion by their children may depend on parent-child transmission of norms-laden and goals-directing identities.

I emphasize here that it is not just the parents who are critical but the wider family and ethnic community, too. Family aspirations need to be reinforced. Min Zhou's work in New York's Chinatown, using the concept of ethnicity as social capital, shows how the orientation is reinforced by the whole community in all kinds of ways (Zhou 1997, 2005). One of these is the protection of children and youth from certain kinds of influences—including street and youth cultures. In contrast, Elijah Anderson's work brings out the difficulties that African-Americans have in avoiding these antischolastic influences (1994; see also Ferguson 2005). Even where parents from different groups may have the same aspirations for their children, they may, independently of class, have access to quite different forms of social capital to materialize their aspirations.

Material resources are important, too. While they relate closely to the class configuration of an ethnic group, it is quite likely that the extent of saving and spending priorities are shaped not just by the availability of resources but by cultural preferences. These preferences are likely to have a class character, but they will also have a significant ethnic dimension. For example, I guess that ethnic minority parents spend a larger proportion of their disposable income on education than white parents. There is no systematic evidence for testing this hypothesis, but the 1998 data on university entrants showed that Indians were slightly more likely than whites to have come from independent schools and the Chinese were twice as likely (Ballard 1999; see also Berthoud et al. 2000, 82). Bearing in mind that these minority groups still have slightly more children per family than whites (Modood et al. 1997, 40–41) and a much higher proportion of the age cohort applying to universities than whites, it means, I estimate, that on a per capita basis, Indians are 2.5 times more likely than whites to be in fee-paying schools and the Chinese five times more so.[6] That's a lot of personal financial investment in educational success, despite the fact that the minority groups not only have lower earnings, as we saw in chapter 3, but also have lower spending power per capita than whites, after one adjusts for pensioner households (Modood et al. 1997). Pakistanis and Bangladeshis do not have the same kind of representation in fee-paying schools, but exactly the same argument about ethnic preferences can be made in their case when one bears in mind that, despite four out of five Pakistani and Bangladeshi households being in poverty (ibid.), these groups produce a larger proportion of university entrants than the white population.

The continuing presence of racial discrimination has also meant that non-white persons have been particularly dependent on qualifications for jobs and economic progression because they lacked the social networks, such as those associated with Oxbridge or certain working-class occupations, to help them get on. Hence, both kinds of factors that I have been referring to, those that are "internal" to the group and those that are "external," have worked together, interacting with and reinforcing each other, to make qualifications and higher education of more value and urgency to ethnic minorities than white people.[7]

Persisting/Growing Polarities

The research frameworks favored by researchers in the 1980s assumed that the African-Caribbean experience would be paradigmatic for children of color (black people). It is, however, more accurately seen as one strand in a multifaceted story (Richardson and Wood 1999).

It is clear, nevertheless, that significant polarities exist among the ethnic minority groups and within specific minority groups. No convincing explanation exists that accounts for both pairs of polar ends. Typically, most researchers focus on one end of one of the polarities and try to explain it, sometimes proceeding as if their chosen end was the whole story. The most polarized groups happen to be the ones that were headlined in the news in 2001 (a year of riots and the start of the "war on terrorism),"[8] the Pakistanis and Bangladeshis. While they continue to be much more likely than all other groups to leave school with no qualifications, before one makes generalizations about the group, it is best to remember that in 40 percent of local education authorities that monitor by ethnic origin, Pakistanis are more likely than whites to attain five A*-C GCSEs[9] (Gillborn and Mirza 2000), and that on a per capita basis there are more Pakistanis than whites at university. Caribbean men, too, are a continuing cause of concern, and if they are less polarized than other groups, it is because they are largely absent at the top end of the pole. Any social inclusion policy needs to target the truly disadvantaged, but it would be no less a mistake to assume that, in relation to educational attainments, any minority group is homogeneous than to assume that an explanation of the educational profile of one minority group explains them all.[10]

Postscript

New data and analyses confirm several of the claims made in this chapter. The 2001 census confirms the general pattern across ethnic groups. Black Africans, Chinese, and Indians are much more likely to have a degree than white British, as are other whites and other Asians and all the mixed categories except white and black Caribbean, who together with the Bangladeshis are the only two groups less likely to have degrees than the white British. The Pakistanis are about as likely as whites to have degrees, and black Caribbeans are slightly more likely. The internal polarities too are apparent, with the Irish (included as a separate census category for the first time), the Pakistanis, and white and black African mixed all having a combination of more of their group with no GCSEs and more with a larger number of degrees than the white British (ONS 2003).

Using Youth Cohort Survey data and controlling for background factors, including a number of class-related variables, Bradley and Taylor (2004) found that Pakistanis, as well as Indians, were 10 percent more likely to get five GCSEs at A*-C than whites in the same circumstances. On the other hand, African-Caribbeans were 8 percent less likely. It does seem that certain ethnicities compound class disadvantage, while others counteract it, when it comes to educational attainment. I have suggested in this chapter that the Asian success is due to the higher valuation placed on academic success, emanating especially from the parents, such that there is little class difference in attitudes to higher education. Considerable support has been found for this idea in the new, and the most extensive yet, study of ethnic minorities and higher education (Connor et al. 2004), though as I say in this chapter, academic goals per se are not as important as the mechanisms to achieve them against sociological predictions, and on this we have no research.

There has also been a development suggesting that some groups have ways of mitigating class disadvantage. For decades Bangladeshis have been at the bottom of all economic and educational tables, as has been shown in this and the previous chapter. This is still the case in relation to adults. The Labour Force Survey for 2002–3 (taking all four quarters together) shows that more than 40 percent of Bangladeshi men in the labor market were without qualifications, compared to 30 percent of Pakistanis (whites, 14 percent). Yet, the National Pupil Database shows that 43 percent of Bangladeshis had more than five GCSEs, A*-C, in 2002 compared to 40 percent of Pakistanis (whites, 51 percent). The Bangladeshi advantage was in both genders, and indeed Pakistani girls equaled the results of white boys (46 percent) while the Bangladeshi girls bettered it (50 percent) (Runnymede Trust 2004). On the other hand, black Africans have moved in the opposite direction, from highly qualified migrants to below-average school results, but with poorly qualified refugees from countries such as Somalia joining an earlier wave of highly qualified Nigerians and Ghanaians, "African" is a far from adequate statistical category.

Part II

The Muslim Challenge

Five

Reflections on the Rushdie Affair: Muslims, Race, and Equality in Britain

"Fight racism, not Rushdie": stickers bearing this slogan were worn by many in 1989 who wanted to be on the same side as the Muslims.[1] It was well meant but betrayed a poverty of understanding. It is a strange idea that when somebody is shot in the leg one says, "Never mind, the pain in the elbow is surely worse." Why should reference to the real problem of racism lessen religious pain? There cannot be much doubt that South Asian Muslims in Britain form a virtual underclass in Britain. Throughout the 1980s, of the nine non-white groups identified in the Labour Force Survey, Pakistanis and Bangladeshis have suffered the highest rates of unemployment, and have the lowest number of educational qualifications and the highest profile in manual work. This is true in each respect not just for women but also for men, and not just for the middle-aged (the first generation) but also the young, as was shown in chapters 3 and 4. They have had the most adverse impact from immigration laws and rules, they have the worst housing, and they suffer from the highest levels of attacks on person and property. Of all groups, Pakistanis are least found in London and the South-East, for they came mainly to work in the rundown mills and factories of the North and Midlands and have in consequence suffered most from the factory closings of the early 1980s and benefited least from the subsequent economic growth. The plight of the Bangladeshis is perhaps worst of all. The scope for improvement is circumscribed by the fact, as a 1990 European Commission survey showed, that while Muslimophobia has not yet reached French proportions Asians are the single most disliked minority in this country (*Today*, March 14, 1990). How can it be that the most socially deprived and racially harassed group should bear all this and explode in anger only on an issue of religious honor? While some commentators have invoked the presence of politically motivated manipulators, there is little evidence that the demonstrations and the book burnings were in the main anything other than spontaneous working-class anger and hurt pride (Ruthven 1990, 97–98).

The root of the failure of understanding is that 1980s antiracism in Britain defined people in terms of their color; most Muslims—suffering all the problems that antiracists identify—hardly ever think of themselves in terms of their color. And so, in terms of their own being, most Muslims feel most acutely those problems that the antiracists are blind to, and respond weakly to those challenges that the antiracists want to meet with most force. And there can be no way out of this impasse if we remain wedded to a concept of racism that sees only color discrimination as a cause and material deprivation as a result. We need, as has been argued in the introduction and chapter 1, a concept of race and racism that can critique sociocultural environments that devalue people not only because of their origins but also because of their membership in a cultural minority and, critically, where the two overlap and create a double disadvantage.

Such a concept should help us to understand that an oppressed group feels its oppression most according to those dimensions of its being that it (not the oppressor) values the most; moreover, it will resist its oppression from those dimensions of its being from which it derives its greatest collective psychological strength. For this and further reasons, Muslims cannot easily, confidently, or systematically assume the moral high ground on the issue of color racism; their sense of being and their surest conviction about their devaluation by others comes from their historical community of faith and their critique of the "West." Authentic "antiracism" for Muslims therefore will inevitably have a religious dimension and take a form in which it is integrated with the rest of cultural concerns. Antiracism begins (i.e., ought to begin) by accepting oppressed groups on their own terms (knowing full well that these will change and evolve), not by imposing a spurious identity and asking them to fight in the name of that. The new strength among Muslim youths in, for example, not tolerating racial harassment owes no less to Islamic reassertion than to metropolitan antiracism: people don't turn and run when something they care about is under attack. The racist taunt "Rushdie!" rouses more self-defense than "black bastard!"[2] British antiracists see the racism but are happy to be ignorant of the living identities that racism obscures. They thus substitute the outsiders' perception for that of the subjects', turning the contingent fact of racism into the essence of being. South Asians who experience racial discrimination are reduced to discriminated beings ("blacks") who happen to be Asians (Modood 1988, 1994c).

Muslims need to be part of the rethinking I speak of and at the same time must admit that they have something not only to teach but to learn from the antiracist, for Muslim thinking too is inadequate to the current situation (Hobohm 1978). The Qur'anic teaching is that people are to be valued in terms of virtue, not color or race. Muslims insist that there is no divinely favored race and that the Qur'an is God's message to the whole of mankind. They take pride in their belief that Islam is a genuine multiethnic religion and point to the fact that one of the first converts to Islam was Bilal, a black slave (Arab trade in black slaves predated the same by Europeans) and that in Muslim history there have been several black rulers and generals in racially mixed societies. This then is the standard Muslim view of racial equality. Like all color-blind approaches it has two weaknesses.

First, it is too weak to prevent racial and ethnic prejudice. While it was strong enough, unlike its Christian and secular Western counterparts, to prevent the development of official and popular ideologies of racism, it is not the case that ethnic bigotry does not exist in the Islamic world. Asians have no fewer racial stereotypes about whites and blacks than these groups have about Asians or about each other.

The second weakness flows from the first. A color-blind approach is unable to sanction any program of positive action to tackle the problem once it is acknowledged to exist. For example, the 1976 Race Relations Act has provisions for employers to identify underrepresentation of racial minorities in the workforce and to target within certain limits those groups for recruitment. Strictly Muslim thinking cannot consistently support this. Some Muslim position statements seem to express reluctance for heightening racial categories, which is essential to positive action. One goes so far as to say, "We believe that it is very unhelpful to look at human relations in Britain on the basis of race" (UKACIA 1989), while another asserts, "There is only one race, the human race" (Akhtar 1989). Muslims (and indeed most other minority communities) do not see themselves in terms of color and do not want a public identity that emphasizes color. The way out is a concept of race that not only allows minorities a purchase on their mode of being but, equally important, also on how British white society defines them—that is to say, on their mode of oppression. While radical anti-racists are religion-blind and culture-blind, a non-white group must recognize the existence of color racism and how it, as well as cultural racism, affects them and their life chances. Not to do so would rob them of effective strategies as well as alliances with other non-white groups to oppose the various dimensions of racism and its effects. To develop such thinking one cannot—*pace* fundamentalism—rely solely on Qur'anic concepts.

Also relevant is the weakness of fundamentalism in dealing with the cultural dimensions of religion. It seems to have escaped many people's attention that the anger over *The Satanic Verses* was not so much a Muslim response as a South Asian Muslim response. If Rushdie had successfully attacked fundamentalism, as I believe he intended, many Muslims would have cheered, and certainly there would not have been the present lines of confrontation. It was not the exploration of religious doubt but the lampooning of the Prophet that provoked the anger. This sensitivity has nothing to do with Qur'anic fundamentalism but with South Asian reverence of Muhammad (deemed by many Muslims, including fundamentalists, to be excessive) and cultural insecurity as experienced in Britain and even more profoundly in India (Modood 1990a). Leaving aside Tehran (which in any case was late on the scene), the demonstrations in Johannesburg and Bradford, Bombay and Islamabad, were all by South Asians. Not only were there no major demonstrations in other Muslim countries, but the only country in Western Europe or North America to have seen ongoing protest was Britain. This cannot be because of the size of Britain's Muslim population (just over a million in 1990), for there are more Muslims in France, Germany, and the United States (two to three million each in 1990). Rather, Britain is the only Western country to have a significant Asian Muslim working class. And while fundamentalism is primarily a movement of the educated middle class, devotion to the Prophet is strongest among the rural peasantry from which Pakistani and Bangladeshi immigrants to Britain, unlike those to the United States, originate. Khomeini's uninvited intervention was purely political. A fatwa is a learned legal opinion; it is not a trial, not a verdict, not a sentence. By turning it into a sentence Khomeini placed himself outside Islamic law, and though by doing so he spoke to the hearts of many Muslims who felt despised, powerless, and without recourse in law, he nevertheless in one stroke jeopardized community relations in Britain. One important aspect of this has been the division that Muslim anger has caused in the race equality constituency and confusion over whether Muslim demands are or are not examples of assertive antiracism of the kind that is okay if made by or on behalf of Jews[3] and blacks. It is therefore important in the context of current thinking to reiterate that, despite some confusion and naïveté in their understanding of race, Muslims are wiser here than radical antiracists: in locating oneself in a hostile society one must begin with one's mode of being, not one's mode of oppression, for one's strength flows from one's mode of being. British thinking on race, following the American lead, has regarded the descendants of African slaves in the New World as the paradigm of a racial group. The claim is that this group is what white society has made them: its mode of being has become virtually identical to its mode of oppression. It is notable, however, that one of the significant strands of the movement by black Americans to achieve dignity and self-respect has been what is understood as at least a partial rediscovery of an ancestral culture, in particular Islam. Not only is there the Nation of Islam, which is not regarded by most Muslims as part of the Ummah (the global Muslim community), in addition there are over a million black American practicing Muslims and the rate of conversion is growing (K. Leonard 2003). The disowning of slave names is a simple but effective illustration of the point I am making: Cassius Clay is the name of the mode of oppression; Muhammad Ali is the name of the mode of being. If dogmatic antiracists continue to define racism and antiracism in terms of the primacy of the mode of oppression, they will shut out Asians and other minorities, fail to understand them, and cut them off from the sources of their group pride (Modood 1988, 1994c).

I believe that we in Britain are slowly learning that our concepts of racial equality need to be tuned not just to guaranteeing that individuals of different hues are treated alike but also to the fact that

Britain now encompasses communities with different norms, cultures, and religions. Racial equality cannot always mean that our public institutions and the law itself must treat everybody as if they were the same—for that will usually mean treating everybody by the norms and convenience of the majority. Local authorities have been discovering this, especially with regard to schools where some attempts have been made, usually in the glare of adverse publicity, to make provision for minority religions and languages, celebrate non-Christian religious festivals, and even to adjust school holidays to coincide with some of them.

More interesting and less publicized are the ways that the law has begun to take cognizance of the new cultural plurality (for details of legal cases mentioned in this paragraph, see Poulter 1986, 1989, 1990). Occasionally this has been at the level of the 1976 statute exempting turban-wearing Sikhs from the legal requirement to wear a crash helmet when riding a motorbike, a principle that was extended to exempt Sikhs from the 1989 compulsory rule that persons on construction sites must wear safety helmets; and the indirect provision in the 1988 Criminal Justice Act for Sikhs to continue to be able to wear their *kirpans* (religious daggers) in public places without being guilty of an offense. More often it is the judiciary that acknowledges the facts of cultural difference. Sometimes this is in the application of the Race Relations Act (1976), such as the House of Lords judgment in the landmark *Mandla v. Lee* (1983) that allows Sikh males to wear turbans in schools (and, by extension, places of work) regardless of the rules of the school (or employer); or the Industrial Tribunal decisions that have allowed, in appropriate circumstances, Asian women to wear trousers at work but not other women; or that a Rastafarian cannot be refused employment merely because he is unwilling to cut off his dreadlocks, though the latter was overturned on appeal. In each of these cases an important aspect of a person's religious or cultural practice was protected by law and made a difference to his or her treatment by the courts. Such a principle can be sharply contrasted with the famous *l'affaire foulard* in France in 1989, which revealed the lack of the right of Muslim girls to wear a headscarf in a state school in France, and which ultimately led to the French Parliament to come down on the side of prohibition by an overwhelming majority in February 2004. When similar conflicts have arisen in England, the schools have been forced to back down by public opinion as well as the force of legal precedent. It is important to note that this religious and cultural protection in Britain is far from comprehensive (the parochialism of the law of blasphemy is a case in point—see chapter 6) and more important that it is indirectly derived from race legislation. Until religious discrimination became an offense at the end of 2003, it was not, for example, the right of Muslim women to wear modest dress at work but the right only of women from those ethnic groups in Britain in which Muslims are a significant number. White Muslim women, for instance, had no rights in this regard, as young converts discovered. The cultural sensitivity of the courts does, however, go beyond merely deciding on cases of racial discrimination. For example, the English courts have been prepared to enforce contracts for the payment of deferred dower *(mahr)* by Muslim husbands upon divorce. In 1990 a High Court judge awarded a divorced Asian woman £20,000 damages against her husband, who had slandered her by suggesting she was not a virgin at the time of her marriage, on the grounds that the insult was very grave in her community.

Each of these examples of statute and judgment is small, but taken together they offer an intimation of a policy approach that might be called equality through pluralism.[4] What I have in mind is not new, not peculiar to Muslims or special to Britain. Indeed, integration through pluralism rather than assimilation, what has been called the "ethnicity paradox," was observed and advocated in the first quarter of this century by the American sociologists Robert E. Park and W. I. Thomas, in respect of the European and Southern black immigration to cities such as Chicago.[5] "Ethnicity paradox" refers to their conviction that allowing ethnic communities to take root and flourish in the new soil was the most satisfactory way of promoting long-term integration and participation in the institutions of the wider American community. They argued that not only did immigrant institutions meet the special cultural needs of a community, but they also provided a basis of continuity for people who were caught in particularly severe and destabilizing change. Even more important, they were a source of an individual's self-esteem and status, which otherwise suffered from the devaluation that the immigrant suffered; moreover, they enabled a group pride and could lead to a rise in status and respect for the group as a whole and, therefore, stem the need to disown one's origins in order to succeed in the new society. They also recognized that ethnic group organizations bring control to areas of urban life that may lack it, and give immigrant groups some control over their own adaptation to the new society and, therefore, allow them to adapt in an atmosphere of relative security as opposed to one of rootlessness and powerlessness, with each individual forced to come to terms with a new society in relative isolation and therefore exclusively on the terms of the majority. Park and Thomas thus noted that "immigrants who began by deserting their group end by attempting to improve the status of these groups . . . seeking to make something with which a man may be proud to identify himself. The fact that the individual will not be respected unless the group is respected becomes thus, perhaps the most sincere source of nationalist movements in America. To this extent the nationalist movements represent an effort to increase participation in American life" (Park and Miller 1921, 143–44).

This, then, is the ethnicity paradox—allowing more space to ethnic minority communities to do their own thing enables them to become a feature of the new society and creates a secure base from which participation in the institutions of the wider society follows. It is interesting that similar arguments surfaced among American black activists and young intellectuals in the late 1960s and 1970s when, after decades in which race egalitarians strenuously denied that there was any such thing as black culture, fearing that an acknowledgment of difference was the thin end of the wedge of inequality, blacks began to celebrate their African roots and what arose from them in the American soil.

Our thinking on equality and pluralism and what may be achieved in Britain is far from clear at the moment, and many voices need to be heard. Some Muslims, for instance, urge some variation of the *millat* system, a form of religious-based communal pluralism in which ethnic minorities ran their own communal affairs with a minimum of state interference, and which reached its height in the Ottoman Empire. The British in India allowed the development of a Muslim family law with its own separate courts, and much the same proposal was put to John Patten, the Home Office minister with responsibility for community relations, by a Muslim delegation at the time of the *Satanic Verses* crisis. The idea, hardly surprisingly, was rejected out of hand, and I do not wish to argue for it. Nevertheless, I do think Britain can usefully consider aspects of Muslim historical experience, for it embodies a record of tolerance of religious and cultural minorities, such as the Jews, which far exceeds that of Christendom and modern Europe.[6] Muslims continue to have a concept not just of tolerance but of respect for the religious beliefs of others, for religion as such, which seems to be disappearing in the West where, as Michael Dummett, one of Britain's leading philosophers, has observed, the assumption among intellectuals is "that religious believers may properly be affronted, indeed deserve to be affronted" (*Independent,* Sunday, February 11, 1990). Once again, dialogue, learning from a variety of traditions, is the way forward, for Muslim views of pluralism are not adequate either. They fail to confer equality of citizenship in some crucial respects. Islam insists on a fundamental equality between all Muslims; it insists on the rights of non-Muslims in a Muslim state to lead their lives according to their own norms and customs; it insists on the right of minorities to enjoy the full protection of the state. It does not, however, even as an ideal, allow them to be senior members of the major branches of the state or propagate an ideology that challenges that of the state, i.e., Islam.[7] Under Jamaat-i-Islami's influence, Zia's Islamicization in Pakistan went even further and created separate electorates so non-Muslims could not influence the election of Muslim legislators. Accordingly, Muslim minorities have historically sought a tolerance-cum-pluralism rather than formal equality; the United Kingdom initially offered its Muslims a formal equality but is not yet willing to acknowledge in its institutional and legal arrangements the existence of a Muslim community that, for instance, can be deeply hurt and provoked to violence by forms of literature that the majority of citizens have become used to tolerating. Is it not obvious that different cultural groups will value irreverent literature in different degrees depending on their history and the vulnerabilities of their position? Some groups may be able to use irreverence positively, while others may be demoralized and disabled by it. If so, equality cannot require everybody to be exposed to the same degree of irreverent literature. Equality, indeed, may best be served by giving a minority group a legal protection that the majority does not want for itself. The general point is that minorities have not merely the negative right of access to what is available to the majority but the positive right to some share of the public domain, including law, in order to live by their communal values even where these run counter to majority values and lifestyles. The question of the interrelationship between equality and pluralism has come to the fore in British race relations and is one on which Muslims have increasingly focused.

However appalled we might be by the "hang 'em and flog 'em" interpreters of the Qur'anic verses, that should not obscure—for any of us, Muslims and non-Muslims—the long-term significance of the Rushdie affair. At issue was not primarily the life of Salman Rushdie, for most Muslims rightly did not mean him physical harm, although they did not believe that the argument ended there; nor was it about freedom of expression per se, for on the one hand most Muslims do not seek to limit freedom of inquiry, and on the other hand just about nobody wants absolute freedom of expression including incitement to racial hatred. It is surely not Muslims alone who oppose the libertarianism that sees the artist as a Nietzschean *Ubermensch,* towering above conventional morality with perfect liberty to publish imaginative explorations regardless of social consequences. Indeed, the artist without social responsibility who provokes anger instead of dialogue threatens the field of discourse itself, as I argue in the next chapter. The ultimate issue that the *Satanic Verses* controversy posed are the rights of non-European religious and cultural minorities in the context of a secular hegemony. It is a time for self-discovery. Is the Enlightenment big enough to tolerate the existence of pre-Enlightenment religious enthusiasm, or can it only exist by suffocating all who fail to be overawed by its intellectual brilliance and vision of Man?

Six

Muslims, Incitement to Hatred, and the Law

There are many ways of considering the Muslim anger and protests against Salman Rushdie's book *The Satanic Verses*. One of the most direct is to ask in what way the Muslim demand for the withdrawal of the book compares and connects with some existing limits to free speech and why these were not adequate to resolve the crisis. Most of the discussion in this respect has focused on the law of blasphemy, and many people, including the Commission for Racial Equality (CRE),[1] the Liberal Democrats, senior politicians in the Labour Party, and most of the broadsheets, have argued that the privileged position that the law gives to Christianity (or perhaps to the Anglican Church only) is incompatible with racial equality and that the law should be abolished or extended to cover other religions (CRE 1991a, 58–61). The law of blasphemy in fact fails to protect Muslims, but it is not the only law to fail them. The Race Relations Acts of 1976 and 2000, including the offense of incitement to racial hatred, do not include religion as a component of the multiform concept of race consisting of differences and inferior treatment perceived to be based on color, race, nationality (including citizenship), or ethnic or national origins. The definition of a racial or ethnic group is wide, but not without limits, and this has meant that some minority religious groups such as Sikhs and Jews enjoy some legal protection against discrimination and incitement to hatred (because they are deemed to meet the criteria of what constitutes an ethnic group), but Muslims do not.[2] This is a significant exclusion, for not only does it weaken the rights of Muslims in employment, housing, and so on, but it also deprives them of a further opportunity of protection against offensive literature. The sense that Muslims have that the existing laws do not adequately recognize them as a group and fail to meet their needs on the issue of group defamation therefore has some justification and needs to be considered in terms of the purpose and nature of incitement to group hatred legislation.

This topic perhaps cannot be discussed without saying where one stands on the Ayatollah Khomeini's infamous fatwa. My view is that natural justice requires that a person cannot be sentenced without a trial, and hence the fatwa cannot be, as its author claimed, a verdict of execution. At best, it is a learned, and for Shia Muslims (not very numerous in Britain) an authoritative *opinion*. It is too readily forgotten in Western discussions that the fatwa of February 14, 1989, was an immediate (indeed, too immediate) and direct response to the deaths of ten anti-*Satanic Verses* demonstrators in Islamabad, Pakistan, on February 12 and five deaths in Srinagar, India, on February 13. The share of responsibility for these deaths by the parties named in the fatwa, the author and publishers of *The Satanic Verses,* is a question I cannot discuss here. Suffice it to say that the Tehran fatwa was cruel and unjust in its method even if one holds, as I personally do not, that the Qur'an sanctions capital punishment for blasphemous literature. I shall endeavor in the rest of this chapter to discuss the issue of group libel as if the fatwa did not exist.[3]

The Law on Incitement to Hatred and Group Defamation

Prior to the existence of any race relations legislation in Britain, hateful speech could be dealt with only under the 1936 Public Order Act: the offense could only be said to occur if the speech actually caused a breach of the peace or in the opinion of the police was likely to do so.[4] Section 6 of the 1965 Race Relations Act broadened this offense by not restricting the criteria to those of outcome. Intending to stir up racial hatred, regardless of the measure of success, became an offense. This in effect meant (and this is how the courts interpreted the few cases that came before them) that stirring up racial hatred could not be construed as an action with an immediate outcome but as something that if not challenged undermined the official commitment to racial equality and led to racial conflict. This offense was further amended by the 1976 Race Relations Act and later incorporated in the 1986 Public Order Act (enacted in Northern Ireland in 1987) so that a person was guilty if, in the use of threatening, abusive, or insulting words or behavior or in the display or distribution of written material,

- He intends thereby to stir up racial hatred (or arouse fear); or
- Having regard to all the circumstances racial hatred is likely to be stirred (or fear is likely to be aroused) thereby. [The words in parentheses are in the Northern Ireland law only.]

The second half of this distinction is important: the offense having been earlier disconnected from any strict likelihood of the breach of the peace, it no longer depends on the speaker's/author's intentions or interpretation of his speech/text but on what a person may reasonably conclude is the likely effect on one or more racial groups, especially the group(s) referred to in the speech/text. If the group is likely to feel that it is being rubbished, that old wounds are being reopened, enmities rekindled, images of domination invoked, then it can legitimately argue that the level of hate is being increased even if that is not the intention of the author and even if no specific act of violence is imminent. If this is a fair reading of the law in question, surely we must conclude that despite the language of causation in which the offense is framed (X incites Y to do something to Z), what is at issue is in fact something akin to group defamation. This is despite the fact that defamation of individuals is a civil, not a criminal offense. It seems to me that if a book uses unambiguously insulting and derogatory language to portray a group, the author could be liable to prosecution on the basis of his insulting portrayal without any special inquiry into the actual consequences.

I am not a lawyer and I could not say with any confidence whether the case I have described is just within or just outside the law (so few cases are brought forward by the attorney general that the discussion is perhaps inevitably somewhat hypothetical). My purpose is to try to bring out the rationale behind the law, and here it is significant that the CRE, almost from its inception in the late 1970s, has been of the view that the law is necessary to avoid the feelings of humiliation, indignity, and insecurity that minority groups would experience if subject to the unchecked use of inflammatory language (House of Commons 1980, 99–101).[5] Similarly, when the Home Office reviewed the Public Order legislation in the 1980s, incitement to racial hatred was viewed in terms of the offense to minority groups occasioned by racialist speech (Home Office 1983, par. 107). The phrases that apply in Northern Ireland, enlarging the focus to include the fear in the breasts of the attacked, as well as the hatred in their potential attackers, are also significant.

The most interesting thing about the comparable offenses in France, Germany, the United States, and Canada is that they cover a wider spectrum of social groups than those defined by race. In each of these countries religious groups are protected, and in Germany the law extends to cover cultural associations and political parties, for the offense is broadly conceived as "an attack on human dignity." In Canada women are included among groups whose dignity is protected by law, and Norway, Sweden, Denmark, and Ireland prohibit incitement to hatred based on sexual orientation (Wintemute 1995).[6] Each of these countries sees the nature of the offense in terms of group defamation. Indeed, in the United States it is treated as a piece of libel, and while libel law is limited by the constitutional right to free speech, nevertheless the Supreme Court in the 1952 decision in *Beauharnais v. Illinois* agreed that since an individual's dignity and reputation was associated with that of the group to which he or she belonged, there was no justification for treating group libel laws differently from the rules of private libel. While the *Beauharnais* decision has been gradually weakened by subsequent decisions, there is some indication of growing public support for the view that "hate propaganda undermines the very values which free speech is said to protect and that the prohibition of such material is not incompatible with the US Constitution" (Board of Deputies of British Jews 1991, 13). In a landmark decision, *R. v. Keegstra,* the Supreme Court of Canada in 1990 found against a high school teacher who was charged and convicted of communicating anti-Semitic statements to his students. The court argued, by a majority of five to four, that multiculturalism was an important political objective for which it was sometimes reasonable to restrict the expression of hatred against identifiable cultural groups, and that in any case hate propaganda contradicted all the values, such as quest for truth, promotion of self-development, public debate, and democratic participation that supported freedom of expression. One other point to notice is that the laws of group defamation in Germany and France are more widely drawn, at least in the protection of the Jews, than in Britain, for the offense is not limited to abusive, insulting, and threatening language but outlaws at least one proposition regardless of the manner in which it is put forward. This is the proposition that six million Jews did not die in Nazi gas chambers, the propounding of which has been a criminal offense in both countries for some time, punishable by imprisonment in the case of Germany and in France, too, since 1990 (Marnham 1990, 17).

It seems then that the United Kingdom is in an anomalous position among liberal democracies in confining its group libel laws only to racial groups and in not including religious groups (except in Northern Ireland where groups defined by reference to religious beliefs have been covered since 1970) (Lee 1990a, 13–16; see also Lee 1990b). The distinction, however, is not a clear-cut one. As British courts recognize religious minorities such as Sikhs and Jews as ethnic groups, it has been argued that "the advocacy of hatred against the Jewish community on account of its *religious beliefs* would amount to the stirring up of racial hatred against the Jewish community as a group"; the critical legal point is not that the hatred be directed to the racial features of a group but that it be directed to any distinctive feature of a group defined in law as a race (Board of Deputies of British Jews 1991, 46; my emphasis). Nevertheless, the greater protection afforded to (some) groups in France and (West) Germany comes as a double surprise. First, this restriction on hate literature, especially in connection with the Holocaust, coexists with a virtual absence of antiracial discrimination legislation and racial equality promotion (there is no equivalent, for instance, to Britain's Commission for Racial Equality); second, it belies the impression created by some commentators, such as the *Observer* and *New Statesman and Society,* that the reason why in 1989 the French and German governments took a more severe stand against protesters of *The Satanic Verses* than did the British is that there is a greater libertarianism in the intellectual sphere in those countries. I would like to underline the point that legislation in other countries confirms and makes explicit what in Britain is perhaps only implicit, that the rationale of such legislation is not the danger of some immediate violence or breach of the peace but group defamation.

The above discussion, I think, helps us to see that the aim of this kind of law may at times be narrowly conceived, but it tends toward and its rationale depends on a wider conception. The concern of the legislation may initially be limited to some of the earlier of the following points, but the concept of incitement to hatred leads to a concern with them all:

1. An immediate breach of the peace.
2. The aggressive intent of the speaker/author in the context of a possible breach of the peace.
3. The stirring up of racial hatred and antagonisms that if left unchecked could lead to serious social conflict and an eventual breakdown of public order.
4. Speech and writing that have the same effects as (3) even if the speaker/author had not intended it.
5. Group defamation as "an attack upon human dignity."

While point 1 represents the position in Britain before 1965, when there was no incitement to racial hatred offense as such and when it was simply a public order concern, 2 constitutes the 1965 position, 3 and 4 represent the explicit context of the 1976 Act, and finally 5 represents what I take to be implicit in the use of that act as opinion has developed on the matter so that it represents where we are today, or where we have nearly reached, and where other liberal democracies and Northern Ireland have already reached.

Muslim Honor and Liberal Legislation

It was noticeable from the placards of the anti–*Satanic Verses* demonstrators and from those interviewed on television at the time that, in trying to convey the nature of the insult and their hurt, words such as "honor" and "dignity" were more commonly used than "blasphemy." Similarly, Shabbir Akhtar, described by the *Guardian* and the *Independent* as the most formidable Muslim fundamentalist intellectual ranged against Rushdie, began his critique, titled *Be Careful with Muhammad!* by reminding all that one of the most basic duties of Muslims is to guard the honor of their Prophet (Akhtar 1989, 1); and it is interesting that when Akhtar discusses the question of legal remedies he concludes that "it may well be that, in a secular society like Britain, the Muslims' best bet is to campaign for a law making certain kinds of conduct or publication socially unacceptable as opposed to religiously offensive" (Akhtar 1990b, 24). The honor and dignity that Muslims feel to be at stake may be located in their religion but cannot be understood as a narrowly theological matter. Malise Ruthven has tried to bring out this aspect by describing it as a form of *izzat* (1990, 73–75). Izzat is a form of honor important to Muslims, usually associated with the social standing or respectability a family may enjoy. The issue here, however, is *ghairat*: while izzat is about the respect others accord to one, ghairat is about the quality of one's pride or love—pride in one's religion or the Prophet. While izzat is something to be maintained, ghairat is something to be tested.[7] *The Satanic Verses* was for many Muslims an unavoidable challenge to demonstrate their attachment to and love for their faith: their *imani ghairat*. And naturally the more the book was lauded as a literary masterpiece and so on, the greater the challenge, and the greater the response required.

It may perhaps be clear how the honor of the Prophet is linked to the dignity of the followers, and so to group defamation, but I think it would be best to explore this a bit further by comparing it with cases of racial defamation that contemporary Western societies are more familiar with. Consider the following propositions:

1. Six million Jews did not die in Nazi gas chambers.
2. American blacks have a lower IQ than American whites.

Each of these is regarded by many people, at least officially, as statements that are false or highly misleading, grossly disrespectful to a minority who have a right to be angry, perhaps inevitably violently so, because the statements belong to an ideology of domination and exploitation. Some would doubt whether these statements can have any place in legitimate intellectual inquiries and, as we have seen, to argue the first proposition in Germany and France is to risk imprisonment.

Consider another proposition, which led to a successful legal prosecution in Britain in 1977:[8]

3. Jesus Christ was a homosexual.

Many people who strongly object to the propagation of 1 and 2 would not want the law to interfere with 3. The difference would lie in some or all the following features:

A. The proposition is about an individual, not a group.
B. The proposition disputes a religious belief and does not defame a group.

C. There is not a historical or contemporary oppression linked to the proposition.

D. Some Christians do not mind if the proposition was true, and many of those who do mind yet believe that those who wish to say such things have the right to do so.

How do these four differentiating features compare with

4. Prophet Muhammad was a lewd, dishonest, dissembling power seeker.

Feature A applies to proposition 4, and the charge against the individual in question is considerably more serious than in 3. Feature B also seems to carry over to 4, but I think we need to question whether it makes a valid distinction. It certainly does not sufficiently distinguish 4 from 1 and 2 if it is the case, as indeed it is, that there is a historical oppression linked to the proposition. Proposition 4 has been very much part of the medieval and early modern Christian diatribes against Islam and Muslims (Daniel 1961, 1967; Armstrong 1988), who have subsequently been dominated by the West, and in contemporary Britain find themselves, as argued in the earlier chapters, suffering much anti-Muslim as well as racial prejudice, and of all minority groups are the worst off as measured by the usual indices of discrimination and disadvantage. As for feature D, Muslims cannot view the truth of proposition 4 with any kind of equanimity, though, like contemporary Christians with 3, most are sufficiently confident of its falsehood to allow it to be a subject of reasoned inquiry as opposed to parody and unsubstantiated claims.

The similarity of type between proposition 4 and the first two propositions lies in showing that a defamation of the Prophet is indeed a defamation of Muslims. The link is the belief that the honor and good name of Muslims depends on upholding the honor of the Prophet. For some liberals, willing to give oppressed minorities a sympathetic hearing but on guard to prevent unnecessary restrictions on free speech, this mediating belief is one belief too many. Michael Ignatieff, for example, has argued that it is important to distinguish between two incompatible conceptions of freedom: one that protects beliefs and ultimately leads to a theocratic state, and the other that protects individuals against expressions of hatred such as racial defamation. His view is that liberals cannot countenance the use of law to protect beliefs from insult, even though those beliefs may be central to a group of people, a religion, or a way of life, but he would protect the individuals who happen to be members of that religion or way of life. He, therefore, would not have the honor of Muhammad or any other Muslim conceptions enjoy any kind of legal immunity from insult, but he would support a law to prosecute those who would shout "you filthy Muslim" at Muslims (Ignatieff 1989, 1990). This distinction between beliefs and the individuals who may or may not hold those beliefs may normally work, but there is at least one type of belief where it does not hold: beliefs that form the self-definition of a group, for there cannot be membership of a group without some idea of the relevant groupness. Even those groups who are identified in terms of physical features, such as skin color or sex, can only exist as groups as long as members actually hold the belief that the physical attributes in question are what define them. If all black people or all women ceased to define themselves in terms of their skin color or sex, black people and women would cease to be groups, unless others, white people and men, had the power to maintain these groups; but, again, they could only do so by acting on a set of beliefs. A group exists only while some persons identify themselves and others in certain ways, and this cannot be done without beliefs.

This is not a trivial logical point. Besides beliefs that I might call part of the primary self-definition of a group, there are other beliefs that, as it were, have got historically or sociologically stuck on a group because they are involved in its oppression, in its relationship with the oppressor. That piece of history, that piece of oppression, can become so central to the psyche, to the life and continuing vulnerability of that group, that it can become part of its mode of being (Modood 1992). This is the case with the Holocaust to modern Jewry, and racial slavery to the African diaspora. Hence, to protect those groups the liberal state must uphold the truth of and commitment to certain beliefs and protect them, if not from critical inquiry that promises to be respectful, at least from gratuitous and blatantly offensive attack; the beliefs in question are the negation of propositions 1 and 2.

And how are Muslims to be protected? Is not the reaction to *The Satanic Verses* an indication that the honor of the Prophet or the imani ghairat is as central to the Muslim psyche as the Holocaust and racial slavery is to others? Ignatieff's reservations, and I am sure that he is not alone, seem to be that the honor of the Prophet is not relevant to the prejudice, discrimination, and harassment that Muslims experience in Britain; that it is not a focus of oppression and violence; so that however offended Muslims may be by abuse of the Prophet, it is not likely to make them feel physically insecure. He infers, therefore, that while "you filthy Muslim" harms them, abuse of the Prophet only insults them and does not warrant legal intervention. Muslims will argue, however, that, historically, vilification of the Prophet and of their faith is central to how the West has expressed hatred for them and has led to violence and expulsion on a large scale. It may be that the West thinks in a more secular mode now, but Muslims are fearful of what a revival of that old provocation can lead to. They are also mindful of how medieval religious anti-Semitism provided much of the imagery and folk memory that nourished modern racial anti-Semitism, and believe that religious Islamophobia will reinforce secular anti-Muslim racism if left unchecked. The numerous attacks on mosques, the appearance of graffiti such as "Gas the Muslims" (in Bradford, Yorkshire) and "Kill a Muslim for Christmas" (London) and cases of discrimination in employment against Muslims at the time of the *Satanic Verses* affair suggests indeed that Muslims qua Muslims had become a target for secular racism by the early 1990s.[9]

Since then, and especially since 9/11, this has multiplied and indeed has been joined by a prominent religious Islamophobia, especially among the Christian Right in the United States. The Runnymeade Trust Commission on British Muslims and Islamophobia (2004) cites two examples. In November 2001, in a speech on NBC *Nightly News*, Rev. Franklin Graham, the son and assistant to the famous evangelist and confidant of President G. W. Bush, Billy Graham, claimed that "Islam is a very evil and wicked religion." Rev. Jerry Vines, past president of the largest Christian organization in the United States, the Southern Baptist Convention, told the Convention in June 2002 that "Muhammad was a demon-possessed paedophile"—an image right out of *The Satanic Verses*!

In any case, no matter what the nature of the more usual defamation and discrimination may be, in order to resist it, as argued in the previous chapter, Muslims have to draw strength from the sources of their group pride, that is to say, from nonsecular roots. An attack on those roots, even if it is not the most typical of the harassments Muslims currently experience, is the more devastating, for it hits the group in a way that does most damage and undermines its strength as a group to resist attacks from any direction. For these reasons as well as imani ghairat, given the choice between having to suffer a secular-ized "you filthy Muslim" (one that was not shorthand for "you filthy follower of the lewd, and so on, Prophet") and insults on the Prophet, many Muslims would prefer to have to live with the former—just as Jews might prefer to suffer contemporary insults rather than allow anything that defiles the memory of those who suffered and died in the Holocaust. Of course, not all Muslims are active believers, and they may not weigh the two sorts of insult in the same way as some believers. But they know that an abusive attack on the believers by non-Muslims or in a non-Muslim society ultimately affects the digni-ty, pride, social status, and safety of Muslims as a group and therefore of all Muslims. Under such an attack many nonpracticing or lapsed Muslims, as happened with the *Satanic Verses* affair, instinctively rally round in community solidarity. The effect is just the same as when in Northern Ireland lapsed Catholics, who among themselves may be irreverent about their community's dogmas and rituals, are provoked to anger and community defense when Protestants or oth-ers taunt believers with images of the Virgin Mary as a whore. Such taunts are not part of the healthy clash of ideas that all beliefs ought to be subject to; they are an incitement to community hatred based on an intimate knowledge of what will hurt and set the communities apart. It is for this reason that in Northern Ireland, though not in the rest of the United Kingdom, incitement to religious hatred is a crimi-nal offense. If Muslims and other minorities are to be welcomed as a constituent community of Britain, they will need similar protection against group defamation (Lee 1990c).

Liberals may well prefer, given the history of Europe out of which liberalism has arisen, that minority groups should not identify them-selves so closely with a religion, that religion should not be a form of group self-definition. But is this anything more than an antireligion prejudice? It is now widely acknowledged that, despite how others may see them, many Muslims do not primarily see themselves in terms of color or race and that religion is central to their ethnicity, to their group-beingness, and to how they relate to other groups (see chapters 6 and 8; Modood et al. 1997, ch. 9; Jacobson 1997; Saeed, Blain, and Forbes 1999). Muslims are not alone in this: a similar situation holds not just with Jews and Catholics in some contexts, but also with Sikhs and Hindus. Whatever reservations liberals may have about giving public recognition and legal protection to religious groups, an antireligion prejudice can itself be a form of racial discrimination, for religion is currently of greater personal and community importance to non-white than to white people in this country; hence, however racially neutral the principles of secularism may be in their formulation, they will affect different groups in unequal ways. Muslims in particular feel that they suffer a double discrimination: they do not enjoy the legal protection favored on the majority religion, and, not being a racial group, they are not recognized as a group protected by the incitement to racial hatred offense. The *Satanic Verses* crisis was not a clash "between incompatible conceptions of freedom." It was an attempt by Muslims, however inept in terms of public relations and callous as regards the author of that book,[10] to press their claim to be recognized as an oppressed group in British society, as a group whose essential dignity must be respected by the rest of society. The important question then is, who is to be protected by law? Muslims believe that they are worthy enough to merit legal protection against group defamation, in addition to the groups that already enjoy this protection. The Muslim protests were not so much a refusal to come to terms with modern creative literature and humanistic irreverence, not some form of opting out of the country that they have made their home, but a demand to be incorporated with the same kind of legal protection as other oppressed groups—a demand for a full membership in which society makes clear through law and other institutional means that gross defamation will not be tolerated.

Free Speech and Free Discourse

> Space is not often given—it has to be taken. You have to create it, and when a group of people appears to be intolerant, to be demanding that the established norms be opened up a little, it is also a demand to *create a space in which a dialogue is possible.*[11]

The above quote from Bhikhu Parekh—in a piece rich in insights into the dynamics of multiculturalism—links the intolerance of which campaigns for rights can be guilty with the objective that we should all have before us, a space in which dialogue is possible. R. G. Collingwood, when forced to justify what was superior about liberal democracy compared to the Nazis, placed the commitment to political debate, to the politics of persuasion, at the heart of his understanding of liberalism (Collingwood 1942). Free and open debate on all matters of public concern did not mean what some currently call "freedom of expression." Free debate is structured by a goal and by an important restraint. The goal is that all speech, all discourse, should use every opportunity to convert nonagreement into at least some possibility of meaningful exchange: to avoid the *eristic* in favor of the *dialectic*. The paradigmatic examples of eristic reasoning are the early Socratic dialogues where no effort is made by Socrates to understand his opponent, to help his opponent reach greater understanding, or to seek some constructive common ground; instead, the logos is used to break up the opponent's understanding, to demonstrate Socrates' intellectual superiority and to exert intellectual power over his opponent. None of these dialogues leads anywhere; they all break down in bad temper. When students of philosophy are first introduced to these works, most are dismayed that philosophy can be so barren and surprised that Socrates does not sometimes get a physical beating. The dialectic, on the other hand, as demonstrated in the main part of Plato's *Republic*, uses questioning and criticism carried out cooperatively and constructively. Its ideal is to share understanding and through creative difference to improve understanding. The restraint that dialogue must work with is that arguments must not be pressed or criticisms ignored in a way that threatens the possibility of discourse. Collingwood recognizes that the principal risk to civilized discourse is one party rousing anger or fear or some other powerful disabling emotions in another, such that the latter is unable to exercise rational control over himself or herself, and the dialogue collapses into uncivil conflict; indeed, Collingwood calls such a provocation the use of "force" and believes that it is essential to civilized relations that individuals do not provoke such conduct (the gradual elimination/reduction of force from our relations with each other being the mark of civility) (Collingwood 1942, par. 35.41–35.45).

Of course, social life is not like a philosophy seminar, the law should not be used to make it so, and Collingwood did not intend it so. The point is that the ideal of civilized discourse has built-in restraints, and in the extreme case liberals may have to use law (where nothing else will do) to prevent the kind of abuse and provocation that would lead to a breakdown. As Susan Mendus has put it: "Where free speech is employed in such a way as to destroy the possibility of communication, and of mutual understanding, then its *raison d'etre* is destroyed" (1990, 16). She sees in this idea a basis of a socialist conception of tolerance, of appreciating that people's existing ethnic and other group loyalties have to be respected, indeed welcomed, if they are to feel a sense of belonging and common citizenship that socialist solidarity seeks to create (1989, 154–62).

Appeals to solidarity can sometimes lead to undue restrictions on free speech. I personally think that the National Union of Students' campaign of No Platform for Racists and Fascists in the 1980s is an example.[12] Yet some socialists responded to the Rushdie affair by asserting libertarianism. The authors John Mortimer and Hanif Kureishi are two who declared that they could no longer support an incitement to racial hatred statute except where the incitement could be shown to lead directly to violence (i.e., the pre-1965 position), and others have made comments in the heat of the *Satanic Verses* conflict as if that were their position too.[13] The libertarianism, whether genuine or born out of a moral panic or simply out of solidarity for a fellow artist, is out of character with all the mainstream British political philosophies that, at least since the time of T. H. Green, have been committed to balancing the rights of individuals with the good of the community. It is only in the context of shared conventions and responsibilities that rights arise and can be met, and just as unbridled economic individualism can destroy the ethical base on which it depends for the continuation of a public order, so similarly the artist without social responsibility, who provokes anger where there can be no dialogue, threatens the field of discourse itself. Twentieth-century liberal politics have successfully resisted the individualism of Herbert Spencer and John Stuart Mill, of Max Stirner and Nietzsche, and recognized that where internalized restraints break down, social harmony and other goals must be protected by means of law. In the 1980s we saw the rise and later to some extent the reining in of the latest brand of economic individualism; we should not succumb to the libertarianism that sees the artist as a Nietzschean *Ubermensch,* towering above conventional morality with perfect liberty to publish imaginative explorations regardless of social consequences. In most cases the necessary inhibitions will be acquired through habit, principle, sympathy, and public censure, but where they are lacking and civility is threatened, the law may be the only recourse available.

The Need for Public Accountability and Equality

Some people who may accept the substance of the foregoing arguments still believe that the best way to deal with most or all forms of group defamation is by nonlegal means (Lee 1990a, 17; P. Jones 1993). Of course, the law can only deal with the most extreme cases, and even there its legitimacy depends on cultural attitudes, forms of self, and social restraint that have a much wider scope than the law itself. For the law to have any support at all, challenges to it must be relatively few; moral disapproval, public censure, acceptance by the political parties, the education system, the mass media, artists, publishers, and so on is crucial. But for any of this to take place, at least two conditions have to be fulfilled in connection with any group:

- Its condition is thoroughly publicized and its sensibilities are widely understood.
- It can exercise sufficient pressure when rallied to prevent the defamation from being published.

In the absence of these two conditions, especially the second, the more powerful and more established groups will be able to manage without recourse to legal action, while weaker groups will be forced to put up with the libel or make a lot of protest and noise, make a nuisance of themselves, and risk being labeled as intolerant in the process and thereby lose what public sympathy they initially had. And is not this more or less what happens? A Jewish lobby was able to stop the stage production of Jim Allen's *Perdition* at the Royal Court Theatre with little adverse publicity; they were able to postpone twice a BBC Desert Island Discs interview with Lady Moseley; according to some press reports they were a contributory factor in the banning of the anti-Rushdie video *International Guerrillas*. British blacks do not have anything like the same influence, though many public libraries and schools are careful not to give offense, and the publisher of Noddy books about the time of the *Satanic Verses* protests succumbed to black protests and banished golliwogs (a grotesque black doll) from Toytown, a major toy store. American blacks are a more substantial lobby and were able in October 1989 to get an association of advertising agencies to collectively refuse to handle a $25-million advertising campaign by Benetton because they thought it evoked images of black slavery. In 1967 Allen Lane, the owner of

Penguin (which was to publish *The Satanic Verses* two decades later), surreptitiously burned the entire stock of Siné's *Massacre* because some Christian booksellers found it deeply offensive (Webster 1990, 26–27). Nine years later, plans for *The Many Faces of Jesus,* a film on the sex life of the hero, had to be abandoned in the face of protests including those of the queen and the prime minister of the day. If some of these examples are thought to belong to the pre–*Satanic Verses* era, one should also consider the banning of the anti-Semitic *Lord Horror,* a novel based on the life of the traitor Lord Haw-Haw (*Sunday Telegraph,* September 8, 1991, 3); the withdrawal and pulping of the graphic novel *True Faith* by one of Robert Maxwell's companies because he learned that it caused offense to some Christians (*Muslim News,* April 19, 1991, 3); the decision by the BBC to cancel the screening of *The Last Temptation of Christ* (a film banned from cinemas by many local authorities);[14] the seizure by Scotland Yard of records by Niggas with Attitudes on the grounds that the rap music "could provoke racial hatred against whites and police" (*Daily Mail,* June 5, 1991, 5); the virtual banning of Robert Crumb's comic book, *My Troubles with Women,* by the refusal of his usual distributors to handle it because "it is degrading to women" (*Independent on Sunday,* October 14, 1990). These are all British examples, but similar examples of state censorship by the powerful and censorship through pressure groups can be found in each of the countries in which Muslims are vilified as being uniquely illiberal, though often they receive little or no publicity (*Independent Magazine,* September 7, 1991).[15] It is indeed remarkable that in the same period of time that liberal intellectuals rallied round "I am not anti-Muslim but . . ." speeches, they have endorsed a rising tide of politically correct censorship, particularly on American campuses, without any sense of hypocrisy. Muslims, understandably, complain of double standards; far from taking exhortations to freedom of expressions to heart, perhaps they should be encouraged by what is possible.

Because the absence of a law or some other publicly accountable procedure is inegalitarian and tends toward creating confrontational situations, the issue of group defamation cannot be left entirely to the process of informal pressure and public indignation. Perhaps a combination of a minimalist legal framework and a voluntary code of practice regulated by a semiofficial body is a happy compromise. I am thinking of something like the equivalent of the Press Council. While that particular body has not been notably successful in its aims, perhaps in the less rough world of books a Writers Council may be adequate (Weale 1990, 58). Group defamation could be explicitly added to the following statement from the charter of PEN, the World Association of Writers, which could be used as a basis of its objectives:

> Since freedom implies voluntary restraint, members pledge themselves to oppose such evils of free press as mendacious publication, deliberate falsehood and distortion of facts for political and personal ends.

Such restraint cannot in my view be entirely a matter of individual conscience. There has to be some public forum where these issues are discussed, principles laid down, specific charges examined, defenses heard, apologies and retractions made, and commitments about future behavior given. In this way groups who feel despised or powerless can have their case heard and the same standards applied to all groups. One has to be very careful, of course, in being able to distinguish defamation from legitimate criticism, for while freedom of expression is too gross a right and has to be seriously qualified by the protection of minorities and other civilized values, freedom of inquiry is too precious to lose. It is for this reason that I think the Anglo-Saxon instinct is to be preferred to the German or French mode of protection. Defamation should ideally be confined to "threatening, abusive, or insulting" language or images, not to the presentation of arguments, however outrageous, in the context of ongoing debates. I appreciate that this is something of an ideal and could not always be adhered to, and that a debate itself is something that needs to be created and is at least partly dependent on social equality and access to education, research, the media, publishers, and so on. Yet ideals are important, for without them we are left uncertain as to what is at issue in a particular conflict and the direction we need to be moving in. Where reasoned discussion is possible, where dignity and mutual understanding can be maintained through sympathy and intellectual discipline in which insults have no place, then, in my opinion, even outrageous arguments amount to something less than defamation and must be, because they can be, replied to differently than by proscription. This applies to arguments that embody the four sample propositions above—though the four should be treated equally. Where the content of an argument is unpalatable, special attention needs to be given to its form and mode of presentation. The form of the argument must aspire to dialogue: it must be an argument *with* not *about* the minority group in question, and reasoned refutation must be possible. The ideal, as far as free speech is concerned, ought to be to create the conditions for *dialectical* inquiry and to prevent those conditions that lead to the breakdown of rational discourse into *eristical* conflict. This is the liberal ideal, not the impossible utopia offered by literary libertarians where everyone is free to abuse and insult everybody else because words cease to wound and insults cease to hurt.

Postscript

The law on incitement to hatred in the United Kingdom has developed somewhat since the *Satanic Verses* affair. A new offense has been created that does not depend on intention and so indirectly gives "incitement" the meaning that I have argued is implicit in key policy discourses and in the law of various countries. Moreover, religion in some contexts is becoming entwined with race. The 1998 Crime and Disorder Act introduced the concept of a "racially aggravated" offense that covers the intention of an act and its consequences as well. It relates primarily to acts of violence but also to amendments to the section of the 1986 Public Order Act that deals with threatening, abusive, or insulting behavior. The latter behavior is not determined by intentions alone. Following 9/11, an Anti-Terrorism, Crime, and Security Act was quickly passed and extended the phrase "racially aggravated" to "racially or religiously aggravated." In 2003, the High Court upheld the conviction in the *Norwood* case, arguing that displaying a British National Party poster bearing the words "Islam out of Britain" and "Protect the British People" accompanied by a picture of the 9/11 attack on the Twin Towers amounted to an offense because it caused alarm or distress. The High Court argued that evidence of actual alarm or distress was not necessary if it was determined that "any right thinking member of society" is likely to be caused harassment, alarm, or distress. It concluded, therefore, that the poster was racially insulting and, additionally, religiously aggravated. It seems then—though this is only on the basis of one case—that Muslims in Britain may have some legal protection against a version of incitement to religious hatred (for further details see *Norwood v. DPP* [2003], which is discussed in Runnymede Trust Commission 2004).

Seven

Multiculturalism, Secularism, and the State

Recent migrations have created new multicultural situations in Western Europe and elsewhere. At the center of this are religious groups. I want to address the question of whether the new plurality of faiths requires a deepening of the institutional separation between private faith and public authority. I shall suggest that the political project of multiculturalism, with its reappraisal of the public/private distinction, particularly the relationship between ethnicity and citizenship, poses a challenge to the taken-for-granted secularism of many theorists of multiculturalism.

I shall argue that the strict division between the public and privates spheres as argued by some multiculturalists does not stand up to scrutiny and, more particularly, does not adequately take into account the interdependence that exists between the public and private spheres. Moreover, the assertion of a strict divide between the public and private spheres, far from underpinning multiculturalism, will work to prevent its emergence. In the light of the interdependence between the public and private spheres, the call for the development of a "politics of recognition" becomes more intelligible: it explains why minority groups, among others, are calling for the appropriate public recognition of their private communal identities. A brief consideration of how different kinds of states may or may not be able to facilitate this recognition forms the basis of the penultimate section of this chapter. And finally, I shall conclude by arguing that a moderately, rather than a radically, secular state is the best mechanism through which the claims for recognition put forward by contending religious groups can be satisfied.

Multiculturalism and the Strict Division between Public and Private Spheres

There is a body of theoretical opinion that argues that the public/private distinction is essential to multiculturalism. John Rex, for example, distinguishes between plural societies such as apartheid South Africa and the multicultural ideal. He contends that the fundamental distinction between them is that the latter restricts cultural diversity to a private sphere so all enjoy equality of opportunity and uniform treatment in the public domain (1986, ch. 7). Immigrants and minorities do not have to respect the normative power of a dominant culture, but there must be a normative universality in relation to law, politics, economics, and welfare policy.

An important assumption contained in this way of seeing the public/private distinction is found in a discussion by Habermas. Although he maintains that a recipient society cannot require immigrants to assimilate—immigrants cannot be obliged to conform to the dominant way of life—he also contends that a democratic constitutional regime must seek to "preserve the identity of the political community, which nothing, including immigration, can be permitted to encroach upon, since that identity is founded on the constitutional principles anchored in the political culture and not on the basic ethical orientations of the cultural form of life predominant in that country" (1994, 139). But is this distinction between the political and cultural identities of a society valid? Politics and law depend to some degree on shared ethical assumptions and inevitably reflect the norms and values of the society they are part of. In this sense, no regime stands outside culture, ethnicity, or nationality, and changes in these will need to be reflected in the political arrangements of the regime. Indeed, Habermas seems to concede this when he states that "as other forms of life become established (i.e., following immigration) the horizon within which citizens henceforth interpret their common constitutional principles may also expand" (139–40). But this concession begs the question of the coherence of his initial distinction. If the political identity of the regime is determined by reference to the "constitutional principles anchored in the political culture," how can the articulation, interpretation, and, therefore, operation of these constitutional principles not be subject to the "basic ethical orientations" of new (religious) citizens, given these orientations provide the fundamental interpretative horizons for these principles? As the fundamental interpretative horizons of the citizenry "expands" through the immigration of peoples with religions new to that society, so too the political identity of the regime is inevitably altered. Moreover, the interdependence between the political and the cultural, the public and the private, is not confined to the level of ethical generalities. On a practical level, as Rex recognizes, religious communities may look to the state to support their culture (e.g., through support for religious schools and other educational institutions), and the state may, reciprocally, look to religious communities to inculcate virtues such as truth telling, respect for property, service to others, and so on, without which a civic morality would have nothing to build on.

Furthermore, if the public and private spheres mutually shape each other in these ways, then however abstract and rational the principles of a public order may be, they will reflect, to use Rex's term, the "folk cultures" out of which that particular public order has grown. If this is the case, then there can be no question of the public sphere being morally, ethnically, or religiously neutral. Rather, it will inevitably appeal to points of privately shared values and a sense of belonging found within the (religious and nonreligious) communities that make up society, as well as to the superstructure of conventions, laws, and principles that regulate it. And this will have the further important implication that those citizens whose moral, ethnic, or religious communal identities are most adequately reflected in the political identity of the regime, those citizens whose private identity fits most comfortably with this political identity, will feel least the force of a rigidly enforced public/private distinction. They may only become aware of its coercive influence when they have to share the public domain with persons from other communities, persons who may wish the identity of the political community to reflect something of their own community, too.

There is, therefore, a real possibility that the elaboration of a strict public/private distinction may simply act to buttress the privileged position of the historically integrated folk cultures at the expense of the historically subordinated or newly migrated folk. In this context, therefore, a strict interpretation and application of the public/private distinction, far from underpinning multiculturalism, will work to prevent its emergence.

Public/Private Interdependence and the Politics of Recognition

If we recognize that the public sphere is not morally neutral, that the public order is not culturally, religiously, or ethnically blind, we can begin to understand why oppressed, marginalized, or immigrant groups may want that public order (in which they may for the first time have rights of participation) to "recognize" them, to be "user-friendly" to the new folks. The logic of demanding that public institutions acknowledge their ways of doing things becomes readily intelligible, as does the whole phenomenon of minorities seeking increased visibility, of contesting the boundaries of the public, of not simply asking to be left alone and to be civilly tolerated.

The content of what is claimed today in the name of equality is more than what would have been claimed in the 1960s. Iris Young expresses well the new political climate when she describes the emergence of an ideal of equality based not just on allowing excluded groups to assimilate and live by the norms of dominant groups, but also on the view that "a positive self-definition of group difference is in fact more liberatory" (1990, 157). She cites the examples of the black power movement, the gay pride assertion that sexual identity is a matter of culture and politics, and a feminism that emphasizes the positivity and specificity of female experience and values. (These movements have not had the same impact in Europe as in parts of North America, but are nevertheless present.)

The shift in the content of these claims is from an understanding of equality in terms of individualism and cultural assimilation to a politics of recognition, to equality as encompassing public ethnicity, that is to say, equality as not having to hide or apologize for one's origins, family, or community, but requiring others to show respect for them and adapt public attitudes and arrangements so that the heritage they represent is encouraged rather than ignored or expected to wither away.

There seem to be two distinct conceptions of equal citizenship, each based on a different view of what is public and private. Broadly speaking, the first equates to the content of the claims for equality proffered in the 1960s; the second accords more fully with the content of the claims presented by contemporary proponents of a politics of recognition. These two conceptions of equality may be stated as follows:

1. The right of assimilation to the majority/dominant culture in the public sphere and toleration of "difference" in the private sphere.
2. The right to have one's "difference" (minority, ethnicity, and so on) recognized and supported in the public and the private spheres.

These are not mutually exclusive; in my view, multiculturalism requires support for both. The assumption behind the first conception is that participation in the public or national culture is necessary for the effective exercise of citizenship (the only obstacles to which are the exclusionary processes preventing gradual assimilation). The second conception assumes groups excluded from the public or national culture have their citizenship diminished as a result but proposes to remedy this by offering the right to assimilate while, at the same time, agreeing to widen and adapt the public or national culture (including the public and media symbols of national membership) to incorporate the relevant minority ethnicities.

It may be thought that the second conception of equality involves something of a contradiction: it accepts that participation in national or shared culture(s) is necessary for effective equality but encourages individuals to cultivate minority identities and practices. There is indeed a genuine tension here, and perhaps it can only be resolved in practice through finding and cultivating points of common ground between dominant and subordinate cultures, as well as new syntheses and hybridities. For an effective multicultural interaction, the important thing is this tension should not be heightened by the burdens of change—or the costs of not changing—all falling on one party to the encounter.

The Multicultural State

Having suggested that a strict division between the public and private spheres does not stand up to scrutiny, and having briefly set out in what sense the call for recognition of minority groups (including religious groups) can be seen to be reasonable given the interdependence between the public and private spheres, let us briefly examine the types of conceptions of the individual, community, and the state that are consistent with these views, for that may illuminate what is at issue and the sources of disagreement—not least *among* advocates of multiculturalism. More particularly, I suggest that how we interpret and apply the public/private distinction will depend on the extent to which one believes individuals, (ethnic) groups, and the (nation-)state form coherent unities, are the bearers of ethical claims, and can be integrated with each other. I offer below five ideal types, marking five possible ways in which one could respond to the contemporary challenge of diversity consequent upon immigration in Europe.[1]

The Decentered Self

Some theorists describe the present condition as "postmodern." Among the many things meant by this term is the assertion that, due to factors such as migration and the globalization of economics, consumption, and communications, societies can no longer be constituted by stable collective purposes and identities organized territorially by the nation-state. In its most radical version, this view rejects not only the possibility of a politically constituted multiculturalism, but also the idea of a unified self per se:

> If we feel we have a unified identity . . . it is only because we construct a comforting story or "narrative of the self" about ourselves. . . . The fully unified, completed, secure and coherent identity is a fantasy. Instead, as the systems of meaning and cultural representation multiply, we are confronted by a bewildering, fleeting multiplicity of possible identities, any one of which we could identify with—at least temporarily. (Hall 1992b, 277)[2]

The radical multiple self has a penchant for identities but prefers surfing on the waves of deconstruction to seeking reconstruction in multiplicity. It is a post-self rather than a multi-self. Even in less radical versions, the self is no more connected to one location/society/state than another, any more than the typical consumer is connected to one producer or the goods of one country. Reconciled to multiplicity as an end in itself, its vision of multiculturalism is confined to personal lifestyles and cosmopolitan consumerism; more significantly, its vision of multiculturalism does not extend to the state, which it confidently expects to wither away.

Under this scheme, therefore, the call for recognition and the contention of the interdependence between the public and private spheres have little meaning. At most, multiculturalism can mean the development of ever more different (even bizarre) "life-style enclaves" where the postmodern self can find or lose itself without (much) reference to the character of the public sphere (Bellah et al. 1985, 72). So long as the public culture does not use coercive force to prevent the fluidity and multiplicity of the postmodern person, he or she can have no need or desire to influence the character of the public culture. The decentered self is at its most happily apolitical where the state is punctiliously culturally neutral.

The Liberal State

In contrast, the liberal theorist expects the integrity of individuals (though not necessarily large-scale communities) to survive the social changes that are in motion. Individuals may temporarily become disoriented, bewildered by the multiplicity of identities, decentered, but the liberal theorist confidently believes they will soon recenter themselves. Lifestyles in their neighborhoods may change as persons of exotic appearance, large families, and pungent-smelling foods move in. The old residents and the new have to adjust (perhaps gradually, certainly repeatedly) their sense of self, community, and country as these changes occur, but the liberal theorist contends that no major political project other than the elimination of discrimination is required to achieve this. The state exists to protect the rights of individuals, but the question of recognizing new ethnic groups does not arise, for the state does not recognize any groups. Individuals relate to the state as individual citizens, not as members of the group. The state is group blind, it cannot "see" color, gender, ethnicity, religion, or even nationality. In the parlance of North American political theorists (it is certainly easier to see the United States than any European state as approximating to this liberal ideal), the just state is neutral between rival conceptions of the good. It does not promote one or more national cultures, religions, ways of life, and so on. These matters remain private to individuals in their voluntary associations with each other. Nor does the state promote any syncretic vision of common living, of fellow feeling, between the inhabitants of that territory other than the legal entitlements and duties that define civic membership.

In a liberal regime, therefore, there is no need to recognize the particular identity of ethnic or religious groups. Their equal citizenship is assured, and their equality is determined by reference to an overarching political viewpoint whose legitimacy is determined without reference to the particular "basic ethical orientations" of any or all of the groups within society.[3] Even if it could be shown that a liberal regime was not morally, ethnically, or religiously neutral in its effect, this would be considered by the liberal theorist to be of no consequence: it would not impinge on the claim to neutrality presented by the liberal regime. Any regulatory regime will affect diverse groups differently: what is important to the liberal theorist is the neutrality of the procedure to decide between the various individuals and groups within society, not the neutrality of the outcomes (Ackerman 1990, 39; Rawls 1993, 194; Larmore 1987, 44). Liberals argue that even if the effect of a liberal regime may be to bolster dominant groups, its neutrality is not compromised because *in intention* it does not seek to prejudice any group (Nagel 1991, 166). In the light of this, the question of the public recognition of private communal identities, and so on, does not arise; the liberal state can remain indifferent to such claims. Whatever the coherence of the distinction between neutrality in intention and neutrality in effect, it is naive to expect that those who are not satisfied by the outcomes that are generated will not question the legitimacy of the procedures that systematically prevent the outcomes that their conception of the good directs them toward.

The Republic

The ideal republic, like the liberal state, does not recognize groups among the citizenry. It relates to each citizen as an individual. Yet, unlike the liberal state, it is amenable to one collective project; more precisely, it is itself a collective project, a project that is not reducible to the protection of the rights of individuals or the maximization of the choices open to individuals. The republic seeks to enhance the lives of its members by making them a part of a way of living that individuals could not create for themselves; it seeks to make the individuals members of a civic community. This community may be based on subscription to "universal" principles such as liberty, equality, and fraternity; to the promotion of a national culture; or, as in the case of France, to both. In a republic, the formation of public ethnicity by immigration or in other ways would be discouraged, and there would be strong expectation, even pressure, for individuals to assimilate to the national identity. In such a situation, it would be difficult to see how the call for public recognition by minority ethnic and religious groups can get off the ground.

The Federation of Communities

In contrast to the first three responses to multicultural diversity, this option is built on the assumption that the individual is not the unit (or at least not the only unit) to which the state must relate. Rather, individuals belong to and are shaped by communities, which are the primary focus of their loyalty and the regulators of their social life. Far from being confined to the private sphere, communities are the primary agents of the public sphere. Public life in fact consists of organized communities relating to each other, and the state is therefore a federation of communities and exists to protect the rights of communities.

As with all of the ideal types listed here, one can think of a more radical or extreme version of the model and a more moderate version, which balances the rights of communities with the rights of individuals, including the right to exit from communities. The *millet* system of the Ottoman empire, harking back to Prophet Muhammad's Constitution of Medina in the seventh century, which has been called "the first plural society in history" (Badawi 2003, 18), delegated some powers of the state to Christian and Jewish communities. Their power to administer personal law within their communities in accordance with their own legal system is an example of this model of the multicultural state and has occasionally been invoked in Britain as an example to emulate. The *millet* system offered significant autonomy to communities but, of course, did not offer equality between communities or any conception of democratic citizenship. The problem with this system of political organization is not that it is unable to give suitable cognizance to the call for recognition by minority ethnic and religious groups, but rather the fact it is likely to remain an unattractive proposition to many unless a democratic variant can be devised. The system of pillarization in the Netherlands or Belgium, a moderate version of this type of institutionalized communal diversity within a democratic framework, may be favored by some.[4]

The Plural State

A more promising conception of the organization of the multicultural state is provided by the notion of the plural state. In this model, again an ideal type of which there can be strong and weak forms, there is a recognition that social life consists of individuals and groups and both need to be provided for in the formal and informal distribution of powers—not just in law, but in representation in the offices of the state, public committees, consultative exercises, and access to public fora. There may be some rights for all individuals as in the liberal state, but mediating institutions such as trade unions, churches, neighborhoods, immigrant associations, and so on may also be encouraged to be active public players and fora for political discussion and may even have a formal representative or administrative role to play in the state. The plural state, however, allows for, indeed probably requires, an ethical conception of citizenship and not only an instrumental one as in the liberal and federation-of-communities conceptions. The understanding that individuals are partly constituted by the lives of families and communities fits well with the recognition that the moral individual is partly shaped by the social order constituted by citizenship and the publics that amplify and qualify, sustain, critique, and reform citizenship.

If the state should come to have this kind of importance in people's lives, it is most likely they will, as in a republic, emotionally and psychologically invest in the state and its projects. The most usual form of this emotional relationship is a sense of national identity. In an undiluted form national identity, like most group identifications, can be dangerous and certainly incompatible with multiculturalism. On the other hand, assuming a plurality of identities and not a narrow nationalism, the plural state, unlike the liberal state, is able to offer an emotional identity with the whole to counterbalance the emotional loyalties to ethnic and religious communities, which should prevent the fragmentation of society into narrow, selfish communalisms, while the presence of these strong community identities will be an effective check against monocultural statism.

For the plural state, the challenge of the new multiculturalism is the integration of transplanted cultures, heritages, and peoples into long-established yet ongoing historic national ones. It is about creating a cultural synthesis in both private and public spaces, including education and welfare. Above all, proponents of the new multiculturalism are anxious to find new ways of extending, reforming, and syncretizing existing forms of public culture and citizenship. This is not about decentering society or deconstructing the nation-state; rather it is concerned with integrating difference by remaking the nation-state. In contrast to common political parlance, "integration" here is not synonymous with "assimilation." Assimilation is something immigrants or minorities must do or have done to them, whereas integration is interactive, a two-way process: both parties are an active ingredient and so something new is created. For the plural state, then, multiculturalism means re-forming national identity and citizenship.

Secularism and Multiculturalism

If, as I argue, the plural state provides a good model for a viable multicultural state, the question remains whether such a state must inevitably exclude religious communities qua religious communities from participating in the political life of the state. More particularly, should the multicultural state be a radically secular state? Or alternatively, can religious communities play a central role in the political life of a multicultural state?

In examining these questions, we must not be too quick to exclude particular religious communities from participation in the political debates, and so forth, of a multicultural state. Uncompromising secularism should not be embraced without careful consideration of the possibilities for reasonable dialogue between religious and nonreligious groups. In particular, we must beware of an ignorance-cum-prejudice about Muslims that is apparent among even the best political philosophers (Modood 1996b, 178–79).

Charles Taylor makes this mistake in his argument for a politics of recognition. In contrast to Iris Young, he presents a moderate version of a "politics of difference," and part of his moderation consists in his recognition that not everybody can join the party: there are some groups to whom a politics of recognition cannot be extended within a liberal polity, such as mainstream Muslims. While he refers to the controversy over *The Satanic Verses*, the only argument he offers for the exclusion is: "For mainstream Islam, there is no question of separating politics and religion the way we have come to expect in Western liberal society" (1994, 62). I believe this is an odd conclusion for at least two reasons.

First, it seems inconsistent with the starting point of the argument for multicultural equality; it is mistaken to separate culture and politics. More to the point, it all depends on what one means by separation. Two modes of activity are separate when they have no connection with each other (absolute separation), but activities can still be distinct from each other even though there may be points of overlap (relative separation). The person who denies that politics and religion are absolutely separate can still allow for relative separation. In contemporary Islam there are ideological arguments for the absolute subordination of politics to religious leaders (e.g., Khomeini; even then the ideology is not always deemed practical), but this is not mainstream Islam, any more than the model of politics in Calvin's Geneva is mainstream Christianity.

Historically, Islam has been given a certain official status and preeminence in states in which Muslims ruled (just as Christianity or a particular Christian denomination had preeminence where Christians ruled). In these states Islam was the basis of state ceremonials and insignia, and public hostility against Islam was a punishable offense (sometimes a capital offense). Islam was the basis of jurisprudence but not positive law. Legislation, decrees, law enforcement, taxation, military power, foreign policy, and so on were all regarded as the prerogative of the ruler(s), as political power, which had its own imperatives, skills, and so on, and was rarely held by saints or spiritual leaders. Moreover, rulers had a duty to protect minorities.

Just as it is possible to distinguish between theocracy and mainstream Islam, so it is possible to distinguish between radical or ideological secularism, which argues for an absolute separation between state and religion, and the moderate forms that exist throughout Western Europe except France. In nearly all of Western Europe there are points of symbolic, institutional, policy, and fiscal linkages between the state and aspects of Christianity. Secularism has increasingly grown in power and scope, but it is clear that a historically evolved and evolving compromise with religion is the defining feature of Western European secularism, rather than the absolute separation of religion and politics. Secularism today does enjoy a hegemony in Western Europe, but it is a moderate rather than a radical, a pragmatic rather than an ideological, secularism. Paradoxical as it may seem, Table 11 shows that mainstream Islam and mainstream secularism are philosophically closer to each other than either is to its radical versions. Muslims then should not be excluded from participation in the multicultural state because their views about politics are not secular enough. There is still a sufficient divide between private and public spheres in the Islamic faith to facilitate dialogue with other (contending) religious and nonreligious communities and beliefs.

Table 11. Islamic and secularist views regarding the separation of religion and the state.

Religion-State	Radical secularism	Radical Islam	Moderate secularism	Moderate Islam
1. Absolute separation	Yes	No	No	No
2. No separation	No	Yes	No	No
3. Relative separation	No	No	Yes	Yes

There is an alternative argument, however, for a multiculturalism that explicitly embraces radical secularism. Versions of this argument are quite popular with reformers as well as academics in Britain at the moment (Modood 1994a, 1997). This argument recognizes that, in a country like Britain, religion and state are not separate; the constitution gives the Church of England (and Scotland), with its links with the monarchy and Parliament, a privileged position, often referred to as "establishment." Moreover, it is asserted that an institutional privileging of one group is ipso facto a degrading of all the others, allowing them only second-class citizenship: establishment "assumes a correspondence between national and religious identity which marginalizes non-established churches, and especially non-Christians as only partial members of the British national collectivity" (Yuval-Davis 1992, 283). It is maintained that if we are to take multicultural equality seriously, the Church of England ought to be disestablished: public multiculturalism implies radical secularism, regardless of whatever compromises might have been historically required.

This argument relies on three different assumptions that I will consider in turn.

Neutrality

It seems to be assumed that equality between religions requires the multicultural state to be neutral between them, as derived from Rawls's contention that the just state is neutral between "rival conceptions of the good." It is, however, an appeal to a conception of neutrality that theorists of difference disallow, for they argue that the state is always for or against certain cultural configurations: impartiality and openness to reason, even when formally constituted through rules and procedures, reflect a dominant cultural ethos, enabling those who share that ethos to flourish while hindering those who are at odds with it (Young 1990).

This objection seems to apply to secularism in particular; even where it is not avowedly atheistical, it seems not to be neutral between religions. For some people, religion is about the inner life or personal conduct or individual salvation; for others, it includes communal obligations, a public philosophy, and political action (for example, the Christian socialism favored by the British Labour prime minister, Tony Blair, not to mention the various Christian Democratic parties in Western Europe). Radical secular political arrangements seem to suit and favor private religions but not those that require public action. It is surely a contradiction to require both that the state should be neutral about religion and that the state should demand that religions with public ambitions give them up. One way out of this difficulty is to restrict neutrality to certain kinds of cases. Thus, for example, it has been argued that the liberal state is not and ought not to be neutral between communalistic and individualistic conceptions of the good; liberals should use state power to encourage individualistic religions over those oriented to shaping social structures—they ought to be neutral only between the various individualistic religions (Waldron 1989, 78–80). But then why should nonliberals, in particular those whose conception of the good is not confined to forming a coherent individual life for themselves, be persuaded that the liberal state is the just state; and, if they are not, and the pretence of meta-neutrality is dropped, how is the liberal state to secure its legitimacy? Even this, however, is a less arbitrary use of the idea of liberal neutrality than found among multiculturalists such as Taylor or Amy Gutmann. After recognizing that multicultural equality between groups can take a neutralist or interventionist version, Gutmann suggests that the former is more suited to religious groups and the latter to nonreligious educational policy (1994, 10–12). Yet she offers no justification for this differential approach other than that it reflects U.S. constitutional and political arrangements.

It has been argued that even where absolute neutrality is impossible one can still approximate to neutrality, and this is what disestablishment achieves (A. Phillips 1997). One could just as well maintain that though total multicultural or multifaith inclusiveness is impossible, we should try and approximate to inclusiveness rather than neutrality. Hence, an alternative to disestablishment is to design institutions to ensure that those who are marginalized by the dominant ethos are given some special platform or access to influence so their voices are nevertheless heard. By way of illustration, American secularism is suspicious of any state endorsement of religion, but Indian secularism was designed to ensure state support for religions in addition to those of the majority. It was meant not to deny the public character of religion but to deny the identification of the state with any one religion. The latter is closer to what I am calling moderate rather than absolute secularism. In the British context, this would mean pluralizing the state-religion link (which is happening to a degree), rather than severing it. It is interesting that Prince Charles has let it be known he would as a monarch prefer the title "Defender of Faith" to the historic title "Defender of *the* Faith" (Dimbleby 1994, 528).

Autonomy of Politics

Implicit in the argument for the separation of the spheres of religion and politics is the idea that each has its own concerns and mode of reasoning and achieves its goals when not interfered with by the other. (I am here concerned only with the autonomy of politics.) The point is that politics has limited and distinctive goals and methods that relate only to a dimension of our social world and can best be deliberated in their own terms, not derived in a lawlike way from scriptures, dogmas, or theological arguments. The focus of political debate and of common political action has to be defined so that those of different theologies and those of none can reason with each other and can reach conclusions that are perceived to have some legitimacy for those who do not share a religious faith. Moreover, if people are to occupy the same political space without conflict, they mutually have to limit the extent to which they subject each other's fundamental beliefs to criticism. I think such arguments became particularly prominent in seventeenth-century Western Europe as people sought to put to an end the religious wars of the time.

I have already suggested that this idea of relative autonomy has shaped statecraft both in the Muslim world and in the constitutional structures of contemporary European states. Nevertheless, I do not think the autonomy of politics is (or could be) absolute or that it supports radical (as opposed to moderate) secularism. This view of politics is not just the result of a compromise between different religions, or between theism and atheism, but is part of a style of politics in which there is an inhibition, a constraint on ideology. If politics is a limited activity, it means political argument and debate must focus on a limited range of issues and questions rather than on general conceptions of human nature, of social life, or of historical progress. Conversely, to the extent politics *can* be influenced by such ideological arguments—for example, by their setting the framework of public discourse or the climate of opinion in which politics takes place—it is not at all clear that religious ideologies are taboo. The distinction, on the one hand, between the practical and reasonable nature of politics and, on the other hand, between the totalizing and dogmatic nature of religion is in effect a distinction between politics and ideology. While it is a contingent matter as to what kinds of ideologies are to be found at a particular time and place, it is likely that ideologically minded religious people will be most stimulated to develop faith-based critiques of contemporary secularism where secular ideologies are prevalent and, especially, where those ideologies are critical of the pretensions of religious people.

Of course, we cannot proscribe ideology, secular or religious. My point is simply that the ideological or ethical character of a politics allied to a religion is not by itself a reason for supposing religion should have no influence on politics. Rather, institutional linkages between religious conscience and affairs of state (as through the twenty-six bishops who by right sit in the House of Lords at Westminster) are often helpful in developing politically informed and politically constructive religious perspectives that are not naively optimistic about the nature of politics.

Democracy

Proponents of a radically secular multicultural state maintain that establishment, even a reformed establishment (e.g., a Council of Religions), is a form of corporatist representation and is therefore open to the charge of being undemocratic. Advocates of multicultural equality are skating on thin ice here, for it is not uncommon for them to argue for special forms of minority representation. While in practice this often means special consultative committees, the preferred method is usually some form of constraint on an electoral process (for example, reserving certain seats for women or a minority in a decision-making forum). In any case, there is no reason to be a purist in polities where mixed forms of representation are the norm and are likely to remain so. We are, after all, talking about bodies with very little power. One would have to take a practical view of how damaging it would be for an institution with such little power to remain independent of the franchise. There are certainly advantages in allowing organized religion corporatist influence rather than encouraging it, or obliging it, to become an electoral player. Some examples of when a religion deprived of state influence seeks an electoral intervention and joins the party competition—such as Pat Buchanan's bid for the Republican Party presidential nomination in the United States, the emergence of Islamist parties in various countries, or the effects of electoral Hindu chauvinism on the Indian state—suggest the radical secularist's concern with democratic purity may in the end be counterproductive (Sandel 1994). Of course, one could argue that organized religion should not be allowed to support electoral candidates (Audi 1989), but advocates of this restriction typically fail to explain why churches and other religious organizations are significantly different from businesses, trade unions, sport and film stars, and so on. It is also difficult to see how such restrictions are democratic: denying religious groups corporate representation while at the same time requiring them to abstain from electoral politics—all in the name of democracy and so that "the non-religious will not feel alienated or be denied adequate respect" (Audi 1989, 295)—seems to more seriously compromise democracy than the maintenance of the current weak forms of corporate representation.

The goal of democratic multiculturalism cannot and should not be cultural neutrality but rather inclusion of marginal and disadvantaged groups, including religious communities in public life. Democratic political discourse perhaps has to proceed on the assumption that, ideally, contributions should, in principle, be seen as relevant to the discourse by any member of the polity. This may mean that there is a gravitational pull in which religious considerations come to be translated into nonreligious considerations or are generally persuasive when allied with nonreligious considerations. It does not warrant the relegation of religious views to a private sphere. I neither intend nor expect the demise of secularism. The argument for inclusion is aimed at keeping open the possibility of dialogue and mutual influence. It does mean, as pointed out by Graham Haydon, that there is no reason to assume that religious points of view must entirely give way to secular ones. The entry of nonsecular views into the debate does at least make it more possible for secular thinkers to appreciate the force that other points of view have for those who adhere to them.

Secular thinkers may pragmatically be willing to make some accommodation to the views of religious thinkers: movement need not be all the other way (as it would be, by default, if religious viewpoints were to remain only in a private realm) (Haydon 1994, 70).

In arguing that corporate representation is one of the means of seeking inclusiveness, I am not arguing for the privileging of religion but recognizing that, in the context of a secular hegemony in the public cultures of contemporary Western Europe, some special forms of representation may be necessary and more conducive to social cohesion than some other scenarios.

One such proposal is to be found in the recommendations of the Royal Commission on the Reform of the House of Lords (2000). It argued that the Lords, the UK upper chamber, should be "a relatively non-polemical forum for national debate, informed by the range of different perspectives which its members should have." Members should, among other things, have "the ability to bring a philosophical, moral or spiritual perspective to bear." It believed that it was time to end the hereditary principle of membership of the House, but it did not recommend a wholly elected chamber. It thought that its ideals would be better met if part of the House continued to be unelected. The latter includes one of the elements of establishment, the right of twenty-six Anglican bishops to sit in the Lords. The Royal Commission endorsed this principle but argued that the number of Anglican bishops should be reduced to sixteen and that they should be joined by five representatives of other Christian denominations in England, five representatives of other Christian denominations in the rest of the United Kingdom, and five representatives of non-Christian faiths. Hence, the Royal Commission sought to make up the democratic deficit that arises when national fora are completely dominated by party politicians by proposing an increase not just in the width of religious representation but also in the number of seats, from twenty-six to thirty-one.

Such proposals might be regarded as a form of reforming or pluralizing establishment without abolishing it. It suggests that weak establishment can be the basis for moving toward multicultural equality without constitutional disestablishment (cf. Bader 2003). I am not contending that some version of establishment (weak or plural) is the only way or the best way of institutionalizing religious pluralism in Britain or similar countries. My point is that a reformed establishment can be one way of institutionalizing religious pluralism. In certain historical and political circumstances, it may indeed be a good way: we should be wary of arguments from democratic multiculturalism that rule it out.

Conclusion

The strict divide between the public and private spheres suggested by some theorists of multiculturalism is overplayed. There is an interdependence between the public and private spheres that must be taken into account in any adequate characterization of a multicultural state. In particular, I contend that there is a theoretical incompatibility between multiculturalism and radical secularism. In a society where some of the disadvantaged and marginalized minorities are religious minorities, a public policy of public multiculturalism requires the public recognition of religious minorities and the theoretical incompatibility becomes a practical issue. In such situations moderate secularism offers the basis for institutional compromises. Such moderate secularism is already embodied in the church-state relations in Western Europe (France being an exception). Rather than see such church-state relations as archaic and as an obstacle to multiculturalism, we should be scrutinizing the compromises that they represent and how those compromises need to be remade to serve the new multicultural circumstances. Multiculturalism may not always require a break from the past but may reasonably be pursued as an extension of ideas associated with the plural state.

Since September 11, the case for a mutually informed moderate secularism and moderate multiculturalism has become even more difficult to make. The dominant noise in the aftermath of the tragic terrorist attack has not been about just Islamic terrorism but also about a global clash of civilizations and the death of multiculturalism at home. In the moral panic about Muslims, there are wild generalizations about the tendencies to violence inherent in political Islamism, even in Islam itself. Sensible commentators realize that such essentialist portrayals of a complex and diverse world religion are not just intellectually indefensible but highly dangerous in the present climate, reinforcing the perception of Muslims as a radical and inferior "Other." Even so, many such commentators argue that civil peace and democracy require a robust secularism, forgetting that for every religious fanatic that they cite, a secularist counterpart is easy to find. In the modern period, the secularists have used state power to mobilize populations in the name of orthodoxy, to crush dissent, and to engage in mass slaughter—Nazi Germany, Soviet Russia, and Communist China are only the most prominent. Even in the democratic polities of Western Europe, it has been Marxist (e.g., the Baader-Meinhof gang, the Red Brigade) or nationalist (e.g., the IRA in Northern Ireland and ETA in the Basque country) terrorism that has claimed the lives of civilians and necessitated repressive security measures. All ideologies, secular and religious, are capable of fundamentalism, and the resort to violence is often due to specific political and social conditions rather than a belief system per se. If we forget such elementary truths and insist on imposing a secular straitjacket on the new Muslim populations of Europe and North America, we retreat from multiculturalism without gaining any extra civic inclusivity. Indeed, we risk creating the polarization that we all seek to avoid.

Eight

Muslims and the Politics of Multiculturalism

The large presence of Muslims in Britain today (1.6 million in the 2001 census, more than half of South Asian, primarily Pakistani, origins) is a result of Commonwealth immigration from the 1950s onward. This was initially male labor from rural small farm–owning and artisan backgrounds seeking to meet the demand for unskilled and semiskilled industrial workers in the British economy, with wives and children arriving from about the 1970s. The proportion of urban professionals among South Asian Muslims was small, though it increased with the arrival of political refugees from East Africa in the late 1960s and 1970s (the majority of this group were Hindus and Sikhs). Britain, particularly London as a cosmopolitan center, has been very attractive to some of the rich and the professional classes from the Middle East, especially since the 1970s, and many of them have large investments in property in the city. During this period there have also been waves of political refugees from other parts of the Muslim world; Somalia, Bosnia, and Afghanistan are among the notable cases.

Racial Equality Movements

The presence of new population groups such as these has made manifest certain kinds of racisms in Britain, and antidiscrimination laws and policies began to be put into place in the 1960s. These laws and policies, initially influenced by contemporary thinking and practice in relation to antiblack racism in the United States, assume that the grounds of discrimination are color and ethnicity. Muslim assertiveness has become a feature of majority-minority relations in the last decade or so, but prior to this, racial equality discourse and politics was dominated by the idea that the dominant postimmigration issue was color racism (Rex and Moore 1967; CCCS 1982; Sivanandan 1985; Gilroy 1987). This perspective was epigrammatically expressed by the writer Salman Rushdie: "Britain is now two entirely different worlds and the one you inherit is determined by the colour of your skin" (1982). He, together with most antiracists, has come to adopt a more pluralistic perspective, one in which the Muslim presence is seen as a fact to be ignored at one's peril. Nevertheless, in a pure or in a mixed form, the U.S.-derived racial dualism continues to be an influential force in British social science and radical politics (Luthra 1997; Alexander 2002). One consequence of this is that the legal and policy framework still reflects the conceptualization and priorities of racial dualism.

Until December 2003 it was lawful to discriminate against Muslims qua Muslims because the courts do not accept that Muslims are an ethnic group (though, oddly, Jews and Sikhs are recognized as ethnic groups within the meaning of the law); on that date an offense of religious discrimination was created but confined to employment. While initially unremarked upon, this exclusive focus on race and ethnicity, and the exclusion of Muslims but not Jews and Sikhs, came to be a source of resentment among Muslims. Muslims did, however, enjoy some limited indirect legal protection qua members of ethnic groups such as Pakistanis, Arabs, and so on. Over time, groups like Pakistanis have become an active constituency within British race relations (Middle Easterners tend to classify themselves as white, as in the 1991 and 2001 censuses, and to date have not been at all prominent in political activism of this sort, or in domestic politics generally). One of the effects of this politics was to highlight race.

A key measure/indicator of racial discrimination and inequality has been numerical underrepresentation in prestigious jobs, public office, and so on. Hence people have had to be (self-)classified and counted, and group labels, and arguments about which labels are authentic, have become a common feature of certain political discourses. Over the years it has also become apparent that by these inequality measures it is Asian Muslims, and not African-Caribbeans as policy makers had originally expected, who have emerged as the most disadvantaged and poorest group in the country (Modood et al. 1997). To many Muslim activists the misplacing of Muslims into race categories and the belatedness with which the severe disadvantages of the Pakistanis and Bangladeshis have come to be recognized by policy makers means, at best, that race relations are an inappropriate policy niche for Muslims (UKACIA 1993) and, at worst, are a conspiracy to prevent the emergence of a specifically Muslim sociopolitical formation (Muslim Parliament of Great Britain 1992). To see how such thinking has emerged, we need to consider the career of the concept of racial equality.

The initial development of antiracism in Britain followed the American pattern, and indeed was directly influenced by American personalities and events (see chapter 1). Just as in the United States the color-blind humanism of Martin Luther King Jr. came to be mixed with an emphasis on black pride, black autonomy, and black nationalism as typified by Malcolm X, so also in the United Kingdom (both these inspirational leaders visited Britain). Indeed, it is best to see this development of racial explicitness and positive blackness as part of a wider sociopolitical climate that is not confined to race and culture or non-white minorities. Feminism, gay pride, Quebecois nationalism, and the revival of Scottishness are some prominent examples of these new identity movements that have come to be an important feature in many countries, especially those in which class politics has declined. This means, as was argued in the previous chapter, that our basic concept of civil rights or civic equality has been supplemented by the concept of equality as difference, by the right to have one's difference recognized and supported in the public sphere.

Beyond a Liberal Politics

This new, emergent notion of equality creates some dissonance with preexisting political concepts. It does not easily fit with, for example, a Tory British nationalism, and it is at odds with some of the center-left ideas that underpinned the earlier notion of racial equality (Goulbourne 1991a, 1991b). The politicization of racial and ethnic groups (and women and homosexuals) is taken to introduce particularism into universalistic conceptions of justice defined by meritocratic individualism, liberal citizenship, or socialist equality. (Why class solidarity or national citizenship is universalistic and identification with the female half of the species or black internationalism is particularistic I personally fail to understand.) The success of the new concept of multicultural equality, at least on the left, has been made possible because it was not anomalous but fitted in with wider challenges to liberal individualism. For example, it was consistent with feminist arguments that ostensible gender-neutral conceptions of the political, of citizenship, of the domain of law and of legal norms, as well as a host of substantive laws and policies were in fact covert but systematic expressions of male perspectives and ignored the needs and capacities of women (Pateman 1988; Young 1990). The abstract, rational individual of liberal politics and jurisprudence was a man, as evidenced by the fact that this individual didn't seem to have any domestic or child-rearing obligations, and the definition of the political, the activities appropriate for public discourse, political campaigns, and legal control favor male interests, leaving male power in domestic and sexual relations unchallenged—hence the alternative politics born out of the slogan "the personal is the political."

The politics that I have just mentioned is both a theoretical, discursive politics and a politics of institutional reform, competition for office, and social policies. My concern here—as a way of coming to approach the political-normative climate of opinion in which British Muslims can and are mounting a case for Muslim rights—is particularly with the theoretical dimension of the politics of difference as a critique of the 1960s notions of liberal equality. It is therefore worth mentioning some other theoretical sources of this politics in order to emphasize how important it has become among center-left egalitarians, especially in book-writing and book-reading circles, in Britain and elsewhere. It is a politics that gets considerable underpinning from the rise of philosophical antiessentialism in the social sciences (Modood 1998a). Originating from the—very different—work of thinkers such as Nietzsche, Heidegger, and Wittgenstein, given a certain indeterminate radicalism in the hands of more recent theorists like Foucault and Derrida, antiessentialism in one form or another has been used to critique hegemonic ideas such as nation-state, community, class, and even counterhegemonic notions such as woman, black, and so on (Fuss 1989). This has been taken to such an extent that an appreciation of perspectivism, of the essentially contested nature of concepts, of fluidity and multiplicity of meanings, of cultural pluralism, and perhaps even of aporia, has quickly established itself as an orthodoxy in social theory.

Of relevance here is how this antiessentialism, when married to a theory of political equality as participation in a discursive public space (Arendt 1963, 1968; Habermas 1984, 1987), can define inclusion into a political community not in terms of accepting the rules of the existing polity and its hallowed public-private boundary lines (as many European politicians do as regards Muslims), but the opposite. Public space is defined as essentially contested and indeed created through ongoing discursive contestation and political struggles, where the rules of what are appropriate concerns, and the terms of politics, far from being fixed in advance, are an object of political discourse (Benhabib 1992; Fraser 1992). Typically, on these accounts, the public-private distinction works as a gag rule to exclude matters of concern to marginalized and subordinated groups, and the political integration of these minorities on terms of equality inevitably involves their challenging the existing boundaries of publicity. Integration flows from the process of discursive engagement as marginal groups begin to confidently assert themselves in the public space and others begin to argue with and reach some agreement with them, as well as with the enactment of new laws, policies, and so on. Indeed, laws and policies may be of lesser importance, for these theories explicitly repudiate the classical liberal identification of the political with the realms of law and the state. A more expansive understanding of the political is more compatible with the idea of shifting boundaries and politics as debate and allows for the changing of certain attitudes, stereotypes, stigmatizations, media images, and national symbols as primary political goals. Hence, it should now be clear why I believe that in the 1990s we were dealing with a new concept of equality, one in which the issues of representation are not just the numbers of various categories of people in certain jobs or positions of power but the public imagining of groups qua groups (Hall 1992a).

Racialization and Identity

This may seem all rather abstract and as no more than the preoccupations of a few academics and their students, but in my opinion it is an important part of the story of the emergent politics of Muslim identity in Britain. In any case, it is time to briefly mention some of the events that took place "on the ground." The minorities politics, the cutting-edge antiracism that developed in Britain in the 1970s and early 1980s (first in radical activism and ultraleft corpuscles, then, following the Brixton riots of 1981, in some local governments, trade unions, radical public sector professional associations, and the Labour Party), was based on a concept of political blackness. The British population was divided into two groups, black and white. The former consisted of all those people who were potential victims of color racism, though in both theory and practice they were assumed to disproportionately have the characteristics of the African-Caribbean population (Modood 1994c).

This political movement has played an important part in opening up the question of race in Britain and has come to define the identity of many people (less so now than at its height in the mid- to late 1980s). Whether at any point this political identity was embraced by the majority of South Asians or Muslims is an open question (I personally think not). Two things, however, are clear. First, this identity was embraced by Asian political activists in the 1980s, especially those whose activism was concerned with mainstream British society rather than the organization of their own communities. Second, from the late 1980s onward, if not earlier, most Asians were emphasizing a more particular ethnic or religious identity than this all-inclusive non-whiteness. Several factors were at play here, for example, time, numbers, and confidence. As the Asian communities became more settled and thought of themselves less as sojourners, as they put down familial and community roots, and as some Asian groups, especially African Asians, began to acquire a prosperity and respectability that most Asians sought, they began to express their own identities rather than the borrowed identity of blackness, with its inescapable African-Caribbean resonances. Movements outside the United Kingdom were relevant (for example, the Sikh battle for Khalistan, the growth of Hindu cultural nationalism, the rise of Islamism in various parts of the world). Additionally, the multicultural climate I have described played an important part in encouraging people to define themselves and publicly project themselves in terms of authenticity, difference, and victimhood and gave them the confidence to reject opposing arguments (such as that newly settled groups should be seen and not heard; that when in Rome do as the Romans do). This was probably especially the case with middle-class professional people who had some choice in emphasizing integration or difference in their public discourse and political persona.[1]

Political blackness was, therefore, unraveling at a grassroots level at the very time when it was becoming hegemonic as a minority discourse in British public life (1980s). The single event that illustrated this most dramatically was the battle over *The Satanic Verses* that broke out in 1988–89 (see chapter 5). This was seen by all concerned as a Muslim versus the West battle. On the Muslim side, it generated an impassioned activism and mobilization that no previous campaign against racism had been remotely able to stir. Many lapsed or passive Muslims (Muslims, especially the nonreligious, for whom hitherto their Muslim background was not particularly important) (re)discovered a new community solidarity. What was striking was that when the public rage against Muslims was at its most intense, Muslims neither sought nor were offered any special solidarity by any non-white minority. Some white liberal Anglicans tried to moderate the hostility against the angry Muslims, and interfaith fora rather than political-black organizations tried to create space where Muslims could state their case without being vilified. Political blackness—up to then considered the key formation in the politics of postimmigration ethnicity—was seen as irrelevant to an issue that many Muslims insisted was fundamental to defining the kind of respect or civility appropriate to a peaceful multicultural society, that is to say, to the political constitution of difference in Britain (see chapter 5).

The fundamental problem for political blackness came from the internal ambivalence I mentioned earlier, namely, whether blackness as a political identity was sufficiently distinct from and could mobilize without blackness as an ethnic pride movement. This black identity movement, in a growing climate of opinion favorable to identity politics of various kinds, was successful in shifting the terms of the debate from color-blind individualistic assimilation to questions about how white British society had to change to accommodate new groups. But its success in imposing or making a singular identity out of a diverse ethnic minority population (unlike black America or South Africa) was temporary (probably at no time did a majority of Asians think of themselves as part of a positive black identity). What it did was pave the way to a plural ethnic assertiveness, as Asian groups, including Muslims, borrowed the logic of ethnic pride and tried to catch up with the success of a newly legitimized black public identity.

An oppositional identity depends on emotionally welding together a disparate population; to do so one must draw on the traditions and beliefs of the oppressed, especially in a way that is readily communicable to the ordinary mass of people. Where the relevant population embodies one or more major historical cleavages, the task is difficult. For example, in British India the mobilization of the Indian masses required an appeal to past Hindu glories, to Hindu symbols and customs, in short, to a form of Hindu nationalism. But the beating of that drum led through group competition and a me-too attitude to a rival oppositional identity, a Muslim nationalism, and eventually the creation of Pakistan, which, the more populist it had to be, that is to say, the more it had to mobilize mass action, the more religious it became in rhetoric, imagery, and so on. If the matter could have been left to an Anglicized Indian elite, communal passions would not have been aroused; but the politics of anti-imperialism required the mobilization of the masses, and the political struggle had to be couched in terms that made sense to the masses and could elicit their support and sacrifices.

I hope the point of the historical illustration is clear: just as the development of an Indian oppositional identity was confused with Hindu nationalism, so it is not surprising that the development of a contemporary British black (i.e., non-white) oppositional identity was confused with the development of a black ethnic pride (African roots) movement and triggered off other ethnic assertions, such as Asian, Muslim, and so on, and reduced a political black to an ethnic blackness.

Not only have British ethnic minorities not united under a single identity capable of mobilizing them all, but the number of identities that generate intensity of commitment and community mobilization grows all the time. Of course, much of this has to do with context and in particular with what one feels one needs to react against. Pakistanis were black when it meant a job in a racial equality bureaucracy, Asian when a community center was in the offing, Muslim when the Prophet was being ridiculed, Kashmiris when a nationalist movement back home had taken off and blood was being spilt. These identities are pragmatic moves, and they define the field in which the moves are made. And yet all this leaves unanswered the question, why is it that ethnic (i.e., regional and national origins) and religious identities have come to be politically prominent among South Asians in Britain instead of other group identities, most notably, a color-based identity?

At a time when social theory and research is dominated by constructivism and antiessentialism of various sorts, it is with some trepidation that I raise the question whether, among alternative identities, certain ethnicities or collectivities may be more real than others, have a greater durability or ability to resurface—in short, whether they may not have some characteristics that cannot be accounted for by radical constructivism.

When I try to explain to myself why Pakistanis mobilize around "Muslim" with a conviction, intensity, and solidarity that they do not around "black," I use the distinction between a group's mode of oppression and mode of being, as in chapter 5. Even if white British society sees and treats Muslims as a "colored Other," it doesn't follow that Muslims accept that description of themselves. Excluded groups seek respect for themselves as they are or aspire to be, not simply a solidarity on the basis of a recognition of themselves as victims; they resist being defined by their *mode of oppression* and seek space and dignity for their *mode of being.* All the identities that are being discussed here are in some sense reactive and are shaped by a situation that the minorities do not control (though I am impressed by the degree to which the minorities are active in these identity formations). I am not contrasting situationally or politically constructed identities with something primordial. My point is that a minority will respond to some forms of exclusion or inferiorization and not to others. It will respond to those that relate in some way to its own sense of being. Again, this sense of being is not atemporal and can change, but it does mean that neither the oppressor nor the oppressed are totally free to set the terms of a reactive identity—the oppression must speak to the oppressed; it must reach their sense of being.

So, part of the answer as to which identity will emerge as important to a group at a particular time lies in the nature of the minority group in question. That the Caribbeans have mobilized around a color identity and the South Asians around religious and related identities are not chance or just a construction but based on something deeper about these groups. That Muslims in their anger against *The Satanic Verses* found a depth of indignation, a voice of their own, in a way that most had not found in relation to events and in mobilization in the previous decades cannot be explained just in terms of issues related to political leaderships, rivalries, tactics, and so on. Certainly, some individuals and organizations exploited the situation, but they could not have done so if there was not a situation to exploit.

Muslim Identity Politics

Once out, the genie has not been recorked. In a very short space of time "Muslim" has become a key political minority identity, acknowledged by right and left, bigots and the open-minded, the media and the government. It has become integral to local community politics and yet thrives through romantic, global solidarities as wars and massacres in Palestine, Bosnia, Kosovo, the Gulf, Chechnya, Kashmir, India, and so on fill our newspapers and television screens and lead some young British-born Muslims to reinvent the concept of the *umma*, the global community of Muslims, as global victims. This politics has meant a recognition of not just a new religious diversity in Britain but a new or renewed policy importance for religion. Recent empirical evidence shows overwhelmingly that the religion of one's family is the most important source of self-identity among people of South Asian origin, especially Muslims. The Fourth National Survey of Ethnic Minorities, a large, nationally representative survey (as described in chapter 3, n. 2) found that rather than skin color, which was prominent in the self-descriptions of Caribbeans, religion was most prominent in the self-descriptions of South Asians (Modood et al. 1997, ch. 9). This owes as much to a sense of community as to personal faith, but the identification and prioritization of religion is far from just a nominal one. Very few Asians marry across religious and caste boundaries and most expect that their children will be inducted into their religion. At a time when a third of Britons said they do not have a religion, nearly all South Asians said they have one, and 90 percent said that religion was of personal importance to them (compared to 13 percent of whites). While about a quarter of whites attend a place of worship once a month or more, over half of Hindus and seven out of ten Sikhs attend once a month or more, and nearly two-thirds of Muslims attend at least once a week. Even among the young, expressions of commitment were exceptionally high: more than a third of Indians and African Asians, and two-thirds of Pakistani and Bangladeshi sixteen- to thirty-four-year-olds said that religion was very important to how they led their lives compared to 5 percent of whites (nearly a fifth of Caribbeans took this view) (ibid.).

There are two important points to make here about these identities, especially Muslim. First, they cannot be characterized as belonging to private life and irrelevant to public policies and resources.

For example, half of the Muslims interviewed said that there should be state funding for Muslim schools. Second, religious and ethnic identities were not simply an expression of behavior, of participation in distinctive cultural practices, for, across the generations and in relation to time spent in Britain, there was a noticeable decline in participation in the cultural practices (language, dress, attendance at place of worship, and so on) that go with a particular identity. Yet the decrease in self-identification with a group label (black, Muslim, and so on) was relatively small (Modood et al. 1997). For example, there are people in Britain who say of themselves that they are Muslim but may not be religious at all.

In one sense, there is nothing new or peculiar about the above distinction. In another sense, it marks a new conception of ethno-religious identities, for we are not talking about passive or fading identities. That would be to overlook the pride with which they may be asserted, the intensity with which they may be debated, and their capacity to generate community activism and political campaigns. People may still feel passionate about the public recognition and re-sourcing of aspects of their community identity, even though as individuals they may not wish that resource for themselves. For example, the demand for public funding of Muslim schools has been a source of Muslim grievance, with some secular as well as religious Muslims highlighting the injustice of a system that funds Christian and Jewish but not Muslim schools. Yet in the Fourth Survey only half of those Muslims who supported funding of Muslim schools said that if they had the choice they would prefer to send their own child to a Muslim school; once again, the young were not much less likely to want the funding but were much less likely to want to take up the option for their own (future) children (Modood et al. 1997, 324–25). Muslim purists might disparage these ambivalences, but in fact the success of the Muslim campaign partly depends on the political support of the Muslims who do not fully practice their religion, on the extensive mobilization of the Muslim community. Hence, it would be wrong to think of nonreligious Muslims as only token or symbolic Muslims (Rex 1996, par. 4.13).

Religious Equality

One of the current conceptions of equality is difference-affirming, with related notions of respect, recognition, and identity—in short, what I understand by political multiculturalism. What kinds of specific policy demands are being made by or on behalf of religious groups, and Muslim identity politics in particular, when these terms are deployed?

I suggest that these demands have three dimensions, which get progressively "thicker"—and are progressively less acceptable to radical secularists.

No Religious Discrimination

One Muslim organization concerned with these issues is the Forum Against Islamophobia and Racism (FAIR). Set up in 2000 "for the purpose of raising awareness of and combating Islamophobia and racism, monitoring specific incidents of Islamophobia and racism, working toward eliminating religious and racial discrimination, campaigning and lobbying on issues relevant to Muslim and other multi-ethnic communities in Britain," its mission statement sets out this first dimension of equality.

The very basic demand is that religious people, no less than people defined by race or gender, should not suffer discrimination in job and other opportunities. For example, a person who is trying to dress in accordance with their religion or who projects a religious identity (such as a Muslim woman wearing a headscarf, a *hijab*), should not be discriminated against in employment. Till the end of 2003 there was no legal ban on such discrimination in Britain, and the government argued that the case for it was not proven. This was despite the kind of evidence referred to in the introduction and chapter 1, for that was taken to be anti-Asian rather than anti-Muslim, racial rather then religious prejudice and bias.

The legal system thus left Muslims particularly vulnerable because, while discrimination against yarmulke-wearing Jews and turban-wearing Sikhs was deemed to be unlawful *racial* discrimination, Muslims, unlike these other faith communities, were not deemed to be a racial or ethnic group nor were they protected by the legislation against religious discrimination that did exist in one part of the United Kingdom: explicitly designed to protect Catholics, it covers only Northern Ireland. The best that Muslims were able to achieve was to prove that the discrimination against them was indirectly against their ethnic characteristics: that they suffered discrimination by virtue of being, say, a Pakistani or an Iraqi.

While it is indeed the case that the discrimination against Muslims is mixed up with forms of color racism and cultural racism, the charge of race discrimination will provide no protection if it is clearly the individual's religion, not their race, that has led to the discrimination. Moreover, some Muslims are white and so do not enjoy this second-class protection, and many Muslim activists argue that religious freedom, being a fundamental right, should not be legally and politically dependent on dubious concepts of race and ethnicity. The same argument applies to the demand for a law in Britain (as already exists in Northern Ireland) making incitement to religious hatred unlawful, to parallel the law against incitement to racial hatred. (The latter extends protection to certain forms of anti-Jewish literature, but not anti-Muslim literature—though see the "Postscript" section in chapter 6.)

After some years of arguing that there was insufficient evidence of religious discrimination, the hand of the British government was forced by Article 13 of the EU Amsterdam Treaty (1999), which includes religious discrimination in the list of the forms of discrimination that all member states are expected to eliminate. Accordingly, the British government, following a European Commission directive—which not all member states have rushed to implement—outlawed religious discrimination in employment, beginning in December 2003. This is, however, only a partial catching-up with the existing antidiscrimination provisions in relation to race and gender. It does not extend to discrimination in provision of goods and services, and will not require employers to take steps to promote equality of opportunity.

Parity with Native Religions

Many minority faith advocates interpret equality to mean that minority religions should get at least some of the support from the state that longer-established religions do. Muslims have led the way on this argument, and have made two particular issues politically contentious: the state funding of schools and the law of blasphemy. After some political battle, the government has agreed in recent years to fund a few (so far, five) Muslim schools, as well as a Sikh and a Seventh Day Adventist school, on the same basis enjoyed by thousands of Anglican and Catholic schools and some Methodist and Jewish schools. (In England and Wales, over a third of state-maintained primary and a sixth of secondary schools are run by religious groups—but all have to deliver a centrally determined national curriculum.)

Some secularists are unhappy about this. They accept the argument for parity but believe this should be achieved by the state withdrawing its funding from all religious schools. Most Muslims reject this form of equality in which the privileged lose something but the underprivileged gain nothing. More specifically, the issue between equalizing upward and equalizing downward is about the legitimacy of religion as a public institutional presence.

Muslims have failed to get the courts to interpret the existing statute on blasphemy to cover offenses beyond what Christians hold sacred, but some political support exists for an offense of incitement to religious hatred, mirroring the existing one of incitement to racial hatred. The government inserted such a clause in the post–9/11 security legislation in order to conciliate Muslims who, among others, were opposed to the new powers of surveillance, arrest, and detention. As it happened, most of the latter was made law, but the provision on incitement to religious hatred was defeated in Parliament. It was reintroduced in a private member's bill from a Liberal Democrat, Lord Avebury, which also sought to abolish the laws governing blasphemy. Although unsuccessful, in 2004 the government announced its intention to create an offense of incitement to religious hatred, though some government supporters continued to express their opposition. In any case, it may be that a recent High Court judgment has created a form of indirect protection against anti-Muslim incitement, as explained in the "Postscript" section of chapter 6.

Positive Inclusion of Religious Groups

The demand here is that the category of religion in general, or at least "Muslim" in particular, should be used to judge the inclusiveness of social institutions, as they increasingly are in relation to race and gender. For example, employers should have to demonstrate that they do not discriminate against Muslims by explicit monitoring of Muslims' positions within the workforce, backed up by appropriate policies, targets, managerial responsibilities, work environments, staff training, advertisements, outreach, and so on.[2] Similarly, public bodies should provide appropriately sensitive policies and staff in relation to the services they provide, especially in relation to (non-Muslim) schools and social and health services; Muslim community centers or Muslim youth workers should be funded in addition to existing Asian and Caribbean community centers and Asian and black youth workers.

To take another case, the BBC currently believes it is of political importance to review and improve its personnel practices and its output of programs, including its on-screen representation of the British population, by making provision for and winning the confidence of women, ethnic groups, and young people. Why should it not also use religious groups as a criterion of inclusivity and have to demonstrate that it is doing the same for viewers and staff defined by religious community membership?

In short, Muslims should be treated as a legitimate group in their own right (not because they are, for example, Asians), whose presence in British society has to be explicitly reflected in all walks of life and in all institutions, and whether they are so included should become one of the criteria for judging Britain as an egalitarian, inclusive, multicultural society. There is no prospect at present of religious equality catching up with the importance that employers and other organizations give to sex or race. A potentially significant victory, however, was made when the government agreed to include a religion question in the 2001 census. This was the first time this question had been included since 1851 and was largely unpopular outside the politically active religionists, among whom Muslims were foremost. Nevertheless, it has the potential to pave the way for widespread religious monitoring in the way that the inclusion of an ethnic question in 1991 has led to the more routine use of ethnic monitoring.

These policy demands no doubt seem odd within the terms of the French or U.S. separation between the state and religion, and may make secularists uncomfortable in Britain, too. But it is clear that they virtually mirror existing antidiscrimination policy provisions in the United Kingdom.

In an analysis of some Muslim policy statements in the early 1990s, following the activism stimulated by the *Satanic Verses* affair, I argued that the main lines of arguments were captured by the following three positions:

- a color-blind human rights and human dignity approach
- an approach based on extension of the concepts of racial discrimination and racial equality to include anti-Muslim racism
- a Muslim power approach

I concluded that these "reflect not so much obscurantist Islamic interventions into a modern secular discourse, but typical minority options in contemporary Anglo-American equality politics, and employ the rhetorical, conceptual and institutional resources available in that politics" (Modood 1993a, 518).

All three approaches are present today. For example, the Muslim Council of Britain (MCB), stating that its aim is to "make Britain a successful multi-faith and multi-cultural society," has said that its three key domestic policy concerns are "the need to outlaw religious discrimination; measures to tackle high levels of poverty and social exclusion and concern about the curtailment of civil liberties and the targeting by the authorities of Muslim organisations" (MCB press release, October 1, 2003).[3] At the same time, some high-profile radicals have made a Muslim power approach more prominent, in a manner not dissimilar to the rise of black power activism after the height of the civil rights period in the United States. This approach is mainly nourished by despair at the victimization and humiliation of Muslims in places such as Palestine, Bosnia, Kashmir, and Afghanistan. For many British Muslims, such military disasters and humanitarian horrors evoke a strong desire to express solidarity with oppressed Muslims through the political idea of the *umma*, which must defend and restore itself as a global player. To take the analogy with U.S. black power a bit further, one can say that as black nationalism and Afrocentrism developed as one ideological expression of black power, so, similarly, we can see political Islamism as a search for Muslim dignity and power.

Muslim assertiveness, then, though triggered and intensified by what are seen as attacks on Muslims, is primarily derived not from Islam or Islamism but from contemporary Western ideas about equality and multiculturalism. While simultaneously reacting to the latter in its failure to distinguish Muslims from the rest of the black population and its uncritical secular bias, Muslims positively use, adapt, and extend these contemporary Western ideas in order to join other equality-seeking movements. Political Muslims, therefore, have an ambivalence in relation to multicultural discourses. On the one hand, as a result of previous misrecognition of their identity and existing biases, there is distrust of the race relations industry and of liberals; on the other hand, the assertiveness is clearly a product of the positive climate created by liberals and egalitarians.

This ambivalence can tend toward antagonism, as the assertiveness is increasingly being joined by Islamic discourses and Islamists. Especially, as has been said, there is a sense that Muslim populations across the world are repeatedly suffering at the hands of their neighbors, aided and abetted by the United States and its allies, and that Muslims must come together to defend themselves. Politically active Muslims in Britain, however, are likely to be part of domestic multicultural and equality currents—emphasizing discrimination in educational and economic opportunities, political representation, and the media, working against Muslim-blindness in the provision of health care and social services, and arguing for remedies that mirror existing legislation and policies in relation to sexual and racial equality (Modood and Ahmad forthcoming).

A Panicky Retreat to a Liberal Public-Private Distinction

If the emergence of a politics of difference out of and alongside a liberal assimilationist equality created a dissonance, as indeed it did, the emergence of a British Muslim identity out of and alongside ethnoracial identities has created an even greater dissonance. Philosophically speaking, it should create a lesser dissonance, for it seems to me that a move from the idea of equality as sameness to equality as difference is a more profound conceptual movement than the creation of a new identity in a field already crowded with minority identities. But to infer this is to naively ignore the hegemonic power of secularism in British political culture, especially on the center-left. While black and related ethnoracial identities were welcomed by, indeed, were intrinsic to, the rainbow coalition of identity politics, this coalition is deeply unhappy with Muslim consciousness. While for some this rejection is specific to Islam, for many the ostensible reason is that it is a religious identity. In this latter objection, if it is taken at its face value, the difference theorists, activists, and paid professionals must revert to a public-private distinction that they have spent two or three decades attempting to demolish. The unacceptability, the bad odor, of Muslim identity no doubt partly arises from the conservative views on gender and sexuality professed by Muslim spokespersons, not to mention issues with freedom of expression as they arose in the Rushdie affair, discussed in chapter 6. But these are objections to specific views, and as such they can be argued on a point-by-point basis[4]—they aren't objections to an identity. The fundamental stated objection to Muslim identity is that it is a politicized religious identity.

In the previous chapter I discussed this view and how some multiculturalists have concluded that religion belongs to the private sphere and is not a legitimate basis for a political identity; rather, the inclusion of religious minorities, like Muslims, into the British polity requires the abolition of the Church of England's constitutional privileges and the severance of any relationship between the state, local or central, and religion. One explicit implication of this would be the phasing out of state funding for denominational schools, of which there are thousands (two Muslim private schools joined these ranks for the first time in 1997, with a further three approved since).

Initially, few members of religious minorities joined this discussion, and so the secular multiculturalists were taken to be speaking for the marginal religious minorities. More recently, spokespersons of a number of non-Christian religious minorities have argued for the importance of maintaining a symbolic and substantive link between religion and the state (Modood 1997). In fact, somewhat surprisingly, besides arguing for various benefits for the minority religions and the importance of religious discrimination legislation to complement that on racial discrimination, they have not challenged the Anglican privileges or even the conception that Britain is/ought to be a Christian country (ibid.).

It is once more worth emphasizing that the panic among secular multiculturalists caused by the rise of Muslim assertiveness has resulted in knee-jerk reactions and inconsistencies (Women Against Fundamentalism 1990; Yuval-Davis 1992; Saghal and Yuval-Davis 1992). By forcing the debate about religion and politics into the polar options of establishment-disestablishment, they have obscured other options such as replacing the Anglican/Christian link with the state by a pluralized religions-state link or by developing other forms of institutionalization that would give political and administrative expression to a multifaith society. Nor have they suggested any lay or secular forms of representation for Muslims and related groups. In fact, the latter would be just as or more consistent with the ethos of Sunni Islam. Most mosques in Britain are run by local lay committees, and the mullah or imam is usually a minor functionary. At the national level, too, very few of those who aspire to be Muslim spokespersons and representatives have religious authority and are not expected to have it by fellow Muslims. So the argument is as much about the recognition and support of communities as about ecclesiastical or spiritual representation in political institutions.

These debates are more consistent with the notions of group recognition and of publicity that currently inform much multiculturalist

thinking. By suggesting that if a religious denomination is not established then it effectively is a matter of private religious observance and
conscience and has no place among public, political identities, multicultural disestablishmentarians are applying different standards of
publicity to religion than they apply to ethnic and other identities. We
thus have a mixed-up situation where secular multiculturalists may
argue that the sex lives of individuals—traditionally, a core area of
liberal privacy—is a legitimate feature of political identities and public discourse (and the sexualization of culture is generally welcomed,
if not the prurient interest in the sexual activity of public characters),
while on the other hand religion—a key source of communal identity
in traditional, nonliberal societies—is regarded as a private matter,
perhaps as a uniquely private matter. Most specifically, Muslim identity is seen as the illegitimate child of British multiculturalism.

The Rushdie affair made evident that the group in British society
most politically opposed to (politicized) Muslims wasn't Christians
or even right-wing nationalists but the secular, liberal intelligentsia.[5]
While hostile press reporting and inflammatory headlines about black
people are more characteristic of the tabloids than the broadsheets,
with the latter usually castigating such journalism, Muslims are frequently criticized in the op/ed pages of the broadsheets in a way that
few, if any, other minority groups are. Muslims often remark that if
in such articles the word "Muslims" was substituted for "Jews" or
"blacks," the newspapers in question would be attacked as racist and
indeed risk legal proceedings (cf. Runnymede Trust 1997). The large
Fourth Survey found that nominal Christians and those without a
religion were more likely to say they were prejudiced against Muslims
than those Christians who said their religion was of importance to
them (Modood et al. 1997, 133–34). Just as the hostility against Jews,
in various times and places, has been a varying blend of anti-Judaism
(hostility to a religion) and anti-Semitism (hostility to a racialized
group), so it is difficult to gauge to what extent contemporary British
Islamophobia is religious and to what extent racial. It is generally
becoming acknowledged that of all groups Asians face the greatest
hostility today, and Asians themselves feel this is because of hostility
directed at Muslims (Modood et al. 1997). These matters are not easy
to disentangle, have hardly been researched at all, and anti-Muslim
racism is only just beginning to be recognized by antiracists. One has
also to acknowledge that there must be analytical space for forthright

criticism of aspects of Muslim doctrines, ideologies, and practice without dismissing it as Islamophobia—this being a parallel problem to, say, distinguishing anti-Zionism and anti-Semitism.

I want to step back a little now from debates around the emergent Muslim politics and discuss aspects of a broader normative vision in which such politics is being theorized. In the "Conclusion" I will return to the political debates about the Muslim political challenge when I consider it in the light of 9/11 and its aftermath and of wider questions about British identity.

Nine

Rethinking Multiculturalism and Liberalism

Multiculturalism emerged as a policy idea in Britain in the 1970s and 1980s, especially in education. It gave way, however, under pressure from the right, from antiracists who criticized it as obscuring racism and subordination, and from post-antiracists who argued that it essentialized cultures and ethnic groups (Modood 1998a). In recent years it has made a comeback. This time it is much more likely to be employed by political theorists, and its use in Britain owes much to its growing centrality in current anglophone political philosophy. Indeed, this latest use is largely imported from Canada and the United States. Several Britons have made notable contributions to this new theorizing but none more so than Bhikhu Parekh. In a long string of journal articles, book chapters, and conference papers, he has developed a point of view that has benefited not only from his wide reading in political philosophy—historical and contemporary, Western and Indian—but from his ongoing political engagement with the issues of equality and minorities in Britain and India. These resources have enabled him to develop a distinctive voice that is a counterpoint to North American academic liberalism. *Rethinking Multiculturalism* (2000), his first book-length statement on the subject, exemplifies all these strengths. It is profound, original, and wide-ranging, yet accessible to nonspecialists.

Parekh's concern is not with difference as such. The diversity he is interested in is not confined to a limited deviation from prevailing norms (as in the case of a subculture of homosexuality), but one that embodies a complex of alternative cultures sustained by distinct communities (Parekh 2000, 3–4). This communal diversity in the contemporary period, Parekh believes, is typified by the arrival and settlement of migrant groups from outside the West into Western societies, each of which has historically thought of itself as united by a single national culture and which has often enjoyed ties of colonial domination with the sending country. Most of Parekh's theorizing and detailed discussions relate to this postwar phenomenon. The book's greatest virtue, however, is the connections it makes between metaphysics, moral philosophy, political theory, and public policy, which makes it, as far as multiculturalism is concerned, unique.

Beyond Liberalism

Parekh rejects the dominant philosophical traditions that assert or imply that only one way of life is fully human. This moral monism is found among even those liberals who are best known as celebrators of diversity. J. S. Mill, for example, cherished individuality, not cultural diversity, and was prone to assume superiority over non-Western cultures, leading to justifications of "paternal despotism" and imperialism in Asia and Africa (2000, 45). Parekh recognizes that contemporary liberals are concerned to remedy these historic liabilities and engages at some length with the key ideas from John Rawls, Joseph Raz, and Will Kymlicka. He concludes that while liberalism is the political doctrine most hospitable to cultural diversity, we need to go beyond it. I would identify two moves here in Parekh's thinking: we need to make a more radical break with moral monism, and we need to take a less liberal view of culture.

Liberalism takes a clear, individualist view of what is the ultimate good for human beings and uses it as a standard to judge all actual and possible societies. It thus universalizes itself while relativizing all other cultures and societies. All other ways of living become particular, historical, and contingent, of value to some at a moment in time or as a means to individual autonomy, but not a universal good. It may be much more open, minimalist, and thus less judgmental and more inclusive than many other monisms, but it nevertheless operates with a uniform view of human nature. And in a "the West and the rest" manner, it divides all societies and perspectives into those that are acceptable to liberals and those that are not. Hence, for liberals the multicultural question is, how is liberalism to cope with non-liberal groups (in American political theory usually and quite unself-consciously referred to as "illiberal groups")? Parekh's solution is to relativize liberalism by seeking a higher philosophical vantage point from which liberalism is no less particular than its rivals.

Second, he urges us to take a less instrumental view of culture. Considering a culture in terms of options and choices is an inadequate characterization of how we are constituted by and relate to our own culture. Some people would say they love their culture and are not sufficiently detached from it to evaluate it in terms of its functions. "Obviously love of one's culture should not blind one to its faults, but that is very different from making it a function of its desirable quali-ties" (99). Moreover, in what is probably his most specific original contribution, he points out that liberal arguments about why culture matters to individuals cannot reach the purported conclusion that cul-tural diversity matters. It can make the majority aware that minority cultures matter to their members, but that is only an indirect argument for diversity. For Parekh, multiculturalism is not about the rights of minority cultures but about the value of cultural diversity. The value of the presence of a variety of cultures in a society cannot be under-stood as increasing our options, for other cultures are rarely options for us. Rather, their sense of contrast gives us a deeper understanding of our own culture and makes us reflect and learn about the diversity of humanity.

Hence, Parekh is committed to a universalism but it is not liber-alism; it is a metaethical commitment to the cultural diversity that constitutes humanity, an understanding of humanity that eludes every culture but is glimpsed in the dialogue between cultures. It is an understanding of a humanity that is much bigger than any "-ism" and is hinted at in Oakeshott's "conversation of mankind" (Oakeshott 1962). Parekh distinguishes his humanism from moral monism by arguing that human nature is always mediated by a culture; the inter-action of human nature and culture is such that we can never isolate an aspect of personality or a cultural practice and say *that* is human nature. Moreover, human nature might consist of certain tendencies and aversions, but they can be shaped by culture and manifest themselves in quite different ways and so by themselves can never explain human behavior or justify a way of life.

Parekh does, however, think that some kind of moral universalism follows. On the whole he thinks it will be relatively minimal and will consist of fairly general abstract concepts, such as human rights, which are susceptible to different interpretations within different moral traditions and societies. He thinks, of course, that such universal values cannot be worked out within one moral tradition, such as liberalism, but necessarily entail a dialogue of equals between all moral traditions. This is a difficult and complex enterprise that requires considerable self-humility and sensitivity to the views of cultures other than one's own. The current circumstances of Western hegemony are not conducive to it, but he thinks it is achievable and instances the 1948 UN Declaration of Human Rights as a document that approximates to his dialectical and pluralist form of minimal universalism (2000, 133–34). Readers of Parekh's previous work on multiculturalism may be surprised to the extent that universalism features in his larger philosophy, but they may also feel that it is a very thin universalism. For example, Parekh clearly sides with those exponents of "Asian values," such as the signatories of the Bangkok Declaration of 1993, who argue that human rights have to be defined and applied in the light of local history, culture, and religious backgrounds. In particular, he argues that human rights should not always be legal rights against the state, but can be realized within a communitarian moral framework based on mutual concern and solidarity (135–36), and that morally justifiable trade-offs between human rights and, say, filial piety and good neighborliness are compatible with universalism, even though some cultures may not produce the moral balance that liberals would.

Political Multiculturalism

For Parekh, then, multiculturalism is a form of (highly qualified) universalism. Its primary political implication is that liberals need to go beyond toleration and accommodation of other cultures to a dialogue with them, and this dialogue has to be institutionalized. The political structure of each just society will vary, for it ought to reflect and be a product of an equal dialogue of the diverse cultural communities within that society. Among its preconditions are "freedom of expression, agreed procedures and basic ethical norms, participatory public spaces, equal rights, a responsive and popularly accountable structure of authority, and empowerment of citizens" (Parekh 2000, 340). It is also likely to require giving encouragement and support, through public resources, to minority cultures, which may be suffering from oppression and marginalization, to rebuild confidence in themselves, resist the pressures of assimilation, enjoy equal cultural citizenship, and through interaction with dominant cultures enrich society for all (108). This last point is important. The public policy benefit of supporting minority cultures is not just its effects on members of that minority but on the whole of society (196).

Using this perspective, Parekh argues that the modern state is too homogenizing and insistent on a symmetrical federation because it privileges territorial identity. Yet provinces like Quebec and Kashmir represent cultural communities that may need special status. Parekh takes this idea further to sever the link between territory and representation, arguing that there may sometimes be a need for a culturally based federal structure when cultures within a polity cannot neatly be demarcated by territory. He is careful to stress that a multicultural society has to make provision for fostering unity as well as diversity. At one level this is achieved through the creation of a common culture, in which all should enjoy the right and opportunity to participate, but which will inevitably reflect the bias of the long-established culture (Parekh 2000, 221). A common culture cannot be officially engineered, but Parekh distinguishes his view from those he calls "civic assimilationists" by emphasizing that a common culture will necessarily be found in both the public and the private realms (219–24). A common belonging, however, lies primarily in the evolution of a national identity. It too cannot be culturally neutral and should have the power to evoke deep historical memories while including minorities within it (235). He believes, however, that national identity is exclusively located in a society's political culture, not its habits, temperament, attitude to life, sexual practices, customs, family structure, body language, hobbies, and so on (231–32).

I think this is too restrictive of the meaning of a national identity. It would mean that the idea of developing a British Islam or an Indian Islam, an Islam that was adapted to the culture of a particular country, would seem difficult to conceptualize. Yet this kind of separation between culture and politics seems to be out of character with Parekh's philosophy as a whole. If national identity is located in the political structure and not in ethnocultural terms, then how can ethnic identities be included in the definition of a national identity, as Parekh strongly recommends? Moreover, his view seems to make it difficult to make assertions such as that the French language is part of French national identity, or that the Welsh had a national identity before devolution. Similarly, I think more ethnic minority persons in Britain want to be part of a British identity in a nonassimilationist way than want to reduce British identity to the political. Here Parekh seems to be using a civic-ethnic/cultural distinction that for the most part he is opposed to.

Besides outlining the general features of a political theory of multiculturalism, Parekh devotes over a quarter of the book to elaborating his theory through real multicultural dilemmas. A dozen that are evoked to illustrate the logic of intercultural evaluation are listed (2000, 264–65), but these far from exhaust the cases that are discussed in this and other parts of the book. This way of grounding political theory is one I much sympathize with, but space does not permit me to elaborate on Parekh's discussion. Nevertheless, some general points can be made about his choice of examples. They are mainly to be found in his chapters 8, 9, and 10 and consist of recent and current controversies in the West, especially in Western Europe, mainly arising from the cultural practices or demands of recent migrants from Asia and Africa. The majority of the cases refer to the religion of these people; in more than half the cases the religion is Islam, including the two cases that are given the lengthiest attention, the *Satanic Verses* affair (295–321) and polygamy (262–72). The former is a crisis that Parekh played an important part in moderating, but he writes on it here with freshness as well as his previous evenhandedness. He reaffirms that Muslims were right to protest against the book (321) but not to threaten the life of the author, and that they, no less than their critics, failed to be sensitive to the legitimate sensibilities of their opponents. The case is used to illustrate the logic of political discourse and to critique those like Rawls and Habermas who take too cerebral a view of (political) argument (307–11).

The discussion on polygamy is as rare as it is fascinating but perhaps tries to do too much. It starts from asking if any kind of polygamy should be permitted, but soon takes the form of a competition between the virtues of polygamy and monogamy. Parekh does not just dismiss the former if not interpreted as an exclusive male right, but believes nevertheless that it can be clearly contrasted with current Western practices. A more sociological position might suggest that while some Muslims defend polygamy as an article of faith, urban Muslims the world over are in practice among the strictest monogamists. Informal polygamy (what sociologists call multiple partnering) and staggered polygamy (aka serial monogamy), on the other hand, while of many sorts and durations, are a recognizable feature of contemporary Western societies. Parekh's conclusion that even though there is not a decisive case against polygamy, it ought not to be allowed rests on the failure of polygamy to meet the ideals of a gender-egalitarian monogamy. This seems to be a case of double standards, for there is no suggestion that any of the varieties of multiple partnering that are practiced in the West should be outlawed. Parekh is strong in outlining the value of monogamy, less persuasive in showing that it is a "deeply valued liberal practice" that requires the outlawing of polygamy (288). This is perhaps no more than an indication of how difficult these issues are and of Parekh's determination to explore them.

The Minoritization of Religion

Parekh offers one of the most robust normative arguments in the literature on multiculturalism for the public role of religion. He rightly dismisses "strong secularism" (political debate and deliberation should be conducted in terms of secular reasons alone), but I am not sure that his argument is valid. He says that citizens who pass a law for religious reasons are not necessarily imposing any religious beliefs on fellow citizens, who may simply choose to obey the law out of a simple secular duty to respect the authority of the law and ignore the religious motivation (Parekh 2000, 322). But this introduces a dichotomy—the law and its cultural basis—that surely multiculturalists want to bridge. They want to argue that because the law draws its legitimacy from the majority culture, it potentially turns minorities into second-class citizens: people who obey the law without being culturally in sympathy with it (persons who in obeying the law may experience "moral incoherence and self-alienation" [323]). After all, if there is a simple duty to respect the authority of the law, minorities do not need to be given a further reason; they don't need recognition or cultural inclusion. The justification for the partial religious character of the legal and public order is that such orders cannot be culturally neutral. Hence, as I argued in chapter 7, the secularist claim to evenhandedly limit the public scope of all religions amounts to a cultural bias against those religions that want to be public players. Institutionalizing some public space for religious groups in a broadly secular framework (what Parekh calls "weak secularism") is the appropriate multicultural compromise.

I am also not happy with his suggestion that the West encourages groups to dress up their cultural claims as religious ones and that given the relatively nonnegotiable character of religion (more than race?), this sometimes leads to unnecessary political conflict. Despite the fact that an example he cites is the status of the Sikh turban, the sequence of politicization he describes does not fit the British case. In Britain, religion was deliberately left out of the Race Relations Act of 1976, and the Sikh turban has only come to have a protected status through the backdoor of ethnicity; it rests on the House of Lords' legal decision that the Sikhs are not merely a religious but also an ethnic group. It is true that religious identity claims have been encouraged by the present climate, but that is not instead of cultural identity claims. Indeed, a detailed look at the development of minority-majority relations in Britain will show, as suggested in the "Conclusion" of this volume, that it was claims based on race and ethnicity that established the initial and greater legitimacy, with religious claims following on the coattails of the former. It also has to be said that Parekh's political analysis sits oddly with his more theoretical contention that culture tends to be closely connected to religion (2000, 146).

The place of religion in multiculturalism is an extremely neglected topic, and so Jeff Spinner-Halev is to be commended to devoting a book to aspects of it (2000). It is, however, as he acknowledges, a very American book. There is much discussion of real cases, but it all relates to the United States; the key religious groups he is interested in are Protestant fundamentalists, Orthodox Catholics, and Hasidic Jews, predominantly though not exclusively white; there is no discussion of Muslims. Moreover, it assumes a liberal problematic (how is a liberal society to accommodate nonliberals?) and that the answer lies within liberalism, though his task is to show that liberalism can be more inclusive than most liberal theorists allow. Nevertheless, it has something to offer to non-Americans. In many ways this lies in its description of contemporary social dynamics.

Some multiculturalists have a tendency to assume that Western societies consist of minorities pitted against conservative or nationalistic majorities. Spinner-Halev asks us to consider whether it may not be more realistic today that in the United States and elsewhere we have a liberal mainstream and marginalized conservative religious minorities. To some extent this is merely the liberal problematic writ large, but it contains an important insight. While majority cultures are not homogeneous, there is indeed a growing mainstream that cuts across ethnicity and has an inclusive dynamic. This mainstream is individualistic, consumerist, materialist, and hedonistic and is shaped by a globalizing political economy, the media, and commercialized popular culture. This allows it to be pluralistic in terms of accommodating niche markets, lifestyle choices, and subcultures, especially if they are ephemeral and can contribute to a mix-and-match smorgasbord. What it cannot accommodate so easily are minorities who *as groups* reject or are rejected by significant parts of this individualistically diverse mainstream. They don't fit because of their group characteristics, but they are not necessarily ethnic minorities. They may have been, and in some ways may continue to be, racially subordinated, but the liberal dynamic breaks down some of these divisions. In fact, black people, with their physical prowess, music, and style, may even become emblematic of the new diversity. The groups that are likely to (continue to) experience themselves as minorities are those that are opposed to this liberal hedonism, that try to live by rules that do not allow their young to freely taste the smorgasbord. For they represent an alternative, less respected culture; they are most likely to be organized around a religion and to persist where they have the kind of tight rearing, family, and community structures associated with conservative religious groups.

Even if this contrast between liberal mainstream and conservative minorities is too simplistic, Spinner-Halev is able to draw an important implication: members of the latter cannot be characterized as lacking autonomy or "knowing no better." He points out that no one in the United States can be said to be unaware of the existence or the temptations of liberal lifestyles. "The lure of mainstream society is relentless. Living a restricted life takes a depth of commitment, is a matter of constant choice, and, at least sometimes, takes character" (2000, 5). Just because one does not choose individuality does not mean that one is more passive than those shaped by the mainstream.

Spinner-Halev makes the further sociological point that some advocates of diversity are naive about the conditions in which it flourishes, and their advocacy may be reducing rather than enlarging diversity. Main sources of minority formations are exclusion by the majority and internal norms, structures, and relationships that differentiate and separate a group from others, especially the dominant group. If the hopes of liberals and egalitarians are realized, there will be no externally imposed separation. Moreover, there will be considerable restrictions in the forms of authority and hierarchy that minorities can perpetuate, as they are required to adjust themselves to liberal and/or egalitarian norms, for example, in relation to gender roles. Identity theorists speak a language of collectivism but don't appreciate that "if we recognise groups in order to end oppression, group differences will fade in a society where equality reigns. When group boundaries are opaque and shifting, when people are members of different groups, when equality is realized and society's main institutions are inclusive, the individual becomes primary and the group secondary" (Spinner-Halev 2000, 44).

On the basis of these insights, he offers a set of normative principles. I have only space here to mention his key normative point and to query one other principle. His central point is that liberals are right to insist that autonomy is the ultimate political value but wrong to require all communities to put a high value on autonomy (Spinner-Halev 2000, 47). Commitment to a life of restriction and obedience can be worthwhile and ought not to be impeded, as long as it is freely chosen and this last condition is met by the presence of a powerful, welcoming mainstream. The latter ensures that those who choose to stay outside or enter into it on their own terms are doing so in the full knowledge, repeatedly reinforced, that there is an alternative available for them.

Spinner-Halev goes on to offer an interesting discussion of how conservative religious groups can be accommodated in different institutional contexts. He fully appreciates that in the last few decades U.S. courts, guided by academic liberalism, have made some perverse interpretations of the First Amendment (the "no Establishment clause," prohibiting an official state church), so that American jurisprudence on this subject is a mess. Yet, at the end of this discussion he argues that religious people should never be made a special case. "Treating the religious to exemptions from the law that are denied the non-religious would be giving a certain class of people more rights than others" (2000, 208). His solution is that any benefit that accrues to religious people should be made available to everyone. Suppose that employers and schools are required to adjust dress requirements to allow Sikh men to wear the turban; then a corresponding dispensation should be made available to all other employees and students. While this is a well-meaning attempt to maintain the universality of public rules and the law, it seems misguided. His solution fails to show that religious people are not being treated specially. After all, the headdress rule change only occurs because a religious group requires it; whatever the scope of the rule change, its motive is respect for religion. Furthermore, what equivalent can be offered? Spinner-Halev wants fellow employees to be allowed to wear the headdress of their choice—but Sikhs are being granted the right to wear religiously required headdress, not any other headdress. "Because it is required/prohibited by my religion" has a special normative force that obliges us to accommodate it in the way we would not if someone said "because I want to." If we cannot see this, then we do not have a principled reason to accommodate the Sikh turban in the first place, and Spinner-Halev's dilemma does not arise.

Liberal Philosophies and Liberal Practice

Spinner-Halev's approach offers an opportunity to consider to what extent Parekh's approach departs from liberalism. Spinner-Halev is conscious not just of the proper limits to institutionalized cultural hegemony but that something would be lost if certain ways of life—which may not be his—were to be squeezed out. Moreover, he is aware that the existence of nonliberal cultures is a corrective to the excesses of liberal culture and so is a potential resource for those beyond their membership. Yet these values are not derived from liberalism and so are left ungrounded. Parekh has a much broader philosophical vision of equality as difference and not just of equality as sameness and seems to more readily sanction institutional departures from liberal norms. However, as his dialogical multiculturalism seems to presuppose and build on an already existing liberal culture and institutional infrastructure, it is difficult to judge to what extent it is "beyond" liberalism and to what extent, especially in practice, it is a more open and less individualistic liberalism.

Parekh would insist that to describe a whole culture or society as liberal is too simplistic; not only does every society have some liberal elements—where individual choice is given relatively free rein—but no society is only liberal, not simply because it contains nonliberal groups but because liberals cannot be liberal all the time. There are aspects of everyone's life that cannot be properly analyzed in liberal terms. We do not choose our family, community, language, country, and so on, yet these constitute our personality and can be the source of obligations that we may or may not have chosen if we could have invented ourselves. Spinner-Halev makes a similar point but does not conclude that the term "liberal society" is therefore a misnomer. A society cannot be reduced to a single set of principles, but surely it is not an error to characterize it in terms of core or distinctive characteristics as long as the analysis is empirically grounded and not abstractly constructed.

This is what Adrian Favell does. His book on "actually existing liberalism" argues that the ways France and Britain have managed immigration and integration are based on their respective national philosophies and demonstrate that liberalism can take different, incompatible forms that do not bear any resemblance to American theorizing. The contrast is of a "France emphasising the universalist idea of integration, of transforming immigrants into full French *citoyens;* Britain seeing integration as a question of managing public order and relations between majority and minority populations, and allowing ethnic cultures and practices to mediate the process" (2001, 4). Using the concept of path dependency, Favell argues that each approach is imprisoned by its presuppositions and so produces "pathologies" that it is unable to deal with. The British approach, based on diffusing color racism and meeting postimperial obligations is, for example, unsuited for dealing with the demands of Muslims and of refugees and asylum seekers who are not "colored" or have no historic connections with this country. What is missing in the French intellectual project of "universalism in one country" and the British "multiculturalism in one country" is a universal standard of rights and policies that can be harmonized across Europe, for a common European policy can no longer be avoided. For him, the fact that the

British understanding of unity and plurality is distinctive has itself become a pathology (201).

Favell's book is in many ways an excellent analysis that takes national political culture seriously and throws new light on immigration and race in Britain and France, making each country illuminating to itself as well as to the other. In his Europeanist solution to national pathologies, however, sober analysis gives way to wishful thinking. He dismisses the idea of change/progress as internal and organic, calling it a self-flattering British myth, even though the motor of change in Britain is mainly our own debates. Two important recent reports (Macpherson 1999; and CMEB 2000, the latter chaired by Parekh) are creative yet distinctly British. While not narrowly national, they owe little to mainland European thinking or practice. Similarly, despite his gloss, the ethnic minority social and political advances that Favell points to rarely have anything to do with European institutions. The future may be European but not because we cannot diagnose and cure our own pathologies. We would do well to prepare for European infections as well as medicine.

The question of empirical fit can be raised with Parekh, too. He offers a philosophical perspective within which to approach the practical issues of multiculturalism, but it is not obvious that one of his major foci of interest, the postimmigration multiculturalism in Western Europe, sits squarely within this perspective. As the second and third generations become the majority within their groups, these may depart from being "organised communities entertaining and living by their own different systems of beliefs and practices" (Parekh 2000, 3). There are at the moment at least two simultaneous trends: the development of hybrid lifestyles and hyphenated identities that approximate to what Parekh understands as subcultures and the development of ethnoreligious communities. This suggests that Spinner-Halev's model of "liberal mainstream and conservative religious minorities" may turn out to have more relevance, when integrated with analyses of ethnicity and racism, than "dialogue among diverse cultures." Such minorities are of course likely to feel besieged, and this is unlikely to create the conditions of a dialogue among equals.

Parekh's philosophy may turn out to have more relevance at a global level, offering a basis for what some call a dialogue of civilizations. In any case, his political philosophy is so exceedingly flexible, with its emphasis on culturally mediated interpretations of all universal principles, on asymmetry between citizens and between federal units, and on an open-ended dialogue, that for all its brilliance and empathy, it leaves unclear what exactly it implies in a particular situation and when it is and is not being applied. Perhaps that is the nature of all argument. Certainly, Parekh's book is a major contribution that advances our thinking on all these issues; agree or disagree with him, all will appreciate his clarity and penetration.

Conclusion

Plural Britishness

Contrary to the powerful Atlantocentric idea that racism is basically of one kind (white racism against blacks), we have seen that tensions and dynamics within British society have played an important role in making plural (white) racisms evident to contemporary social science. We have also seen that within this modern narrative of race are a number of contradictions. Some of these have to do with the fact that despite relatively similar starting points toward the bottom of the British economy, non-white groups have not had a uniform trajectory. For example, it was assumed that the black Caribbeans, taken to be like their African-origin peers in urban America, would be the most disadvantaged and lowest earners, but from very early on this position has been occupied by the Pakistanis and Bangladeshis (groups who are quite well placed in the United States). Another example is that Indians (especially those from East Africa) and the Chinese have made remarkable progress and look set to consolidate a more middle-class profile than whites. Thus, in some ways, the color line, a feature of modernity, is in Britain proving to be less intractable than in the United States—mainly because of countervailing features of modernity, such as the acquisition of credentials, relatively open and meritocratic labor markets, and low capital entrepreneurialism.

On the other hand, and this has loomed large in this book, the

Atlantocentric color line, while not likely to disappear, is being eclipsed in importance by a quintessential feature of premodernity, religious identity. Even before September 11, it was becoming evident that Muslims, not blacks, were being perceived as "the Other" most threatening to British society. Hence, the argument of this book has been that what began as a story of an underclass has had to include the (re-)creation of middle-class formations among Indians, and a narrative of racial exclusion and black-white division has been complicated by cultural racism, Islamophobia, and an unexpected challenge to secular modernity.

In claiming that this is how things have developed, I have been criticized for emphasizing culture and religion at the expense of the socioeconomic (e.g., Alexander 2002). It should be clear, for example, from the discussions of chapters 3 and 4 and from Modood et al. 1997 that this is not the case. I am conscious, however, that I have come to be focused on social conflict, change, and reform that are not merely socioeconomic. A related criticism is that I and others emphasize difference and separateness at the expense of commonalities (Alexander 2002). Yet, from quite early publications I have explicitly argued for the fact of existing and emergent commonalities, which politics such as antiracism should not obscure but actively encourage (Modood 1992, ch. 1; Modood 1999), and for policies that eliminate the bases for exclusions and for institutional reforms that bring, for example, potentially antagonistic religious communities into a fraternity at the heart of the state (Modood 1994a). I will acknowledge that commonalities, no less than differences, are not merely given but have to be identified, interpreted, elaborated, and nurtured, and this requires some kind of conceptual-political frame or theory. As there are several such frames, what one sees will depend on which one is operative. The frame within which I have been working has been marginal to British antiracism and sociology, being thought to be both intellectually and politically unsound. I have not used it in a very systematic way, but different analyses in this book and elsewhere in my work are informed by an idea of plural Britishness. In ways to be given more content shortly, this is a compound or, better still, a concrete conception of citizenship and nationality. It is informed by the idea that a study of exclusion and inclusion, of equality and disadvantage, cannot consist of just measurements, and one way of overcoming this is to frame the study in the normative terms of civic inclusion and exclusion—not in terms of mere legalities but in a much more expansive sense of citizenship as a debating community with common concerns that structure a public space and interactions within it. Nor is it an abstract conception of citizenship, sewn together from philosophical reasoning with ethical principles; rather, it is penetrated by a sense of being a particular mixture of people with a particular history and relationships to the rest of the world, and the various senses of inclusion and exclusion that go with that historically derived and continually changing sense of peoplehood. "Britishness" is not just about idiosyncracies, or even merely the normative weight of a changing flow of customs, practices, and discursive images of a collective self and "Others." Rather, it is a complex in which appeals to general principles such as equality and fairness, and how they are to be interpreted, are in dialogical tension with notions of "this is our country" and "this is how we do things here."

One of the perceived inadequacies of any frame that is focused on one country, especially a country that is conceived intersubjectively, is that it may seem appropriate as an object of study but not as a frame of study. It may seem too "particular"; to an earlier (and some of the present) generation of European sociologists and social theorists it is not "universal" enough. The contrast would be with a Weberian or a Marxian notion of class, which by transcending the particularities of a society offers European or international analytical tools. Influenced by this tradition, the study of postimmigration formations in Britain was consciously in a race and class problematic (for a good critical review, see Anthias and Yuval-Davis 1992). Perhaps always considered to be a piece in the story of global capitalism, the tradition has become a contribution to the varied conceptualizations of globalization (see, for example, Hardt and Negri 2000). Another, albeit theoretically very different, concern for antidiscrimination and equal citizenship has grown into theories of human rights and cosmopolitanism of various kinds (Soysal 1994; Held 1995; Banton 2002). Universal or not, what is common to these different kinds of theorizing is that they combine the explanatory and the normative. This, though, is often implicit, and they are frequently presented as being one or the other.

I have not systematically attempted to construct or expound a theory, but to recognize that some kind of theory or frame is being used. My approach is hybrid or, to use a more self-congratulatory term, interdisciplinary. My empirical analyses are sociological of a kind; the loose frame in which they are held together, which I am calling plural Britishness, is more normative than explanatory. While I want to understand and explain events and discourses that I see as important, I identify these through an unhidden normative orientation. I make an effort to discover, highlight, and promote those features of the situation that substantiate the normative perspective and that others, having different perspectives, overlook or give less significance to. The ambition is to be a bridge between political theorists of multicultural citizenship, such as Bhikhu Parekh and Will Kymlicka (but also including political theorists more cautious of multiculturalism, such as Miller [1995] and Raz [1994]), and the sociology of postimperial migrant settlements in Britain, with a view to contributing to public policy (cf. CMEB 2000).

What is elaborated is not normative theory as it is typically discussed by Anglo-American political theorists but the normative challenges as they exist in specific situations. Nor is it the case that normative theory is being "applied" here, as if it was just a matter of delineating the specifics of the situation to which it is supposed to be applied, for that would be to assume an external, contingent relation between norms and situations (Winch 1958; Pitkin 1972). It is to assume that the meaning and the normative charge of an idea is clear and derives from the logic of a theory; any cases that are referred to are mere illustrations, logically independent of the theory. It is true that normative theory is sustained by an eclectic appeal to illustrative empirical examples, but these are dealt with cursorily, with virtually no attention to issues of interpretation and comparative method (Favell 1998a, 1998b). Typically missing from such theorizing is a context-sensitive argument that shows that the examples do indeed fit the principle that they are meant to illustrate. This is particularly problematic because theoretical formulations are usually too sharply expressed in terms of opposing principles—which in the real world may never be found in such pure forms or pose such incompatibilities. Inevitably, such a noncontextual approach oversimplifies and distorts issues, making minority behavior serve as exemplars for vices and virtues, where on a more context-informed reading they would not be seen as unambiguous cases. A more context-sensitive approach would bring out, for example, how certain issues of liberal principles become quite different from what they appear when the dimensions of racialized exclusion, socioeconomic equality, and essentialized categorization are taken into account.

Our starting point should be—as it has been in this book—actual societies, actual multicultural situations, actual multicultural crises, actual political institutions, norms, traditions, and so on. Theories that are normatively relevant to, say, actual multicultural situations and multicultural crises must demonstrate that they map on to those situations in a sufficiently accurate way and cannot take for granted that principles derived from abstract theories do indeed fit the situations and do not misread them or distort them through oversimplifications, non sequiturs, and so on (Favell and Modood 2003). Such a normative, context-based inquiry will not be just descriptive/empirical. It must leave space for normative debates, dissent, and reform, but the logic of these will be seen to flow out of the possibilities implicit in the observed contexts. What is being sought, it may be said, is the pursuit of intimations within diverse, internally contested, and mutually interacting traditions (Oakeshott 1962). This will produce political theories of multiculturalism appropriate to specific societies—rather than, for example, importing North American models to Europe—and alerts us in advance that we are not seeking a single theoretical model. The expectation is that multiculturalism will mean different things, though there will be family resemblances between them. It would be foolish to expect a uniformity of meaning or radical diversity in advance of a systematic comparative inquiry of a kind not offered here.

National Contexts

In any case, abstract notions of equality and citizenship are not enough because they never exist as abstract. The specific shape and texture of British citizenship does not simply vary as an instance of citizenship, but is connected to a sense of nationality (complicated by the fact that "British" nests Scottish, Welsh, and English nationalities, and these various nationalities undergo changes in salience and in their relations to each other). At the same time, exactly the same is true of the new migrant groups, the ethnic minorities, for they too each have a specific character and together are a demographic mix that could have been otherwise and indeed is otherwise in other countries. The point can be made comparing France, the former West Germany, and Britain. France and West Germany have, in both absolute and relative terms, a larger foreign-born population and population of non-European origin than Britain. Yet issues of racial discrimination, ethnic identity, and multiculturalism have less prominence in those two countries than in Britain. One aspect of this is that national debates on these topics have a lesser prominence and are less frequently led by non-whites or non-Europeans, who are more the *objects of,* rather than *participants in,* the debates. Another aspect is the relative lack of data about ethnicity and religious communities and, consequently, of research and literature. Yet this is not a simple matter of scale. Each of the countries in the EU has a very different *conception* of what the issues are, depending on its history, political culture, and legal system (Brubaker 1992; Bryant 1997; Favell 2001; Koopmans and Statham 2000; Kastoryano 2002).[1]

The German experience is dominated by the idea that Germany is not a country of immigration, and so those newcomers who can show German descent are automatically granted nationality while the others are temporary guest workers or refugees; none are immigrants. Hence, out of its population of 80 million, Germany has 5 million without German citizenship. This includes about 2 million Turks and Kurds, some of whom are now third-generation residents in Germany but who until recently were excluded from citizenship by German self-conceptions of nationality as *descent*. In contrast, France has a history of immigration that it has proudly dealt with by a readiness to grant citizenship. But it has a republican conception of citizenship that does not allow, at least in theory, any body of citizens to be differentially identified.

In Germany, if you are of Turkish descent you cannot be German. In France, you can be of any descent, but if you are a French citizen you cannot be an Arab. In each case, U.S.-style—and now UK-style—composite identities like Turkish German, Arab French, or British Indian are ideologically impossible. The giving up of pre-French identities and assimilation into French culture is thought to go hand in hand with the acceptance of French citizenship. If for some reason assimilation is not fully embraced—perhaps because some people want to retain pride in their Algerian ancestry or want to maintain ethnic solidarity in the face of current stigmatization and discrimination—then their claim to be French and equal citizens is jeopardized. The French conception of the republic, moreover, also has integral to it a certain radical secularism, *laïcité,* marking the political triumph over clericalism. The latter was defeated by pushing matters of faith and religion out of politics and policy and into the private sphere. Islam, with its claim to regulate public as well as private life, is therefore seen as an ideological foe, and the Muslim presence as alien and potentially both culturally and politically unassimilable. This is most visible in the new French policy to ban "ostentatious" religious symbols in state schools, a measure—so clearly aimed at the use of the *hijab*—that is seen as drawing a "line in the sand" in the containment of Islam.

The British experience of "colored immigration," in contrast, has been seen as an Atlantocentric legacy of the slave trade, and policy and legislation were formed in the 1960s in the shadow of the U.S. civil rights movement, black power discourse, and the inner-city riots in Detroit, Watts, and elsewhere. It was, therefore, dominated by the idea of race, more specifically by the idea of a black-white dualism. It was also shaped by the imperial legacy, one aspect of which was that all colonials and citizens of the Commonwealth were subjects of the Crown. As such they had rights of entry into the United Kingdom and entitlement to all the benefits enjoyed by Britons, from National Health Service treatment to social security and the vote. (The right of entry was successively curtailed since 1962 so that while in 1960 Britain was open to the Commonwealth but closed to Europe, twenty years later the position was fully reversed.)

The British Context

In terms of positive reception of migrants, a commonplace observation is that Britain, like its European neighbors, is an "old" country and not as hospitable to immigrants as, say, Canada, the United States, or Australia, countries that have been historically constituted by immigration. Yet in relation to some groups of immigrants, Britain, in particular cities such as London, has been remarkably receptive and self-transformative. I think this is related to the fact that ethnic minority political mobilization in Britain began with a set of factors that enabled it to reach a degree of ideological assertiveness, prominence, and civic impact in a limited period of time that seems without parallel in Western Europe. I would point to a set of opportunity structures constituted by the following:

- the British imperial connection, felt by many migrants and politically acknowledged by at least some white British

- the sense of having a right to be in Britain and having a British identity
- automatic British citizenship and franchise from day of arrival (later qualified)
- large-scale antiracist struggles elsewhere in the English-speaking world, especially in the United States, in which notions of migrants and hosts were absent and which were borrowed from or emulated in Britain, creating a confidence and assertiveness that among migrants-as-guests would be regarded as intolerable by the hosts

In each of these respects, the West Indians, who thought of themselves as culturally British in the way that New Zealanders arriving in England in the 1950s might have done, took the lead in forging a minority political discourse and assertiveness that South Asians gradually assimilated into, adapted for their own use, or used as a point of departure to press for a less racial, dualist, black-white orientation in favor of an ethnic pluralism (Modood 2004). Once this minority assertiveness is part of a political culture and regarded as legitimate, perhaps even necessary to demonstrate a certain group dignity, then it can take forms that owe nothing to the original source, for example, the form of the Muslim campaign against *The Satanic Verses*, which, as discussed in chapters 5 and 6, to many observers initially bore no relation to antiracism but has increasingly come to be seen in that light.

There is a kind of openness in Britain not found in continental Northern Europe. Northern Europe came to develop the most extensive and generous form of the welfare state and a related political culture has played a major role in defusing the nationalistic conflicts within Western Europe of the first half of the twentieth century. Yet multicultural thinking, including among the progressive opinion, is weak. The Northern European city in which multiculturalism is most a matter of debate and fact is probably Berlin, which has a marked recent American and British influence. The history of Northern Europe has been a regional one, and so its contemporary political openness is focused on the constituent parts of the region. In contrast, Britain has had an oceanic or maritime history that has brought it into contact, for good or for ill, with many parts of the world. The Empire brought the British into contact with a degree of cultural heterogeneity not experienced by Northern Europeans. French history does have parallels with the British, though the comparison only highlights that in both imperial and contemporary settings the French are less tolerant of cultural plurality than the British.

These different histories of contacts and tolerance are part of the explanation of why today London is not simply an English or a British or even a European city, but a world city. And why a characteristic of British culture, despite its self-image of insularity, is the readiness to borrow and mix ideas and influences, as supremely exemplified in the English language. It is perhaps more accurate to say that Britons and mainland Europeans are open to outsiders in different ways. Europeans have sought to put the excesses of nationalism behind them by seeking rapprochement with their neighbors but saw no inconsistency in requiring cultural assimilation from migrants of non-European origin. The British, especially the English, are less open to their European neighbors, but less hostile than most Europeans to multiculturalism and to international exchange (cf. Kumar 2003).

New Ethnicities

The context is not a given, simply lying there for new immigrants and ethnic minorities to step into. In fact, the ethnic minorities have made a major contribution to giving plural Britishness the character it has: the negotiation of change through debate, economic mobility, and a high degree of cultural mixing. This does not come only from the white, indigenous British side. The protests and mobilizations of ethnic minorities have been critical to challenging racism and opening up Britain. Similarly, it has been the hard work and enterpreneurial drive of minorities such as the South Asians and the Chinese and the sociability of the Caribbeans that has made economic mobility and cultural mixing a reality. For example, the presence of racism and the sense of difference has stimulated an ethnic assertiveness, but one that has moved from antiracist oppositional identities to making claims on British national identities, as noted by theorists such as Paul Gilroy and Stuart Hall. Hall has argued that from the mid- to late 1980s "a significant shift has been going on (and is still going on) in black cultural politics" (1992a, 252). Not only does this entail a recognition of a diversity of minority identities, "a plural blackness," but also an understanding that ethnic identities are not pure or static. Rather, they change in new circumstances or by sharing social space with other heritages and influences. Moreover, this also challenges existing conceptions of Britishness (Gilroy 1987). If ethnic minority identities are not simply products of cultures of extra-British origin, but owe something to the stream of British life, then they too contribute to that stream, and so their existence belies the dichotomy of essentially black and essentially British. This has opened the way for talk of "the black Atlantic"—a shared heritage and experience of blacks in Africa, the United States, the Caribbean, Britain, and Western Europe—as a basis for a transnational culture and discourse (Gilroy 1993). In the same period of time there has also emerged an Asian identity based on a hybrid South Asianness rather than a regional, national, caste, or religious identity derived from one's parents, and sometimes directly influenced by or modeled on forms of black pride and black hip-hop or rap music (Baumann 1990). Some, indeed, have argued that the hope for multiculturalism lies in the development of new syncretic and hybrid youth cultures centered on black musical forms like rap and hip-hop and their Asian equivalents (Gilroy 1987).

While acknowledging the insightful and influential ways in which Gilroy and especially Hall have identified new emergent forms of minority identity consciousness and its expressions, particularly the ambivalent relationship to Britishness, I do have some reservations about this new blackness line. My three interrelated criticisms are, first, that these sociocultural theorists invariably focus on African-Caribbeans; second, that they speak of a plural blackness that they expect Asians to fit into but that most Asians are not interested in; third, that they are guilty of a woeful neglect of religion. In each case, Hall has been much more sensitive to social change and allows it to speak in its own voice rather than the voice of political blackness, and so the criticisms are less applicable to his later work (e.g., CMEB 2000, which is discussed in Rojek 2003; Hall 2000).

My criticisms draw on the large Fourth Survey from the mid-1990s.[2] It found that minority ethnic individuals, including those born and raised in Britain, strongly associated with their ethnic and family origins; there was very little erosion of group identification down the generations. Yet despite several decades of various forms of antiracist politics around a black identity—an identity that, as has already been noted, some politicians and theorists have argued is *the* key postimmigration formation—only a fifth of South Asians thought of themselves as black. This is not an Asian repudiation of "the essential black subject" in favor of a more nuanced and more pluralized blackness (Hall 1992a) but a failure to identify with blackness at all.

While skin color was prominent in the self-descriptions of Caribbeans, religion was much more prominent in the self-descriptions of South Asians. As mentioned in chapter 8, no doubt this owes as much to a sense of community as to personal faith, but the identification with and prioritization of religion is substantial. At a time when a third of Britons say they do not have a religion,[3] nearly all South Asians said they have one, and 90 percent said that religion was of personal importance to them (compared to 13 percent of whites). Expressions of commitment were exceptionally high, even among the young: more than a third of Indians and African Asians, and two-thirds of Pakistani and Bangladeshi sixteen- to thirty-four-year-olds, said that religion was very important to how they led their lives, compared to 5 percent of whites (nearly a fifth of Caribbeans took this view) (Modood et al. 1997, ch. 9).

The Fourth Survey does, however, offer for the first time some large data-set evidence that ethnicity is coming to mean new things. While distinctive cultural practices of religion, language, marriage, and so on still command considerable allegiance, there is a visible decline in participation across the generations. This is particularly evident among younger South Asians who, compared to their elders, are less likely to speak to family members in a South Asian language, regularly attend a place of worship, or have an arranged marriage (Modood et al. 1997). Yet, as has been said, this did not mean that they ceased to identify with their ethnic or racial or religious group. In this respect the survey makes clear what has been implicit in recent identity politics: ethnic identification is no longer necessarily connected to personal participation in distinctive cultural practices, such as those of language, religion, or dress. It is fair to say a new conception of ethnic identity has emerged.

Traditionally, ethnic identity has been implicit in distinctive *cultural practices;* this still exists and is the basis of a strong expression of group membership. Additionally, an *associational* identity can be seen that takes the form of pride in one's origins, identification with certain group labels, and sometimes a political assertiveness. Identities in this political climate are not implicit and private but are shaped through intellectual, cultural, and political debates and become a feature of public discourse and policies, especially at the level of municipal government. The identities formed in such processes, as argued in chapter 8, are fluid and susceptible to change with the political climate, but to think of them as weak is to overlook the pride with which they may be asserted, the intensity with which they may be debated, and their capacity to generate community activism and political campaigns.

Britishness

The Fourth Survey uniquely allows us to explore British national identity among non-whites by bringing a large set of data to bear on the question. It is quite clear that the identities already discussed, various as they are, do not necessarily compete with a sense of Britishness. More than two-thirds of Asians said that they felt British, and these proportions were, as one might expect, higher among young people and those who had been born in Britain. The majority of respondents had no difficulty with the idea of hyphenated or multiple identities (see also Runnymede Trust 1998), but there was evidence of some alienation from or rejection of Britishness. For example, over a quarter of British-born Caribbeans did not think of themselves as being British. In separate in-depth interviews it was found that most of the second generation thought of themselves as mostly but not entirely culturally and socially British, but they were not comfortable with the idea of British being anything more than a legal title. In particular, they found it difficult to call themselves "British" because they felt that the majority of white people did not accept them as British because of their race or cultural background. Through hurtful jokes, harassment, discrimination, and violence they found their claim to be British was all too often denied (Modood, Beishon, and Virdee 1994, ch. 6). Of course, "British" is a problematic and declining feature of identification among some white people, too, especially the young; always resisted by many Irish in Britain, it is being eclipsed by "Scottish" in Scotland. Indeed, there seems to be less subjective incompatibility between being British and Pakistani than being British and Scottish, especially among the young. While it seems that Asians in Scotland, like other Scots, are thinking of themselves in terms of Scottishness rather than Britishness (Saeed, Blain, and Forbes 1999),[4] in England, where the whole issue of English identity is full of complexity and ambivalence, of implicit superiority and suspicion of nationalism, "English" has so far largely been treated by the new Britons as a closed ethnicity rather than an open nationality. Hence, while many ethnic minorities have come to think of themselves as hyphenated Brits, they have only recently started to think of themselves as English. For whites too, English as a prominent public identity has only recently begun to be a feature of British cultural life and largely as a reaction to a Scottish disavowal of British. The 2001 census is the first time that a majority of white people in England marked their nationality as English rather than British (National Statistics Online 2004; cf. Curtice and Heath 2000, 158–59). This is an indication of a trend in which ethnic minorities are laggards, despite the fact that, even now, English national identity is most popularly associated with a football team, which places the Caribbeans, who are strongly over-represented as players in the England team, at the center of English national identity. This is one of many examples in which Caribbean people have become an integral feature of popular British culture and the public imagination of self—a remarkable phenomenon, given their disadvantaged socioeconomic profile, not to mention a population size of less than 2 percent.

The Caribbean-white, black-white, social, cultural, sexual, and generational mix is, I believe, very deep in Britain. While the trend in all groups is away from cultural distinctness and toward cultural mixture and intermarriage, it is much more evident among the Caribbeans. Among the British-born in the survey, of those who had a partner, half of Caribbean men and a third of Caribbean women had a white partner compared to a fifth of Indian and African Asian men, a tenth of Pakistani and Bangladeshi men, and very few South Asian women. This has been made possible by the fact that ethnic segregation in Britain is relatively low, not at all approximating to the segregation of African-Americans (Johnston, Forrest, and Poulsen 2002); that the segregation of the Caribbeans is much less than of the South Asians; that the Caribbean migrants started off much closer to the white British, not least in the possession of the English language; and that norms of sexual contact and behavior, as well as of marriage partner selection among Caribbeans, facilitated an easy mixing in radical contrast to the South Asians.

It has been argued that by the mid-1990s "black British culture could be described as confident beyond measure in its own identity" (Hall 1998, 39) and that young black people have made themselves "*the* defining force in street-oriented British youth culture" (40). From being pariahs, many black people have become objects of desire, with many young whites envying and imitating their "style" (cf. Hall in Gates 1997, 196). It is worth emphasizing that this black British cultural success, like some other aspects of Caribbean settlement in

Britain, has been highly inclusive. While born of an assertiveness and a search for dignity, and while sometimes oppositional, it has also been a movement of integration, of wanting to be included into the British mainstream, of sharing and mutual respect (Part 4 of the BBC television series *Windrush,* and Phillips and Phillips 1998, which accompanies the series). It has, inevitably, been largely a black-white relationship, but some young Asians and others have been drawn into it, too. It is particularly important to note that this sociability is not necessarily in a color-blind, assimilationist, "passing for white" context in which racism is ignored. For some young people it can take place in ways in which black ethnicity and antiracism are emphasized—or, indeed, are the point. Black persons can be admired not in spite of but because of their blackness, for their aesthetics, style, and creativity as well as for their antiracist resistance, and sometimes for their outcast or deviant status: for example, at a typical performance of controversial black nationalist rap bands, more than half of the audience will be white.

At a group level, the distinction is not just between Caribbeans and South Asians, but also a contrast among South Asians, namely, between African Asians and Indians (about 90 percent of whom are Hindus and Sikhs), and Pakistanis and Bangladeshis (over 95 percent of whom are Muslims). On a range of issues related to religion, arranged marriages, choice of schools, and Asian clothes, the latter group take a consistently more conservative view than the former, even when age on arrival/birth in Britain and economic position are taken into account. But we should not assume that groups that are most culturally distinct or culturally conservative are least likely to feel British and vice versa. It has already been mentioned that the Caribbeans, of all non-whites the culturally and socially closest to the white British, had the highest proportion who dismissed identification with Britishness—more than the Pakistanis and the Bangladeshis. This should not be taken to imply that the cultural conservatism consists in simply wanting to be left alone as a community and making no political demands on the public space. For example, half of all Muslims wanted state funding for Muslim schools, even though only half of these would actually choose such a school for their own children.[5] The political demands of Muslims such as these are not akin to conscientious objections, to principled exemptions from civic obligations, but, similar to other movements for political multiculturalism, for some small degree of "Islamicization" of the civic—not for getting the state out of the sphere of cultural identities, but for an inclusion of Muslims into the sphere of state-supported culture.

The British political context, the opportunity structures it made available, and the way that ethnic minority groups have responded have allowed for hyphenated or plural Britishness. Increasingly, ethnicity or blackness is experienced less as an oppositional identity than as a way of being British, and I believe that for many Muslims, "Muslim," too, is beginning this transition. These hyphenated or multiple identities that contest and extend what it means to be British are accepted, even welcomed, by some, perhaps many, in the wider British public. They are one of the elements in the rhetoric of the New Labour government, especially in its early phase, which seeks to emphasize the plural and dynamic character of British society by speaking of "Cool Britannia," of "rebranding Britain" (Leonard 1997), of Britain being a "young country" (Tony Blair), a "mongrel" nation (Gordon Brown), and a "chicken tikka masala eating" nation (Robin Cook). This "plural British" rhetoric, and the multicultural trends it is pointing to, has come to be counterbalanced by an integrationist, anti-Muslim rhetoric following the riots of summer 2001, when young Asian Muslim men fought with supporters of the racist British National Party and/or the police in some northern cities (Kalra 2003). The issues raised were far from new, having been made prominent during and after the *Satanic Verses* affair, as discussed in previous chapters. They were, however, considerably reinforced by the reactions to the terrorist attacks in the United States of September 11 and the "war on terrorism" that has followed, which clearly has had and is having major implications for domestic political mutliculturalism.

After September 11

The politics of being Muslim in Britain and the West has, inevitably, come to be dominated by 9/11 and its aftermath. The military and civil liberties aspects of the "war on terrorism," even more so than at the time of the *Satanic Verses* affair, has seen a vulnerable and besieged group assert itself publicly and at times defiantly. The majority of Muslims, while condemning the terrorist attacks on America, opposed the bombing campaign in Afghanistan and the invasion of Iraq. A significant minority of Muslims, however, voiced support for the Taliban, even for bin Laden, and there were media reports that some young men had gone to Afghanistan to fight for the Taliban and that some of them had been killed in the U.S. attacks, though such reports were difficult to confirm. A British Muslim in Pakistan claimed to have helped recruit more than two hundred British volunteers to fight for the Taliban (*Telegraph,* January 8, 2002); a British national was convicted in Pakistan for the murder of the American journalist Daniel Perle. Three of the first fifty captives from Afghanistan, brought to the U.S. prison in Guantánamo Bay, Cuba, were Britons, and eventually they were joined by six others (by mid-2004 none had been charged, and five were released in February 2004). Moreover, the failed "shoe bomber," Richard Reid, was a Briton of Caribbean origin on his father's side. Some British Muslims seem to have been involved in a number of other terrorist incidents in various parts of the world, including a suicide bombing in Israel (*Independent,* March 9, 2004). Under new antiterrorism legislation, 664 persons, mainly Muslims, had been taken into detention by September 2004; only about a sixth had been charged, usually with a minor offense, and over half had been released without charge. The seventeen found guilty of a connection to a terrorist organization were mostly members of Irish paramilitary groups (BBC TV 2004).

Nevertheless, while some Muslims from a variety of Western countries have been drawn into *jihadi* activities, Britons seem to be quite prominent. This may even be a consequence of the political consciousness and assertiveness that are a feature of struggles for multicultural equality. Several commentators have noted that the young Britons who got involved in these international networks were not necessarily from the large Muslim underclass in Britain but were just as or more likely to be students or graduates and professionals (Shaw 2002). This is not in itself surprising and is not inconsistent with the argument of this book that racism and antiracism, broadly conceived, are a primary source of Muslim assertiveness in Britain. Many contemporary equality movements—such as feminism—are led by intellectuals and public sector and media professionals and focus on glass-ceiling and elite issues rather than on severe deprivation. There is also a focus on discursive representations and unconscious racism and sexism, the counterparts of which are likely to be acutely felt by educated Muslims and can be a direct or indirect source for oppositional activism. This is particularly relevant because, as argued in previous chapters, Muslims get self-pride and oppositional energy from their personal faith and collective solidarity. For example, Pnina Werbner has carefully brought out how certain kinds of Islamic millennialism, originating from the Sufism of rural Pakistan, gives succor and redemptive hope in the light of contemporary domestic and international humiliations and powerlessness (Werbner 2001, 2004). Yet she also shows that this discourse, popular among migrants, is not meant to be taken militantly; it does not offer a political agenda. The latter can of course be found in a militant Islamism—journalistically known as "Islamic fundamentalism"—which was absent among Asian Muslim migrants but is increasingly attractive to some of the second generation, especially the better educated. Islamism, then, offers an alternative source of political mobilization to egalitarian multiculturalism or perhaps a complementary one, with the former focused on the international and the latter on the national. It is too early to say what effect the emergence of Islamism will have on the discourse of multiculturalism among British Muslims and among Britons generally. A study of "moderate" Muslim activists and public intellectuals in 2003 found strong support for multiculturalism as long as it included faith as a dimension of difference, with some arguing that the Qur'an, Islam, and Muslim history are powerful sources of multiculturalism and represent a form of multiculturalism superior to that developed elsewhere or available in the contemporary West (Modood and Ahmad forthcoming).[6]

International Islamism and, certainly, terrorism have complicated the case for multicultural equality on the Muslim side, but also on the non-Muslim side. The confused retreat from multiculturalism has been given an enormous impetus by post–September 11 events. There has been widespread questioning, echoing the Rushdie affair, about whether Muslims can be and are willing to be integrated into British society and its political values, paralleling discourses in most of the EU. The New Labour government was at the forefront of this debate, as were many others who are prominent on the center-left and have long-standing antiracist credentials. For example, the Commission for Racial Equality published an article by the left-wing author Kenan Malik in which he argued that "multiculturalism has helped to segregate communities far more effectively than racism" (Malik 2001). The late Hugo Young, the leading liberal columnist of the center-left *Guardian* newspaper, went further and wrote that multiculturalism "can now be seen as a useful bible for any Muslim who insists that his religio-cultural priorities, including the defence of jihad against

America, override his civic duties of loyalty, tolerance, justice and respect for democracy" (November 6, 2001). More extreme again, Farrukh Dhondy, an Asian who pioneered multicultural broadcasting on British television, writes of a "multicultural fifth column" that must be rooted out and argues that state funding of multiculturalism should be redirected into a defense of the values of freedom and democracy (Dhondy 2001).[7] In 2004, Trevor Phillips, the chair of the Commission for Racial Equality, declared that multiculturalism was useful once but is now out-of-date, for it made a fetish of difference instead of encouraging minorities to be truly British (Baldwin 2004).[8]

One of the specific issues, mentioned in chapter 8, that has come to be a central element of this debate is that of faith schools, that is to say, state-funded schools run by religious organizations. While they must teach the national curriculum and are inspected by a government agency, they can give extra space to religious instruction, though not all do so. They are popular with parents for their ethos, discipline, and academic achievements and so can select their pupils, often giving priority to children whose parents can demonstrate a degree of religious observance. Yet the violent disturbances in some northern English cities in the summer of 2001, in which Asian Muslim men had been among the protagonists, were officially blamed in part on segregated communities and segregated schools. Some of these were church-run schools and were 90 percent or more Christian and white. Others were among the most underresourced and underachieving in the country and had rolls of 90 percent or more Muslims. They were called "Muslim schools," even in official reports (Ouseley 2001). In fact, they were nothing of the sort. They were local, bottom-of-the-pile, comprehensive schools that had suffered from decades of underinvestment and "white flight" and were run by white teachers according to a secular national curriculum. "Muslim schools" came to be seen as the source of the problem of divided cities, cultural backwardness, riots, lack of Britishness, and a breeding ground for militant Islam. Muslim-run schools were lumped into this category even though all the evidence suggested that their pupils (mainly juniors and girls) did not engage in riots and terrorism and, despite limited resources, achieved better exam results than local authority secular schools. On the basis of these "Muslim schools" and "faith schools" constructions, tirades were launched by prominent columnists in the broadsheet newspapers against allowing state funding to any more Muslim-run schools or even to church-run schools, and demands were made once again that the British state be entirely secular. For example, Polly Toynbee argued in the *Guardian* that a precondition of tackling racial segregation was that "religion should be kept at home, in the private sphere" (December 12, 2001), utilizing a public-private distinction the political revival of which, as I argue in chapter 8, is a reaction to Muslim assertiveness and Muslim claims on a public policy of multiculturalism.

New Developments

As at the time of the Rushdie affair, the media gave massive and disproportionate coverage to Muslim extremists, regardless of the limited support they enjoyed among Muslims. While the same occurred in relation to more recent controversies, there were at least two new features in the media and political debates after 9/11. First, while in the late 1980s there were virtually no self-identified Muslims (as opposed to persons with a Muslim background) with a platform in the national media, by 2001, partly because Muslims had achieved notoriety as a political problem, there were a couple of Muslim broadsheet columnists. They, together with other occasional Muslim contributors, expressed collective self-criticism. This was absent in the Rushdie affair. While maintaining a strongly anti–U.S. foreign policy stance, they expressed shock at how anger and latent violence had become part of British Muslim, especially youth, culture, arguing that West-hating militant ideologues had "hijacked" Islam and that the moderates had to denounce them.[9] The following quote from Yusuf Islam (formerly the pop star Cat Stevens before his conversion to Islam, and now the head of the Islamia Educational Trust, who had been wrong-footed by the media in relation to Khomeini's fatwa in 1989), nicely captures this shift in the position of the moderates: "I was still learning, ill-prepared and lacking in knowledge and confidence to speak out against forms of extremism. . . . Today, I am aghast at the horror of recent events and feel it a duty to speak out. Not only did terrorists hijack planes and destroy life, they also hijacked the beautiful religion of Islam" (*Independent* [London], October 26, 2001). Other Muslim intellectuals issued fatwas against the fanatics (Ziauddin Sardar, *Observer*, September 23, 2001), described the Muslim revolutionaries as "fascists" (Sardar, *Evening Standard* [London], November 5, 2001) and "xenophobes" (Yasmin Alibhai-Brown, *Independent* [London],

November 5, 2001), with whom they did not want to be united under the term "British Muslims." While in the *Satanic Verses* affair moderate Muslims argued against what they took to be a bias against Muslims—a failure even by liberals to extend the ideas of equality and respect for others to include Muslims—moderates now added to this line of defense an argument about the urgency of reinterpreting Islam. This reinterpretation variously calls for a re-excavation of the Qur'an as a charter of human rights, which, for example, abolished slavery and gave property rights to women more than a millennium before either of these was achieved in the West; a restoration of the thirst for knowledge and rational enquiry that characterized medieval Muslim societies; a recentering of Islam around piety and spirituality, not political ideology; a "reformation" that would make Islam compatible with individual conscience, science, and secularism. Sardar, one of the most prominent of the moderate Muslim intellectuals, said that the failure of the Islamist movements of the 1960s and 1970s was partly responsible for the contemporary distortions of Islam by the militants. Such movements, he argued, had started off with an ethical and intellectual idealism, but had become intellectually closed, fanatical, and violent. Just as today's middle-aged moderates had encouraged the earlier Islamic renewal, they must now take some responsibility for what had come to pass and do something about it (Sardar, *Observer*, October 21, 2001).

A second difference from the *Satanic Verses* affair was that Muslims found that many of their analyses of international developments were shared by non-Muslims, often the majority of Britons, especially the politically minded. While Tony Blair's close support for all U.S. initiatives, especially the invasion of Iraq, deeply alienated most Muslims from the government and the Labour Party[10]—the main forum of Asian Muslim mainstream political activity—the same was true of many non-Muslims. In some countries where U.S. policy, and their government's support for it, was deeply unpopular, as in Italy and Spain, Muslim protests were marginal because Muslims lacked a political presence. But British Muslims were prominent and much more voluble (except for those bound by Labour Party constraints) than their better resourced counterparts in the United States. There was a greater political maturity among British Muslims in comparison to the *Satanic Verses* affair. In terms of elected national politicians and presence in national public bodies and influential nexuses, Muslims continued to be woefully underrepresented (Anwar and Baksh 2003), but there was a new embeddedness in the British political structure. The crucial difference, however, was that Muslims were, virtually for the first time, not isolated, and on some occasions they were part of a broad consensus. There was a near unanimity in the op-ed pages of the national papers that the "price" for the invasions of Afghanistan and Iraq and the rest of the "war on terrorism" was a just solution for the Palestinians, a position that Muslims of all stripes heartily endorsed. This meant that alliances and coalition building were possible in a way denied with the Rushdie affair, and that Muslims were on some occasions part of the political mainstream. For example, the Muslim Association of Britain was one of the three partners that organized a series of mass protest marches in London, including one in February 2003, the largest ever held in that city, and in which—in contrast to most Muslim-organized action hitherto—Muslims formed only a fraction of the gathering of about 2 million.

Reaffirming Multiculturalism

As the *Satanic Verses* affair had done earlier, so the events flowing out of 9/11 are turbulent and testing for political multiculturalism. The watchword, however, has to be "Don't panic." Perhaps we ought to brace ourselves for some excesses: I am reminded of the Marxist radicalism of my student days in the late 1960s and 1970s; as we know, that passed and many a radical now holds high office (and fulminates against young radicals). But we must distinguish between criminal actions and militant rhetoric, between radical Islamists and the wider Muslim opinion; the former, despite the bewitchment of the media, are as representative of Muslims as the Socialist Workers Party is of working-class politics. We must note that, despite the special stresses and strains that arise for Muslims and in relation to Muslims, the situation is not uniquely difficult. It is most likely that Muslims are following a trajectory similar to African-Caribbeans making a claim on Britishness through forms of political self-defense and antiracism. It is important that we not give up on the moderate, egalitarian multiculturalism that has been evolving in Britain and has proved susceptible to gradually accommodating Muslim demands through a process of campaigning, debate, negotiation, and political consensus.

Other than Muslims themselves, a leading actor in bringing Muslim concerns and racial equality thinking into contact has been the

Runnymede Trust, recognizing Islamophobia as one of the chief forms of racism today when it set up its Commission on Islamophobia (Runnymede Trust 1997, 2004). The demand for Muslim schools within the state sector was rejected by the Swann Report on Multiculturalism in the 1980s and by the Commission for Racial Equality even in the 1990s (Swann 1985; CRE 1990b), yet it became government policy in 1997. Adapting the census to measure the extent of socioeconomic disadvantage by religious groups has been achieved, and support has been built up for outlawing religious discrimination and incitement to religious hatred. Talk of Muslim identity used to be rejected by racial egalitarians as irrelevant ("religious not political") and divisive, but in the last few years Muslim organizations, like the Muslim Council of Britain (MCB) and Forum Against Islamophobia and Racism (FAIR), mentioned earlier, have co-organized events and demonstrations with groups such as the National Assembly of Black People and are often supported by the Commission for Racial Equality.

There must, certainly, be an emphasis not just on difference but on commonality too. British antiracists and multiculturalists have indeed been too prone to ignore this, but to do so is in fact less characteristic of Muslims than of the political left (see, for instance, the various statements of MCB from its inception and its choice of motto, "Working for the Common Good"). To take up some recent issues, wanting to be part of British society means having a facility in the English language, and the state must be protective of the rights of those oppressed within their communities, as in the case of forced marriages. But blaming Muslims alone for segregation ignores how the phenomenon in the northern cities and elsewhere has been shaped by white people's preferences as individuals ("white flight") and the decisions of local councilors, not least in relation to public housing, and of employers, again including local councils.

It is foolish to disparage and dismantle the cohesiveness of Muslim communities. We ought to recognize that there is an incompatibility between radical secularism and any kind of moderate multiculturalism in which Muslims are an important constituent. Integration cannot be on a "take it or leave it" basis; we must be willing to redefine Britain in a more plural way. The French approach of ignoring racial, ethnic, and religious identities does not mean that they, or the related problems of exclusion, alienation, and fragmentation, vanish. They are likely, on the contrary, to become more radical, and so the French may actually be creating what they fear, the unraveling of the republic. The recent banning from state schools of the Islamic head scarf, the *hijab*, together with other "ostentatious" religious symbols, will be a test case.

The Future of Multi-Ethnic Britain, the report of the Commission on Multi-Ethnic Britain (2000), is a high-water mark of British thinking on these topics. It tried to answer the question, how is it possible to have a positive attitude to difference and yet have a sense of unity? Its answer was that a liberal notion of citizenship as an unemotional, cool membership was not sufficient; better was a sense of belonging to one's country or polity. The report insisted that this belonging required two important conditions:

- the idea that one's polity should be recognized as a community of communities as well as a community of individuals
- the challenging of all racisms and related structural inequalities (CMEB 2000)

Here we have a much more adequate concept of social cohesion than that which has emerged as a panicky reaction to the current Muslim assertiveness and which runs the risk of making many Muslims feel that they do not belong to Britain. It is a form of social cohesion that makes equality and difference integral to it; it frames social cohesion not only as an embrace of plural, overlapping identities, but also in terms of socioeconomic opportunities and structures (for the complementarity of recognition and redistribution within a concern for equality, see Parekh 2004).

Integration through Assertiveness

The oppositional character of ethnic minority self-concepts has not been at the price of integration per se but, illustrating that integration can take different forms, has been one of the means of integration. Political mobilization and participation, especially protest and contestation, has been one of the principal means of integration in Britain. As activists, spokespersons, and a plethora of community organizations come to interact with and modify existing institutions, there is a two-way process of mutual education and incorporation: public discourse and political arrangements are challenged but adjust to accommodate and integrate the challengers. Political contestation seems to have been an almost necessary stage in the integration process at a time when identities and the solidarities and divisions that they create or constrain are increasingly shaped by public sphere discourses. One of the most profound developments, however, has been that ethnicity or blackness is increasingly experienced less as an oppositional identity than as a way of being British, and something similar is probably happening to the Muslim experience. There is evidence that minority identities, especially among young people, are now less oppositional—perhaps as a result of the success of the oppositional moment. Circumstances are pushing Muslims into being defined and defining themselves in oppositional terms but, considering the wider perspective I have been outlining, give some ground for hope.

A unitary British identity no longer looks feasible (for the moment). This is not a cause for alarm. Contrary to what Enoch Powell and some radical antiracists predicted, there is a desire for a hyphenated Britishness among immigrants and their descendants. At the same time, a new non-right-wing discourse of Britishness has recently emerged (Alibhai-Brown 2000; CMEB 2000). These two developments can be brought together. Each development is somewhat embryonic, and certainly multiculturalism, which so far has been largely a social, bottom-up movement, requires greater mainstream political commitment and leadership than it has received hitherto. The change in attitudes that is required among the white British is a real political challenge. Equally important is the right kind of multiculturalism: a multicultural Britishness that is sensitive to ethnic difference and incorporates a respect for persons as individuals and for the collectivities that people have a sense of belonging to. That means a multiculturalism that is happy with varied hybridities but has space for religious identities. Both hybrid individuals and ethnoreligious communities have legitimate claims to be accommodated in political multiculturalism. The latter are no less hybrid in that their development, too, is a product of British opportunity structures and Asians and Muslims are continuously adapting to British influences. Hybridity and religious communities should not be pitted against each other in an either-or fashion as is done all too frequently by the celebrators of British Asian hybridity (e.g., Rushdie 1991; Kureshi 1995) and by some liberal political philosophers (e.g., Waldron 1992).

The emergence of Muslim political agency has thrown British multiculturalism into theoretical and practical disarray. It has led to policy reversals in the Netherlands and elsewhere, and across Europe has strengthened intolerant, exclusive nationalism and secularism. We should be moving the other way. We should be extending to Muslims existing levels of protection from discrimination and incitement to hatred, and the duties of organizations to ensure equality of opportunity, not simply the watered-down versions of legislation proposed by the European Commission and recently passed by the UK government. We should target more effectively, in consultation with religious and other representatives, the severe poverty and social exclusion of Muslims. We should also recognize Muslims socially and include them in the institutional compromises of church and state, religion and politics, that characterize the evolving, moderate secularism of mainstream Western Europe, resisting the wayward, radical example of France.

Ultimately, we must rethink "Europe" and its changing nations so that Muslims are not a "Them" but part of a plural "Us," not mere sojourners but part of its future. As Du Bois predicted (1995), the twentieth century can be seen as having been dominated by struggles about color, with non-whites resisting the domination of whites. The first years of the new century suggest that similar struggles between non-Muslims and Muslims may define our era. The political integration or incorporation of Muslims—remembering that there are more Muslims in the European Union than the combined populations of Finland, Ireland, and Denmark—has not only become the most important goal of egalitarian multiculturalism but is now pivotal in shaping the security, indeed, the destiny, of many peoples across the globe. This book expresses the optimism that meeting these challenges is not beyond our means. Just as it has been possible to extend antiracism to multiculturalism and expand our sense of what it is to be British, so it is possible to enlarge our antiracism to include anti-Islamophobia and to develop forms of hyphenation and plurality that prevent the latest of a series of familiar identity assertions from becoming walls of separation.

Notes

Introduction

1. The eleven-plus examinations, abolished shortly afterward, were taken at the age of eleven and determined which type of secondary school a child was assigned to.

2. For him Britain was materially brilliant but becoming a morally decadent culture. People like us had to assimilate the former and reject the latter. In his later years he came to think that we had to follow this strategy not just to stay on the "straight path" ourselves but to be an example to the white British in the hope that they may one day learn from us. Among the features of Britain that he continued to respect the most were the sense of honesty and service that informed its institutions and professions and which he thought were more Islamic than their counterparts in the contemporary Muslim world (M. S. Modood 1990).

3. As will be clear from the rest of this book, I do not endorse the view that races are a biological reality. Some authors mark this lack of reality by putting the word *race* in scare quotes. While I occasionally do this, to add quotation marks every time the word is used would make the exercise ritualistic.

2. If Races Do Not Exist, Then What Does?

1. The then chairman of the CRE, Sir Peter Newsam, has subsequently given some indication of the price that advocates of "black" were willing to pay: "I have seen south Asians walk out of CRE meetings because they have been labelled black" (*Independent,* Sunday, April 25, 1993, 25).

2. The socialist author, Tariq Ali, about the time I was writing this chapter, in a conversation said that his only criticism of British imperialism in India was that it did not go far enough in smashing up traditional, feudal, and religious structures (cf. Ali 2002).

3. Ethnic Diversity and Racial Disadvantage in Employment

This chapter is based on work undertaken at the Policy Studies Institute on the Fourth National Survey of Ethnic Minorities. This large project was funded by the Department of Health, Department of Environment, Department for Education and Employment, and the Economic and Social Research Council. I have benefited from the assistance of colleagues and the comments of an advisory group at all stages of the project. For full acknowledgments and details, see Modood et al. 1997.

1. "African Asian" refers to members of the South Asian diaspora in (East) Africa who fled as refugees to Britain in the 1960s and 1970s.

2. The Policy Studies Institute and its predecessor, Political and Economic Planning (PEP), have been conducting surveys charting the changing position of Britain's ethnic minorities about once a decade from the mid-1960s (Daniel 1968; D. J. Smith 1977; C. Brown 1984). The latest in the series, the Fourth Survey, was in the field in 1994. Besides detailed coverage of employment, the survey included many other topics, such as housing, health, racial harassment, and cultural identity (Modood et al. 1997). The survey was based on interviews of about an hour in length, conducted by ethnically matched interviewers, and offered in five South Asian languages and Chinese as well as English. Over five thousand persons were interviewed from the following six groups: Caribbeans, Indians, African Asians, Pakistanis, Bangladeshis, and Chinese. Additionally, nearly three thousand white people were interviewed in order to compare the circumstances of the minorities with that of the ethnic majority. Further details on all aspects of the survey are available in Modood et al. 1997.

3. The scoring schemes used in Figures 1 and 2 inevitably have some degree of arbitrariness. Their main justification is that they reflect the differences in earnings (see Modood et al. 1997, Table 4.23).

4. The low economic participation level and the high unemployment level of Pakistani women probably accounts for their having a job profile different from the men. For example, the Pakistani men's profile relative to Indian men has a much smaller proportion in nonmanual work, but this is reversed in the case of Pakistani women relative to Indian women. This strongly suggests that economic participation by Pakistani women is more likely to take place in the nonmanual sector; their proportionately lower presence in manual jobs was not simply the result of the higher rates of unemployment in manual work because, relative to other groups, the unemployment rate for Pakistani women in nonmanual work is much higher (ibid.). The probable explanation is that Pakistani women who seek paid work outside the home have the language skills, educational qualifications, and career aspirations to make them want nonmanual work, and if they lack these, they are more likely to be keeping house than to be in paid manual work outside the home. Most of the former women are probably from the minority of Pakistani families of urban origin.

5. Compared to the Fourth Survey, the 1991 census reports that women of all ethnic minorities except the Chinese have a greater presence in the top jobs category, with the result that there is little difference between South Asian and white women. The census found also that there was a smaller proportion of Caribbean than other women in the top category, but they are as well represented as white women, and much better than all other groups, among employers and managers in large establishments (3 percent) (OPCS 1993, Table 16; Abbott and Tyler 1995, Table X). South Asian and Chinese women in contrast were more likely to be professional workers. The difference between the 1994 findings and the census may be that that the former

includes more women from the "hard-to-find" categories, such as those with poor facility in English, and as they are more likely to be in manual work (though they are even more likely to be economically inactive), their inclusion will depress the percentage of women of certain minorities in the top category.

6. The respondents were shown a card with sixteen bands of earnings, each labeled with a random letter of the alphabet. They were asked to state the letter of the band in which their gross weekly earnings fell. Although there was a good response from some groups, there was a high refusal rate among South Asians, about a quarter of whom, excluding Bangladeshis, declined to indicate their earnings. The comparative earnings analyses offered here need to be read with this limitation in mind. The nonrespondents in each ethnic group were spread across the job levels, though the relatively few white and Chinese nonrespondents were more likely to be nonmanual employees, and South Asians' rate of refusal was higher when they chose to be interviewed in English only. It is possible, therefore, that the aggregate average earnings presented here are a little reduced as a consequence of the composition of the nonrespondents.

7. It has been argued that the female full-time employees' earnings differentials in the analysis of the 1982 data were misleading, for minority women worked longer hours and were in fact not earning more than white women on an hourly pay comparison (Bruegel 1989, 52; Bhavnani 1994, 84). Maybe this was so in 1982, but the finding of the 1994 survey is that full-time ethnic minority women work fewer hours than whites; an hourly pay analysis would, therefore, widen the gap. The same applies to men.

4. Ethnic Differentials in Educational Performance

1. The generations are (1) the migrants, those who came to Britain over the age of sixteen; (2) the second generation, those who came to Britain under the age of sixteen, and so had some schooling in Britain, or were born in Britain, and were between twenty-five and forty-four years old at the time of the survey; (3) the new generation, between sixteen and twenty-four years old, most of whom were born in Britain and had most if not all of their education in Britain. Strictly speaking, these are not generations as there could be an age overlap between (1) and (2), and the years are not evenly spread across the three categories.

2. For details about the Fourth Survey, see chapter 3, note 2, and Modood et al. 1997.

3. GCSEs are sat on a subject-by-subject basis, typically at the end of compulsory schooling at age sixteen. To possess not even one GCSE is to possess no meaningful scholastic qualification.

4. In practice, three A-levels (or the equivalent) are the minimum entry qualification into higher education, so to possess not even one is at best to be intermediately qualified.

5. Other data suggest that Africans have the highest participation rate of all groups (Berthoud et al. 2000, 9); the Fourth Survey did not include Africans.

6. Thus it needs to be borne in mind that the widening access policy in some prestigious universities that aims to reduce the proportion of entrants from fee-paying schools, if successful, should lower the proportion of Chinese and Indians admitted to those universities, while increasing that of other minority groups. Interestingly, taking the higher education sector as a whole, it has been found that after controlling for A-level scores and a number of other factors, attending an independent school slightly reduced a candidate's chance of admission (Shiner and Modood 2002, 229n8).

7. Whether this investment in education has paid dividends in terms of jobs and incomes is a complex question, but it seems not to have done so at least for the Africans (Berthoud 1999, 2000).

8. These events precipitated a moral panic about "faith schools" without anyone offering any evidence that anyone in Britain involved in the riots or any Islamist organizations had been to a faith school.

9. About half of all sixteen-year-olds take the GCSEs. Nearly all pass them, but only an A*-C pass is regarded as a good pass, and the possession of five A*-C passes in different subjects is generally regarded as the minimum to progress to the next educational level or to obtain a job requiring GCSEs.

10. More detailed support for some of the arguments in this chapter can be found in Modood et al. 1997, ch. 3; and in Modood 1998c.

5. Reflections on the Rushdie Affair

1. In September 1988 Salman Rushdie's novel *The Satanic Verses* was published, and various passages relating to the Prophet Muhammad, his wives, and the Qur'an caused deep offense to many Muslims who mobilized, especially in India, Pakistan, Britain, and South Africa, to have it banned. In Britain, petitions and street marches achieved very little publicity until a copy of the novel was symbolically burned at a mass rally in Bradford. Violent clashes with the police in India and Pakistan led to several deaths and the banning of the novel in those countries and to the Ayatollah Khomeini of Iran issuing a religious edict, a fatwa, proclaiming that it was the duty of all Muslims who had the opportunity to kill the author and publishers. An international crisis ensued, and Salman Rushdie had to go into hiding. There was also a major debate in Britain about the rights and wrongs of this controversy and what it meant for freedom, racial equality, and multiculturalism. This chapter and the next explore some aspects of this domestic political debate. Horton 1993 contains essays exploring aspects that the controversy raises for liberalism and also offers a brief narrative of the main events.

2. This is not surprising in view of the fact that in virtually all Muslim countries colonized by European powers, including India, it was Islam—not race or even secular nationalism—that mobilized the masses in the struggle for independence.

3. The French government, in contrast to the British, was praised for being robustly libertarian and taking a firm stand against Muslim demonstrators in February 1989. It is interesting then that in May 1990 a law was passed in France, following a law of many years' standing in West Germany, prohibiting, by punishment with a prison sentence, statements denying "crimes against humanity" committed by the Nazis against the Jews during the Second World War (see chapter 6). This is a country that experiences intense Islamophobia and anti-Arab racism and yet it has no antidiscrimination legislation to speak of.

4. I appreciate that the term "pluralism" in Western social science discourse usually refers either to societies as conceived by Furnivall, in which communities, socially sealed from each other, come together only in the marketplace; or to Robert Dahl's description of liberal democracy as choice between competing elites. I intend simply to mark out an area of social fact and discussion without wishing to preempt theoretical and political responses. I am using the term following Bhikhu Parekh (1990).

5. The term "ethnicity paradox" is Barbara Lal's, and I am indebted to her for my understanding of Park and Thomas (Lal 1983, 1990).

6. India, of course, is the glaring counterexample to this historical record of toler-

ation, the best examples of which are in the Middle East, Central Asia, North Africa, and Spain, where Christian and Jewish minorities flourished for centuries.

7. See, for example, the account of the minimum principles of an ideal Islamic state agreed to by a 1949 conference of all major sects in Pakistan (Brohi 1979). Interestingly, Mawdudi, with his usual insistence on logical consistency, argues that, given that a "Muslim society" is an ideological not a territorially based society, full citizenship rests on affirming the ideology; moreover, a Muslim, regardless of his origins, is necessarily a full citizen of any Muslim society he enters. This is faultless logic, though not quite the experience of Muslim guest workers in the Gulf.

6. Muslims, Incitement to Hatred, and the Law

1. The Commission of Racial Equality was created by the 1976 Race Relations Act as a permanent body to enforce, review, and make recommendations in relation to antidiscrimination measures and to promote good race relations.

2. As mentioned in chapter 5, the House of Lords judgment on *Mandla v. Lee* (1983) contains the fullest statement of what the law understands to be an ethnic group. Legal judgments have included Sikhs, Jews, Gypsies, Rastafarians, and others within the term, but *Nyazi v. Rymans Ltd* (1988) specifically excluded Muslims. In 1991, the Appeal Court, by a majority decision, overruled the recognition of Rastafarians as an ethnic group, and *CRE v. Precision* (1991) made it clear that direct discrimination against Muslims (as opposed to, say, Pakistanis) is not unlawful. In December 2003 a new offense of religious discrimination was created, see chapter 8.

3. For a defense of the jurisprudential validity of the fatwa, see the introduction to Ahsan and Kidwai 1991; this volume contains a chronology of the affair to February 1991 and an extensive bibliography, though the annotations are of a mixed quality and from a narrowly orthodox Muslim viewpoint. For Muslim criticism of the fatwa, see Sardar and Wyn Davies 1990.

4. I am indebted for the bulk of the factual information on which this section is based to Barendt 1985, 161–67. I have also found helpful Board of Deputies of British Jews 1991.

5. The TUC and the Board of Deputies of British Jews in their oral evidence to the House of Commons Committee explicitly endorsed the CRE's view.

6. In 1989 the Saskatchewan Court of Appeal upheld the judgment against the Engineering Students' Society, University of Saskatchewan, for producing newspapers that "ridiculed, belittled and affronted the dignity of women because of their sex."

7. Allowing for cultural translation, it may be said that the British response to the invasion of the Falklands was a case of national ghairat.

8. *Whitehouse v. Gay News.* Strictly speaking, James Kirkup's poem did not attribute homosexuality to Jesus; rather, it imagined the crucified Christ as a suitable object of homosexual lust.

9. Sometime in 1989, on a domestic British Airways flight, a total stranger, who overheard me talking about *Satanic Verses* to a fellow passenger, interrupted to tell me all Muslims should be gathered together in one place and a nuclear bomb dropped on them.

10. In this regard Western liberals all too readily forget the thirty or so deaths in anti-*Satanic Verses* riots in Islamabad, Srinagar, and Bombay when they assess Muslim attitudes to the author.

11. From a dialogue between Homi Bhabba and Bhikhu Parekh, "Identities on Parade," *Marxism Today,* June 1989, 29; my italics.

12. Over several decades some students have protested against the presence of racist

and other right-wing speakers on campus, and some have disrupted meetings. In the 1980s their national union adopted a policy of excluding such speakers from campuses. In the 1990s the target of such policy became militant Islamists. The students' positions are an illustration of the difficulties and contradictions in some left-wing defenses of freedom of speech.

13. For example, International Committee for the Defence of Salman Rushdie and His Publishers, *The Crime of Blasphemy: Why It Should Be Abolished* (London: International Committee for the Defence of Salman Rushdie and His Publishers, 1989), which includes various black groups among its signatories, insists that there should be no restriction of any kind on the discussion of any subject (6).

14. The BBC denied that the film was withdrawn at the last moment because of a fear of the law. Peter Rosier, head of Corporate Affairs and Press Relations, was quoted as saying: "It is not a legal thing at all. We had a lot of people who have contacted us. It is perfectly plain from the volume of letters and phone calls that we have had that this film will cause some considerable distress to people" (*Muslim News,* no. 33 [November 1991]: 1). This is exactly the sort of sensitivity that was looked for by the sixty thousand British Muslims who signed a petition asking Penguin to withdraw *The Satanic Verses* months before the Bradford book burning, let alone the fatwa.

15. The most bizarre example of pressure-group censorship is the National Stuttering Project having got the U.S. distributors of the British film *A Fish Called Wanda* to cut out a scene in the film in which a character is mocked because of his stutter (The Weasel, "Up and Down the City Road," *Independent Magazine,* September 7, 1991).

7. Multiculturalism, Secularism, and the State

This paper was made possible by the ESRC award R000222124, for which I am grateful. I would also like to thank Nick Trainor of Linacre College, Oxford, for his assistance.

1. These five ideal types and the terms I use to mark them are my own. Given the variety of ways terms like "liberal" and "the plural state" are used, my ideal types do not necessarily correspond with how some others may use these terms, including those who use the terms to designate their own perspective. For a related typology, see CMEB 2000.

2. Hall does not always argue as if the contemporary self was radically decentered. See Hall and Held 1989.

3. Charles Larmore, Joshua Cohen, and Thomas Nagel (in his early work at least) argue that the arguments and reasons advanced in favor of a political regime must be neutral, for if they are not neutral, then these justifications do not (in the words of Larmore) present a solution "to the political problem of reasonable disagreement about the good life. They have themselves become simply another part of the problem" (Larmore 1990, 345). This is not a view held by, among others, John Rawls, who maintains that the arguments in favor of a regime can be non-neutral, though the arguments that are advanced in the operation of the justificatory regime must be in some sense neutral as between different conceptions of the good (1993).

4. "Pillorization" refers to the formal arrangements beginning in the nineteenth century that allowed Protestants and Catholics and different linguistic groups to have state recognition and resources for separate schools, universities, trade unions, civil servants, and so on. It has been in decline in the second half of the twentieth century,

though recently there has been a revival of it in Belgium based on language groups (Flemish and French speakers).

8. Muslims and the Politics of Multiculturalism

1. This was even truer of the Caribbeans than of the South Asians. However, at least superficially, they were able to and did combine an ethnic assertiveness ("black" as pride in African roots) with a wider political solidarity ("black" as inclusive of all non-whites) without a new identity vocabulary.

2. Forum Against Islamophobia and Racism (FAIR), *A Response to the Government Consultation Paper "Towards Equality and Diversity: Implementing the Employment and Race Directives"* (London, 2002); Commission on British Muslims and Islamophobia, *Response to the Commission on Racial Equality's Code of Practice* (London, 2002).

3. For further examples of how a catching-up antidiscrimination and equality agenda has been developing in relation to Muslims, see Runnymede Trust 2004.

4. It is noticeable that Muslim homophobia gets far more condemnation than black homophobia, and Muslim sensitivities against offensive literature gets far less sympathetic treatment than that of radical feminists against pornography and Jews against Holocaust revisionism, not to mention legal restraints against incitements to racial hatred, as mentioned in chapter 6.

5. The feeling is mutual: it is not Christian hegemony but radical secularism and sexual liberalism that Muslims, in private and public, fulminate against.

Conclusion

1. For the basis of at least medium-term pessimism about civic equality and multiculturalism in France and Germany, see Modood 1994b, 87–88.

2. For details about the Fourth Survey, see chapter 3, notes 1 and 2.

3. While this is consistent with many surveys, in the 2001 census, interestingly, only a sixth of whites in England and Wales said they had no religion (but 7.7 percent refused to answer the optional question). On the other hand, the British Social Attitudes Surveys have found that respondents with no religion have increased from 31 percent in 1983 to 44 percent in 1999 (Dirk de Graaf and Need 2000). This suggests not only that the context is critical but that, with the increased saliency in religious minority identities, some white people who do not think of themselves as particularly religious are using "Christian" in some contexts as a cultural identity (for a similar conclusion, cf. Voas and Bruce 2004).

4. Interestingly, non-whites in Scotland and Wales often have a sense of identification with these nations (Saeed et al. 1999), but non-whites in Britain rarely think of themselves as Europeans (Runnymede Trust 1998).

5. This may now have doubled, for a poll by the *Guardian* in March 2004 found that half of Muslims said they would send a child of their own to a Muslim school rather than a state school (Travis 2004).

6. The study found that the term "moderate" was not readily embraced. Even those who did not object to it as a divisive term created by the non-Muslim media and politicians felt that it had unfortunately come to mean "sellout" in the Muslim communities (Modood and Ahmad forthcoming).

7. For a recantation of his Black Panther radicalism, see Dhondy's "A Black Panther Repents," *Times*, June 24, 2002, T2, 2–4.

8. The timing of Phillips's intervention was puzzling given that only a few weeks earlier he had rubbished David Goodhart's widely supported attack on culturally diverse immigration (Goodhart 2004) as genteel xenophobia and liberal racism (Phillips 2004). See also my reply to Phillips (Modood 2004–5).

9. The hijacking theme was most notably introduced by a charismatic, white U.S. Muslim, Hamza Yusuf (who was also consulted by President Bush), and was taken up by the magazine of the young Muslim professionals, *Q News* (e.g., in the November 2001 issue). Dr. Muqtedar Khan, director of international studies, Adrian College, Michigan, had an even more uncompromisingly "moderate" statement in the right-wing tabloid newspaper the *Sun* but was not taken up by British Muslims with a comparable enthusiasm, perhaps because he, unlike Yusuf, did not visit Britain.

10. A poll in March 2004 found that support for New Labour among Muslims had fallen from 76 percent in 1997 to 38 percent (Travis 2004).

Bibliography

Abbot, D. 2002. "Teachers Are Failing Black Boys." *Observer,* January 6. http://observer.guardian.co.uk.

Abbott, P., and M. Tyler. 1995. "Ethnic Variation in the Female Labour Force: A Research Note." *British Journal of Sociology* 46, no. 2: 339–51.

Ackerman, B. 1990. "Neutralities." In *Liberalism and the Good,* ed. R. B. Douglass, G. M. Mara, and H. S. Richardson. London: Routledge.

Ahmad, F., T. Modood, and S. Lissenburgh. 2003. *South Asian Women and Employment in Britain: The Interaction of Gender and Ethnicity.* London: Policy Studies Institute.

Ahsan, M. M., and A. R. Kidwai, eds. 1991. *Sacrilege versus Civility: Muslim Perspectives on the "Satanic Verses" Affair.* Leicester: Islamic Foundation.

Airey, C., and L. Brook. 1986. "Interim Report: Social and Moral Issues." In *British Social Attitudes,* ed. R. Jowell et al., Social and Community Planning Research. Aldershot, England: Gower.

Akhtar, S. 1989. *Be Careful with Muhammad!* London: Bellew Publishing.

———. 1990a. "Is Freedom Holy to Liberals? Some Remarks on the Purpose of Law." In *Free Speech.* London: Commission for Racial Equality.

———. 1990b. "A Faith for All Seasons." *Islam and Western Modernity.* London: Bellew Publishing.

Alexander, C. 2002. "Beyond Black: Re-thinking the Colour/Culture Divide." *Ethnic and Racial Studies* 25, no. 4: 552–71.

Ali, T. 2002. *The Clash of Fundamentalisms: Crusades, Jihads, and Modernity.* London and New York: Verso.

Ali, Y. 1991. "Echoes of Empire: Towards a Politics of Representation." In *Enterprise and Heritage: Crosscurrents of National Culture,* ed. John Corner and Sylvia Harvey. London: Routledge.

Alibhai-Brown, Y. 2000. *Who Do We Think We Are? Imagining the New Britain.* London: Penguin Books.

Amin, K., and R. Richardson. 1992. *Politics for All: Equality, Culture, and the General Election 1992.* London: Runnymede Trust.

Anderson, Elijah. 1994. "The Code of the Streets." *Atlantic Monthly,* May.

Anthias, Floya. 1998. "The Limits of Ethnic 'Diversity.'" *Patterns of Prejudice* 32, no. 4: 5–19.

Anthias, Floya, and Nira Yuval-Davis. 1992. *Racialized Boundaries: Race, Nation, Gender, Colour, and Class and the Anti-racist Struggle.* London/New York: Routledge.

Anwar, M. 1993. *Muslims in Britain: 1991 Census and Other Statistical Sources,* CSIC Europe Papers 9. Birmingham, England: Centre for the Study of Islam and Christian-Muslim Relations.

Anwar, M., and Q. Baksh. 2003. *British Muslims and State Policies.* Centre for Research in Ethnic Relations, University of Warwick, Coventry.

Arendt, H. 1963. *On Revolution.* New York: Viking Press.

———. 1968. *Human Condition.* London: University of Chicago Press.

Armstrong, K. 1988. *Holy War.* London: Macmillan.

Audi, R. 1989. "The Separation of Church and State and the Obligations of Citizenship." *Philosophy and Public Affairs* 8, no. 3.

Back, Les. 1993. "Race, Identity, and Nation within an Adolescent Community in South London." *New Community* 19, no. 2: 217–33.

Badawi, M. A. Z. 2003. "Citizenship in Islam." *Association of Muslim Social Scientists (UK) Newsletter* 6: 17–20.

Bader, V. 2003. "Religions and States: A New Typology and a Plea for Non-constitutional Pluralism." In "Religious Pluralism, Politics, and the State," ed. V. Bader. Special issue, *Ethical Theory and Moral Practice* 6, no. 3: 55–91.

Baldwin, T. 2004. "I Want an Integrated Society with a Difference." *Times,* April 3.

Balibar, Etienne. 1991. "Is There a 'Neo-Racism?'" In *Race, Nation, Class: Ambiguous Identities,* E. Balibar and I. Wallerstein, 17–28. London: Verso.

Ballard, R. 1996. "Islam and the Construction of Europe." In *Islam, Hinduism, and Political Mobilization in Western Europe,* ed. W. Shadid and P. van Koningsveld. Kampen: Kok Pharos.

———. 1999. "Socio-Economic and Educational Achievements of Ethnic Minorities." Paper submitted to the Commission on the Future of Multi-ethnic Britain, Runnymede Trust, London.

Ballard, R., and V. S. Kalra. 1994. *The Ethnic Dimensions of the 1991 Census: A Preliminary Report.* Manchester, England: Census Dissemination Unit, University of Manchester.

Banton, M. 1976. "On the Use of the Adjective 'black.'" *Newtwork* 6: 2–3. Reprinted, *New Community* 5, no. 4 (1977): 480–83.

———. 1979. "It's Our Country." In *Racism and Political Action in Britain,* ed. R. Miles and A. Phizacklea, 223–46. London: Routledge.

———. 1983. *Racial and Ethnic Competition.* Cambridge: Cambridge University Press.

———. 1987. "The Battle of the Name." *New Community* 14, no. 1/2: 170–75.

———. 1988. *Racial Consciousness.* London: Longman.

———. 1991. "The Race Relations Problematic." *British Journal of Sociology* 42, no. 1: 115–29.

———. 2001. "Progress in Ethnic and Racial Studies." *Ethnic and Racial Studies* 24, no. 2: 173–94.

———. 2002. *The International Politics of Race*. Cambridge, England: Polity Press.

Barber, B. R. 1992. *An Aristocracy for Everyone: The Politics of Education and the Future of America*. New York: Ballantine Books.

Barendt, E. 1985. *Freedom of Speech*. Oxford, England: Clarendon Press.

Barker, M. 1981. *The New Racism: Conservatives and the Ideology of the Tribe*. London: Junction Books.

Basit, Tehmina N. 1997. *Eastern Values, Western Milieu: Identities and Aspirations of Adolescent British Muslim Girls*. Aldershot, England: Ashgate.

Baumann, G. 1990. "The Re-invention of *Bhangra*: Social Change and Aesthetic Shifts in a Punjabi Music in Britain." *World of Music*, no. 2, Berlin.

BBC TV. 2004. *The Power of Nightmares*. Part 3. BBC, November 2, 3.

Bellah, R. N., R. Madsen, W. M. Sullivan, A. Swidler, S. M. Tipton. 1985. *Habits of the Heart: Individualism and Commitment in American Life*. Berkeley, CA: University of California Press.

Benhabib, S. 1992. *Situating the Self*. New York: Routledge.

Berthoud, R. 1999. *Young Caribbean Men and the Labour Market: A Comparison with Other Groups*. York, England: Joseph Rowntree Foundation.

———. 2000. "Ethnic Employment Penalties in Britain." *Journal of Ethnic and Migration Studies* 26, no. 3: 389–416.

Berthoud, R., M. Taylor, J. Burton, with contributions by T. Modood, N. Buck, and A. Booth. 2000. "Comparing the Transition from School to Work among Young People from Different Ethnic Groups: A Feasibility Study." Department of Education and Employment, Institute for Social and Economic Research, University of Essex.

Bhavnani, R. 1994. *Black Women in the Labour Market: A Research Review*. Manchester: Equal Opportunities Commission.

Blauner, R. 1972. *Racial Oppression in America: Essays in Search of a Theory*. New York: Harper and Row.

Blum, Lawrence A. 2002. *I'm Not a Racist But—: The Moral Quandary of Race*. Ithaca, NY: Cornell University Press.

Board of Deputies of British Jews. 1991. "A Report on Group Defamation." Unpublished, by a subcommittee of the Law and Parliamentary Committee.

Bonnett, Alastair. 1989. "Urban Struggle in Lanaguage: The Word 'Black.'" Unpublished paper.

———. 1993. *Radicalism, Anti-racism, and Representation*. London: Routledge.

Bradley, S., and J. Taylor. 2004. "Ethnicity, Educational Attainment, and the Transition from School." *Manchester School* 72, no. 3: 317–46.

Brah, Avtar. 1996. *Cartographies of Diaspora*. London: Routledge.

Bright, M. 2004. "Gangsta Culture a Deadly Virus, Says Top TV Presenter." *Observer*, September 12, 1–2.

Brohi, A. K. 1979. "Mawlana Abul Ala Mawdudi: The Man, the Scholar, the Reformer." In *Islamic Perspectives*, ed. K. Ahmad and Z. I. Ansari. Leicester, UK: Islamic Foundation.

Brown, C. 1984. *Black and White Britain: The Third PSI Survey*. London: Policy Studies Institute.

Brown, C., and P. Gay. 1985. *Racial Discrimination: Seventeen Years after the Act*. London: Policy Studies Institute.

Brown, M. 2000. "Religion and Economic Activity in the South Asian Population." *Ethnic and Racial Studies* 23, no. 6: 1035–61.

Brubaker, R. 1992. *Citizenship and Nationhood in France and Germany.* Cambridge, MA: Harvard University Press.

Bruegel, I. 1989. "Sex and Race in the Labour Market." *Feminist Review,* no. 32: 49–68.

Bryant, C. 1997."Citizenship, National Identity, and the Accommodation of Difference: Reflections on the German, French, Dutch, and British Cases." *New Community* 23, no. 2: 157–72.

Cabinet Office. 2003. "Ethnic Minorities and the Labour Market." Final Report, Strategy Unit, London, UK Government.

CCCS (Centre for Contemporary Cultural Studies). 1982. *The Empire Strikes Back: Race and Racism in 70s Britain.* London: Hutchinson.

Cleaver, E. 1968. *Soul on Ice.* New York: McGraw Hill.

Clunis, A. 2002. "Stop Our Failing Children." *Voice* (newspaper), March 25, 20–21.

CMEB (Commission on Multi-ethnic Britain). 2000. *The Future of Multi-ethnic Britain.* London: Profile Books.

Cohen, P. 1988. "The Perversions of Inheritance: Studies in the Making of Multi-racist Britain." In *Multi-racist Britain,* P. Cohen and H. S. Bains. London: Macmillan.

———. 1996. "A Message from the Other Shore." Symposium on Anti-racism in Britain. *Patterns of Prejudice* 30, no. 1: 15–21.

Collingwood, R. G. 1942. *New Leviathan.* Oxford, England: Clarendon Press.

Connolly, P. 1998. *Racism, Gender Identities, and Young Children.* London: Routledge.

Connor, H., C. Tyers, T. Modood, and J. Hillage. 2004. *Why the Difference? A Closer Look at Minority Ethnic Students and Graduates.* Research Report 552. London: Department for Education and Skills.

CRE (Commission for Racial Equality). 1987. *Chartered Accountancy Training Contracts: Report of a Formal Investigation into Ethnic Minority Recruitment.* London: CRE.

———. 1990a. *Free Speech: Report of a Seminar.* London: CRE.

———. 1990b. *Schools of Faith.* London: CRE.

———. 1991a. *Second Review of the Race Relations Act.* London: CRE.

———. 1991b. *Working in Hotels: Report of a Formal Investigation into Recruitment and Selection.* London: CRE.

Cross, M. 1994. *Ethnic Pluralism and Racial Inequality.* Utrecht: University of Utrecht.

Curtice, J., and A. Heath. 2000. "Is the English Lion about to Roar? National Identity after Devolution." In *Focusing on Diversity: British Social Attitudes; The 17th Report,* R. Jowell et al. London: Sage.

Daniel, Norman. 1961. *Islam and the West: Making of an Image.* Edinburgh: Edinburgh University Press.

———. 1967. *Islam, Europe, and Empire.* Edinburgh: Edinburgh University Press.

Daniel, W. W. 1968. *Racial Discrimination in England.* London: Penguin.

Dhondy, F. 2001. "Our Islamic Fifth Column." *City Limits* 11, no. 4.

Dikötter, F. 1990. "Group Definition and the Idea of 'Race' in Modern China." *Ethnic and Racial Studies* 13: 420–31.

Dimbleby, J. 1994. *Prince of Wales: A Biography.* London: Little, Brown.

Dirk de Graaf, N., and A. Need. 2000. "Losing Faith: Is Britain Alone?" In *Focus-*

ing on Diversity: British Social Attitudes; The 17th Report, R. Jowell et al. London: Sage.

Donald, J., and A. Rattansi, eds. 1992. "Race," Culture, and Difference. London: Sage.

Drew, David. 1995. "Race," Education, and Work: The Statistics of Inequality. Aldershot, England: Avebury.

Drew, David, J. Gray, and N. Sime. 1992. "Against the Odds: The Education and Labour Market Experiences of Black Young People." England and Wales Youth Cohort Study, Report R&D no. 68, Employment Department, Sheffield University.

Du Bois, W. E. B. 1995. The Souls of Black Folk. New York: Signet. Originally published 1903.

Esmail, A., and S. Everington. 1993. "Racial Discrimation against Doctors from Ethnic Minorities." British Medical Journal 306 (March): 691–92.

Favell, Adrian. 1998a. "Applied Political Philosophy at the Rubicon: Will Kymlicka's Multicultural Citizenship." Ethical Theory and Moral Practice 1, no. 2.

———. 1998b. "Multicultureel theorie in theorie en pratijk: empirische analyses in de toegepaste politieke filosofie." In Krisis: Tijdschrift voor filosofie, no. 72. English language version kindly supplied by the author.

———. 2001. Philosophies of Integration: Immigration and the Idea of Citizenship in France and Britain. 2nd ed. Basingstoke and London: Palgrave.

Favell, Adrian, and Tariq Modood. 2003. "Multiculturalism and the Theory and Practice of Normative Political Theory." In Contemporary Political Thought: A Reader and Guide, ed. A. Finlayson. Edinburgh: Edinburgh University Press.

Ferguson, R. F. 2005. "Why America's Black-White School Achievement Gap Persists." In Ethnicity, Social Mobility, and Public Policy in the US and UK, ed. G. Loury, T. Modood, and S. Teles. Cambridge: Cambridge University Press.

Fraser, N. 1992. "Rethinking the Public Sphere." In Habermas and the Public Sphere, ed. C. Calhoun. Cambridge: MIT Press.

Frean, A. 2003. "Black Africans in Britain Lead Way in Education." Times, May 8, London. http://www.timesonline.co.uk.

Fredrickson, George M. 2002. Racism: A Short History. Princeton, NJ: Princeton University Press.

Fuss, D. 1989. Essentially Speaking. New York: Routledge.

Gates, H. L., Jr. 1997. "Black London." New Yorker, April 28–May 5.

Gillborn, David. 1990. "Race," Ethnicity, and Education. London: Unwin Hyman.

———. 1996. "Culture, Colour, Power, and Racism." Symposium on Anti-racism in Britain. Patterns of Prejudice 30, no. 1: 22–27.

———. 1998. "Race and Ethnicity in Compulsory Schooling." In Race and Higher Education, ed. T. Modood and T. Acland. London: Policy Studies Institute.

Gillborn, David, and C. Gipps. 1996. "Recent Research on the Achievements of Ethnic Minority Pupils." London: Office for Standards in Education.

Gillborn, David, and H. Mirza. 2000. "Educational Inequality: Mapping Race, Class, and Gender: A Synthesis of Research Evidence." London: Office for Standards in Education.

Gillborn, David, and D. Youdell. 2000. Rationing Education: Policy, Practice, Reform, and Equity. Buckingham and Phildelphia: Open University Press.

Gilroy, P. 1987. There Ain't No Black in the Union Jack: The Cultural Politics of Race and Nation. London: Heinemann.

———. 1990. "The End of Anti-racism." New Community 17: 71–83.

————. 1993. *The Black Atlantic: Modernity and Double Consciousness.* London and New York: Verso.

Glass, R. 1961. *London's Newcomers: The West Indian Migrants.* Cambridge: Harvard University Press.

Glynn, S. 2002. "Bengali Muslims: The New East End Radicals?" *Ethnic and Racial Studies* 25, no. 6: 969–88.

Goldberg, David T. 1993. *Racist Culture: Philosophy and the Politics of Meaning.* Cambridge, MA: Blackwell.

Goodhart, D. 2004. "Horns of the Liberal Dilemma." *Guardian* (London), February 8, 24.

Gordon, P., and F. Klug. 1986. *New Right, New Racism.* London: Searchlight.

Goulbourne, H. 1991a. *Ethnicity and Nationalism in Post-imperial Britain,* Cambridge: Cambridge University Press.

————. 1991b. "Varieties of Pluralism: The Notion of a Pluralist, Post-imperial Britain." *New Community* 17, no. 2: 211–27.

Gutmann, Amy. 1994. "Introduction." In *Multiculturalism: Examining the Politics of Recognition,* ed. A. Gutmann. Princeton, NJ: Princeton University Press.

Habermas, Jürgen. 1984. *The Theory of Communicative Action.* Vol. 1, *Reason and the Rationalization of Society.* Boston: Beacon.

————. 1987. *The Theory of Communicative Action,* Vol. 2, *Lifeworld and System.* Boston: Beacon Press.

————. 1994. "Struggles for Recognition in the Democratic Constitutional State." In *Multiculturalism: Examining the Politics of Recognition,* ed. A. Gutmann. Princeton, NJ: Princeton University Press.

Hagell, A., and C. Shaw. 1996. *Opportunity and Disadvantage at Age 16.* London: Policy Studies Institute.

Hall, Stuart. 1992a. "New Ethnicities." In *"Race," Culture, and Difference,* ed. J. Donald and A. Rattansi. London: Sage. Based on a talk delivered to the "Black Film, British Cinema" conference, Institute of Contemporary Arts, London, February 1988.

————. 1992b. "The Question of Cultural Identity." In *Modernity and Its Futures,* ed. S. Hall and T. McGrew. Cambridge, England: Polity Press.

————. 1998. "Aspiration and Attitude: Reflections on Black Britain in the Nineties." In "Frontlines/Backyards," special issue, *New Formations* 33 (Spring).

————. 2000. "Conclusion: Multi-cultural Questions." In *Un/settled Multiculturalisms: Diasporas, Entanglements, Transruptions,* ed. B. Hesse. London and New York: Zed Books.

Hall, Stuart, and D. Held. 1989. "Citizens and Citizenship." In *New Times: The Changing Face of Politics in the 1990s,* ed. S. Hall and M. Jacques. London: Lawrence and Wishart.

Hardt, M., and A. Negri. 2000. *Empire.* Cambridge, MA: Harvard University Press.

Haydon, Graham. 1994. "Conceptions of the Secular in Society, Polity, and Schools." *Journal of Philosophy of Education* 28, no. 1.

Heath, A., and D. McMahon. 1997. "Education and Occupational Attainments: The Impact of Ethnic Origins." In *Ethnicity in the 1991 Census,* vol. 4, *Education, Employment, and Housing,* ed. V. Karn. London: HMSO.

————. 2005. "Social Mobility and Ethnic Minorities." In *Ethnicity, Social Mobility, and Public Policy: Comparing the US and UK,* ed. Glenn C. Loury, Tariq Modood, and Steven M. Teles. Cambridge: Cambridge University Press.

Heath, A., and J. Ridge. 1983. "Social Mobility of Ethnic Minorities." *Journal of Biosocial Science* suppl. 8: 169–84.

Held, D. 1995. *Democracy and Global Order.* Cambridge, England: Polity Press.

Hobohm, M. A. 1978. "Islam and the Racial Problem." In *The Challenge of Islam,* ed. A. Gauhar, 268–83. London: Islamic Council of Europe.

Home Office. 1983. *Review of the Public Order Act 1936 and Related Legislation.* London: Home Office.

Horton, J., ed. 1993. *Liberalism, Multiculturalism, and Toleration.* Basingstoke, England: Macmillan.

House of Commons. 1969. *The Problems of Coloured School-Leavers.* Vol. 1, Report and Proceedings of the Selection Committee on Race Relations and Immigration. Session 1968–69, report 413-1. London: HMSO.

House of Commons Home Affairs Committee. 1980. *The Law Relating to Public Order,* vol. 11. London.

———. 1983. *Ethnic and Racial Question in the Census.* Vol. 2, *Minutes of Evidence.* London: HMSO.

Iganski, P., and G. Payne. 1996. "Declining Racial Disadvantage in the British Labour Market." *Ethnic and Racial Studies* 19, no. 1: 113–34.

Ignatieff, M. 1989. "Defenders of Rushdie Tied in Knots." *Observer,* April 2.

———. 1990. "Protect People, Not What They Believe." *Observer,* February 11.

Jacobson, J. 1997. "Religion and Ethnicity: Dual and Alternative Sources of Identity among Young British Pakistanis." *Ethnic and Racial Studies* 20, no. 2.

Jasper, L., and T. Sewell. 2003. "Look beyond the Street." *Guardian* (London), July 19. http://www.guardian.co.uk.

Jenkins, Richard. 1986. *Racism and Recruitment.* Cambridge: Cambridge University Press.

Johnston, R., J. Forrest, and M. Poulsen. 2002. "The Ethnic Geography of EthniCities: The 'American Model' and Residential Concentration in London." *Ethnicities* 2, no. 2: 209–35.

Jones, P. 1993. "Respecting Beliefs and Rebuking Rushdie." In *Liberalism, Multiculturalism, and Toleration,* ed. J. Horton. Basingstoke, England: Macmillan.

Jones, T. 1993. *Britain's Ethnic Minorities.* London: Policy Studies Institute.

Kalra, V. 2003. "Police Lore and Community Disorder: Diversity in the Criminal Justice System." In *Explaining Ethnic Differences: Changing Patterns of Disadvantage in Britain,* ed. D. Mason. Bristol, England: Policy Press.

Kastoryano, R. 2002. *Negotiating Identities: States and Immigrants in France and Germany.* Princeton, NJ: Princeton University Press.

Koopmans, R., and P. Statham, eds. 2000. *Challenging Immigration and Ethnic Relations Politics: Comparative European Perspectives.* Oxford: Oxford University Press.

Kumar, K. 2003. *The Making of English National Identity.* Cambridge: Cambridge University Press.

Kureshi, H. 1995. *The Black Album.* London: Faber.

Kymlicka, Will. 1995. *Multicultural Citizenship.* Oxford: Oxford University Press.

———. 2001. *Politics in the Vernacular: Nationalism, Multiculturalism, and Citizenship.* Oxford: Oxford University Press.

Lal, B. 1983. "Perspectives on Ethnicity: Old Wine in New Bottles." *Ethnic and Racial Studies* 6, no. 2: 154–73.

———. 1990. *The Romance of Culture in an Urban Civilisation: Robert E. Park on Race and Ethnic Relations in Cities.* London: RKP.

Larmore, Charles. 1987. *Patterns of Moral Complexity*. Cambridge: Cambridge University Press.

———. 1990. "Political Liberalism." *Political Theory* 18.

Lee, S. 1990a. "First Introductory Paper." *Law, Blasphemy, and the Multi-faith Society*. London: Commission for Racial Equality and the Inter-faith Network for the UK.

———. 1990b. "Law, Respect for Religious Identity, and the Multi-faith Society." In *Law, Respect for Religious Identity, and the Multi-faith Society*. London: Inter-faith Network for the UK and the Commission for Racial Equality.

———. 1990c. "Protecting Both Gods and Books." *Independent* (London), March 9.

Leonard, K. I. 2003. *Muslims in the United States: The State of Research*. New York: Russell Sage Foundation.

Leonard, M. 1997. *Britain TM: Renewing Our Identity*. London: Demos.

Leslie, D., A. Abbott, and D. Blackaby. 2002. "Why Are Ethnic Minority Applicants Less Likely to Be Accepted into Higher Education?" *Higher Education Quarterly* 56, no. 1: 65–91.

Loury, Glenn C., Tariq Modood, and Steven M. Teles, eds. 2004. *Ethnicity, Social Mobility, and Public Policy: Comparing the US and UK*. Cambridge: Cambridge University Press.

Luthra, M. 1997. *Britain's Black Population: Social Change, Public Policy, and Agenda*. Aldershot, England: Ashgate.

Mac an Ghaill, Mairtin. 1988. *Young, Gifted, and Black: Student-Teacher Relations in the Schooling of Black Youth*. Philadelphia: Open University Press.

Macpherson of Cluny, Sir William. 1999. *The Stephen Lawrence Inquiry*. London: Stationery Office.

Maja-Pearce, Adewale. 1990. *How Many Miles to Babylon?* London: Heinemann.

Malcolm X. 1966. *The Autobiography of Malcolm X*. Written with Alex Hailey. New York: Hutchinson and Collins.

Malik, K. 2001. "The Real Value of Diversity." *Connections* (Commission for Racial Equality, London) (Winter).

Marnham, P. 1990. "Just between Friends, Let's Hate Them." *Independent* (London), May 19.

Mendus, Susan. 1989. *Toleration and the Limits of Liberalism*. London: Macmillan.

———. 1990. "The Tigers of Wrath and the Horses of Instruction." *Free Speech*. London: Commission for Racial Equality.

Miles, Robert. 1982. *Racism and Migrant Labour*. London: Routledge.

———. 1987. "Class Relations and Racism in the 1980s." *European Review of International Migration* 3, no. 1/2: 223–28.

———. 1989. *Racism*. London and New York: Routledge.

Miller, D. 1995. *On Nationality*. Oxford: Oxford University Press.

Modood, M. S. 1990. "My Faith: A Personal Statement." In *The Pillars of Islam*, F. Gumley and B. Redhead. London: BBC Books; reprinted in *Searching for Great Ideas*, 2nd ed., ed. T. Klein, B. Edwards, and T. Wymer. New York: Harcourt Brace College Publishers, 1998; and in *My Faith and I Rest Here*, private publication, London, 2003.

Modood, Tariq. 1988. "'Black,' Racial Equality, and Asian Identity." *New Community* 14, no. 3: 397–404.

———. 1989. "The Later Collingwood's Alleged Historicism and Relativism." *Journal of the History of Philosophy* 27, no. 1: 101–25.

———. 1990a. "British Asian Muslims and the Rushdie Affair." *Political Quarterly*

61, no. 2: 43–160. Reprinted in *"Race," Culture, and Difference*, ed. J. Donald and A. Rattansi. London: Sage.

———. 1990b. "Catching Up with Jesse Jackson: Being Oppressed and Being Somebody." *New Community* 17, no. 1: 85–96. Reprinted in *Not Easy Being British: Colour, Culture, and Citizenship*, T. Modood. Stoke-on-Trent: Runnymede Trust, 1992.

———. 1991. "The Indian Economic Success: A Challenge to Some Race Relations Assumptions." *Policy and Politics* 19, no. 3. Reprinted in *Not Easy Being British: Colour, Culture, and Citizenship*, T. Modood. Stoke-on-Trent: Runnymede Trust, 1992.

———. 1992. *Not Easy Being British: Colour, Culture, and Citizenship*. Stoke-on-Trent: Runnymede Trust.

———. 1993a. "Muslim Views on Religious Identity and Racial Equality." *New Community* 19, no. 3: 513–19.

———. 1993b. "The Number of Ethnic Minority Students in British Higher Education." *Oxford Review of Education* 19, no. 2: 167–82.

———. 1994a. "Establishment, Multiculturalism, and British Citizenship." *Political Quarterly* 65, no. 1: 53–73.

———. 1994b. "Ethnic Difference and Racial Equality: New Challenges for the Left." In *Reinventing the Left*, ed. D. Miliband. Cambridge, England: Polity Press.

———. 1994c. "Political Blackness and British Asians." *Sociology* 28, no. 4: 859–76.

———. 1996a. "'Race' in Britain and the Politics of Difference." In *Philosophy and Pluralism*, ed. D. Archard. Cambridge: Cambridge University Press.

———. 1996b. "The Changing Context of 'Race' in Britain." *Patterns of Prejudice* 30, no. 1: 3–13.

———, ed. 1997. *Church, State, and Religious Minorities*. London: Policy Studies Institute.

———. 1998a. "Anti-essentialism, Multiculturalism, and the 'Recognition' of Religious Minorities." *Journal of Political Philosophy* 6, no. 4: 378–99. Reprinted in *Citizenship in Diverse Societies*, ed. W. Kymlicka and W. Norman. Oxford: Oxford University Press.

———. 1998b. "British Multiculturalism: Some Rival Positions and Thoughts on the Way Forward." Seminar paper to the Commission on the Future of Multi-ethnic Britain, London.

———. 1998c. "Ethnic Minorities and the Drive for Qualifications." In *Race and Higher Education*, ed. T. Modood and T. Acland. London: Policy Studies Institute.

———. 1999. "New Forms of Britishness: Post-immigration Ethnicity and Hybridity in Britain." In *The Expanding Nation: Towards a Multi-ethnic Ireland*, ed. R. Lentin. Dublin: Trinity College. Reprinted in *Identity and Integration*, ed. R. Sackman, B. Peters, and T. Faist. 2003. Aldershot, England: Ashgate.

———. 2004–5. "Multiculturalism or Britishness: A False Debate." *Connections*. London: Commission for Racial Equality. Winter.

———. 2005. "Ethnicity and Political Mobilisation in Britain." In *Ethnicity, Social Mobility, and Public Policy*, ed. Glenn C. Loury, Tariq Modood, and Steven M. Teles. Cambridge: Cambridge University Press.

Modood, Tariq, and T. Acland, eds. 1998. *Race and Higher Education*. London: Policy Studies Institute.

Modood, Tariq, and F. Ahmad. Forthcoming. "British Muslim Perspectives on Multiculturalism."

Modood, Tariq, S. Beishon, and S. Virdee. 1994. *Changing Ethnic Identities.* London: Policy Studies Institute.

Modood, Tariq, R. Berthoud, J. Lakey, J. Nazroo, P. Smith, S. Virdee, and S. Beishon. 1997. *Ethnic Minorities in Britain: Diversity and Disadvantage.* London: Policy Studies Institute.

Modood, Tariq, R. Berthoud, and J. Nazroo. 2002. "'Race,' Racism, and Ethnicity: A Response to Ken Smith." *Sociology* 36, no. 2 (May): 419–27.

Modood, Tariq, H. Metcalf, and S. Virdee, 1998. "British Asian Entrepreneurs: Culture and Opportunity Structures." In *Choice and Public Policy,* ed. P. Taylor-Gooby. Basingstoke: Macmillan; New York: St. Martin's Press.

Modood, Tariq, and M. Shiner. 1994. *Ethnic Minorities and Higher Education: Why Are There Differential Rates of Entry?* London: Policy Studies Institute.

Modood, Tariq, and Pnina Werbner, eds. 1997. *The Politics of Multiculturalism in the New Europe: Racism, Identity, and Community.* London: Zed Books.

Mullings, B. 1992. "Investing in Public Housing and Racial Discrimination: Implications in the 1990s." *New Community* 15: 549–64.

Murphy, Dervla. 1987. *Tales from Two Cities.* London: John Murray.

Muslim Parliament of Great Britain. 1992. *Race Relations and Muslims in Great Britain: A Discussion Paper.* London: Muslim Parliament.

Nagel, Thomas. 1991. *Equality and Partiality.* Oxford: Oxford University Press.

Nahdi, F. 1994. "Focus on Crime and Youth." *Q News* 3, no. 3: 15–22.

Nanton, P. 1989. "The New Orthodoxy: Racial Categories and Equal Opportunity Policy." *New Community* 15, no. 4: 549–64.

National Statistics Online. 2004. *Focus on Ethnicity and Identity.* http://www.statistics.gov.uk.

Noon, M. 1993. "Racial Discrimination in Speculative Applications: Evidence from the UK's Top One Hundred Firms." *Human Resource Management Journal* 3, no. 4: 35–47.

Oakeshott, M. 1962. *Rationalism in Politics and Other Essays.* London: Methuen.

Omi, M., and H. Winant. 1986. *Racial Formation in the United States from the 1960s to the 1980s.* London: Routledge.

ONS (Office for National Statistics). 2003. *Focus on Ethnicity.* London: ONS.

OPCS 1993. *1991 Census: Ethnic Group and Country of Birth.* London: OPCS.

Ouseley, H. 2001. *Community Pride, Not Prejudice: Making Diversity Work in Bradford.* Bradford, England: Bradford City Council.

Owen, C., P. Mortimore, and A. Phoenix. 1997. "Higher Educational Qualifications." In *Ethnicity in the 1991 Census.* Vol. 4, *Education, Employment, and Housing among Ethnic Minorities in Britain,* ed. V. Karn. London: OPCS.

Owen, D., A. Green, J. Pitcher, and M. Maguire. 2000. *Minority Ethnic Participation and Achievements in Education, Training, and the Labour Market.* London: Department for Education and Employment.

Parekh, Bhikhu. 1990. "Britain and the Social Logic of Pluralism." In *Britain: A Plural Society,* Commission for Racial Equality, 58–76. London: Commission for Racial Equality.

———. 1994. "Minority Rights, Majority Values." In *Reinventing the Left,* ed. D. Milliband. Cambridge, England: Polity Press.

———. 2000. *Rethinking Multiculturalism: Cultural Diversity and Political Theory.* Basingstoke and London: Macmillan.

———. 2004. "Redistribution or Recognition? A Misguided Debate." In *Ethnicity, Nationalism, and Minority Rights,* ed. S. May, T. Modood, and J. Squires. Cambridge: Cambridge University Press.

Park, Robert E., and Herbert A. Miller. 1921. *Old World Traits Transplanted.* New York: Harper.

Pateman, C. 1988. *The Sexual Contract.* Stanford, CA: University of Stanford Press.

Pathak, S. 2000. "Race Research for the Future: Ethnicity in Education, Training, and the Labour Market." Research Topic Paper, Department of Education and Employment.

Peach, C. 1990. "The Muslim Population of Great Britain." *Ethnic and Racial Studies* 13, no. 3.

———. 1996. *Ethnicity in the 1991 Census.* Introduction to vol. 2, *The Ethnic Minority Populations in Britain,* ed. C. Peach. London: HMSO.

Penn R., and H. Scattergood. 1992. "Ethnicity and Career Aspirations in Contemporary Britain." *New Community* 19, no. 1: 75–98.

Phillips, A. 1997. "In Defence of Secularism." In *Church, State, and Religious Minorities,* ed. Tariq Modood. London: Policy Studies Institute.

Phillips, M., and T. Phillips. 1998. *Windrush: The Irresistible Rise of Multicultural Britain.* London: HarperCollins.

Phillips, T. 2002. "The Time Has Come for Zero-Tolerance." *Mail on Sunday,* February 3, 26.

———. 2004. "Genteel Xenophobia Is As Bad As Any Other Kind." *Guardian* (London), February 16.

Pilkington, A. 1999. "Racism in Schools and Ethnic Differentials in Educational Achievement: A Brief Comment on a Recent Debate." *British Journal of Sociology of Education* 20, no. 3: 411–17.

Pitkin, H. F. 1972. *Wittgenstein and Justice.* Berkeley and Los Angeles: University of California Press.

Poulter, S. 1986. *English Law and Ethnic Minority Customs.* London: Butterworths.

———. 1989. "The Significance of Ethnic Minority Customs and Traditions in English Criminal Law." *New Community* 16, no. 1.

———. 1990. "Cultural Pluralism and Its Limits: A Legal Perspective." In *Britain: A Plural Society,* Commission for Racial Equality. London: CRE.

———. 1991. "Towards Legislative Reform of the Blasphemy and Racial Hatred Laws." *Public Law* (Autumn): 371–85.

Rawls, John. 1971. *A Theory of Justice.* Oxford: Oxford University Press.

———. 1993. *Political Liberalism.* New York: Columbia University Press.

Raz, Joseph. 1994. "Multiculturalism: A Liberal Perspective." *Dissent* (Winter): 67–79.

Rex, John. 1981. "A Working Paradigm for Race Research." *Ethnic and Racial Studies* 4, no. 1: 10–25.

———. 1986. *Race and Ethnicity.* Milton Keynes, England: Open University Press.

———. 1988. "The Urban Sociology of Religion and Islam in Birmingham." In *The New Islamic Presence in Western Europe,* ed. T. Gerholm and Y. G. Lithman. London: Mansell.

———. 1989. Review of A. Shaw, *A Pakistani Community in Britain. New Community* 15, no. 2: 305–6.

———. 1996. "National Identity in the Democratic Multi-cultural State." *Sociological Research Online* 1, no. 2. http://www.socresonline.org.uk/socresonline/1/2/1.html.

Rex, John, and R. Moore. 1967. *Race, Community, and Conflict.* Oxford: Oxford University Press.

Richardson, Robin, and Angela Wood. 1999. *Inclusive Schools, Inclusive Society: Race and Identity on the Agenda.* Stoke-on-Trent, England: Trentham Books.

Robinson, V. 1990. "Roots to Mobility: The Social Mobility of Britain's Black Population, 1971–87." *Ethnic and Racial Studies* 13, no. 2: 274–86.

Rodriguez, Clara E. 1991. "Puerto Ricans: The Rainbow People." In *Rethinking Today's Minorities,* ed. V. N. Parrillo. New York: Greenwood Press.

Rojek, C. 2003. *Stuart Hall.* Oxford, England: Blackwell.

Royal Commission on the Reform of the House of Lords. 2000. *A House for the Future.* London: HMSO, January.

Runnymede Trust. 1997. Commission on British Muslims and Islamophobia. *Islamophobia: A Challenge to Us All.* London: Runnymede Trust.

———. 1998. In partnership with the Commission for Racial Equality. *Young People in the UK: Attitudes and Opinions on Europe, Europeans, and the European Union.* London: Runnymede Trust.

———. 2004. *Islamophobia: Issues, Challenges, and Action.* Stoke-on-Trent, England: Trentham Books.

Rushdie, S. 1982. "The New Empire within Britain." *New Society,* December 9.

———. 1991. "In Good Faith." In *Imaginary Homelands,* S. Rushdie. London: Penguin.

Ruthven, Malise. 1990. *A Satanic Affair.* London: Chatto and Windus.

Saeed, A., N. Blain, and D. Forbes. 1999. "New Ethnic and National Questions in Scotland: Post-British Identities among Glasgow Pakistani Teenagers." *Ethnic and Racial Studies* 22, no. 5: 821–44.

Saggar, S. 1992. *Race and Politics in Britain.* London: Harvester Wheatsheaf.

Saghal, G., and N. Yuval-Davis, eds. 1992. *Refusing Holy Orders: Women and Fundamentalism in Britain.* London: Virago Press.

Said, E. W. 1985. *Orientalism.* Harmondsworth, England: Penguin.

Sandel, M. 1994. "Review of Rawls' Political Liberalism." *Harvard Law Review* 107: 1765–94.

Sardar, Z., and M. Wyn Davies. 1990. *Distorted Imagination.* London: Grey Seal.

Sewell, T. 1997. *Black Masculinity and Schooling: How Black Boys Survive Modern Schooling.* Stoke-on-Trent, England: Trentham Books.

Shaw, A. 2002. "Why Might Young British Muslims Support the Taliban?" *Anthropology Today* 18, no. 1.

Shiner, M., and T. Modood. 2002. "Help or Hindrance? Higher Education and the Route to Ethnic Equality." *British Journal of Sociology of Education* 23, no. 2: 209–30.

Simpson, A., and J. Stevenson. 1994. "Half a Chance, Still? Jobs, Discrimination, and Young People in Nottingham." Nottingham, England: Nottingham and District Racial Equality Council.

Sivanandan, A. 1985. "RAT and the Degradation of the Black Struggle." *Race and Class* 26, no. 4.

Smith, D. J. 1977. *Racial Disadvantage in Britain.* London: Penguin.

Smith, S. J. 1989. *The Politics of "Race" and Residence.* Cambridge, England: Polity Press.

———. 1993. "Residential Segregation and the Politics of Racialisation." In *Racism, the City, and the State,* ed. M. Cross and M. Keith. London: Routledge.

Solomos, J. 1991. "Political Language and Racial Discourse." *European Journal of Intercultural Studies* 2, no. 1: 21–34.

Song, Min. 2004. "Introduction: Who's at the Bottom? Examining Claims about Racial Hierarchy." *Ethnic and Racial Studies* 27, no. 6: 859–77.

Soysal, Y. N. 1994. *Limits of Citizenship: Migrants and Postnational Membership in Europe.* Chicago: University of Chicago Press.

Spinner-Halev, J. 2000. *Surviving Diversity: Religion and Democratic Citizenship.* Baltimore: The Johns Hopkins University Press.

Sudbury, J. 2001. "(Re)Constructing Multiracial Blackness: Women's Activism, Difference, and Collective Identity in Britain." *Ethnic and Racial Studies* 24, no. 1: 29–49.

Swann, M. 1985. *Education for All.* Cmnd. 9453. London: HMSO.

Taylor, Charles. 1994. "Multiculturalism and 'The Politics of Recognition.'" In *Multiculturalism and "The Politics of Recognition,"* ed. A. Gutmann. Princeton, NJ: Princeton University Press.

Taylor, P. 1992. "Ethnic Group Data for University Entry." Project Report for CVCP Working Group on Ethnic Data. Coventry, England: University of Warwick.

Travis, A. 2004. "Desire to Integrate on the Wane As Muslims Resent 'War on Islam.'" *Guardian* (London), March 16.

UKACIA (UK Action Committee on Islamic Affairs). 1989. *The British Muslim Response to Mr. Patten.* London: UKACIA.

———. 1993. *Muslims and the Law in Multi-faith Britain: Need for Reform.* London: UKACIA.

Virdee, S., T. Modood, and T. Newburn. 2000. "Understanding Racial Harassment in School." A Project Report to the ESRC.

Voas, D., and S. Bruce. 2004. "The 2001 Census and Christian Identification in Britain." *Journal of Contemporary Religion* 19, no. 1: 23–28.

Waldinger, R., H. Aldrich, and R. Ward. 1990. *Ethnic Entrepreneurs.* London: Sage.

Waldron, J. 1989. "Moral Neutrality." In *Liberal Neutrality,* ed. R. Goodin and A. Reeve. London: Routledge.

———. 1992. "Minority Cultures and the Cosmopolitan Alternative." *University of Michigan Journal of Law Reform* 25, no. 3/4: 751–93.

Weale, A. 1990. "Freedom of Religion?" *Free Speech.* London: Commission for Racial Equality.

Webster, R. 1990. *A Brief History of Blasphemy.* Southwold, England: Orwell Press.

Weldon, F. 1989. *Sacred Cows.* London: Chatto and Windus.

Werbner, Pnina. 2001. "Divided Loyalties." *Times Higher Education Supplement* 14 (December).

———. 2004. "The Predicament of Diaspora and Millennial Islam: Reflections on September 11, 2001." *Ethnicities* 4, no. 4: 451–76.

Willis, P. 1977. *Learning to Labour.* Aldershot, England: Gower.

Winch, P. 1958. *The Idea of Social Science and Its Relation to Philosophy.* London: Routledge and Kegan Paul.

Wintemute, R. 1995. *Sexual Orientation and Human Rights: United States Constitution, the European Convention, and the Canadian Charter.* Oxford, England: Clarendon Press.

Wittgenstein, L. 1968. *Philosophical Investigations.* Trans. G. E. M. Anscombe. Oxford, England: Blackwell.

Women Against Fundamentalism. 1990. "Founding Statement." *Women Against Fundamentalism Journal* 1, no. 1: 1.

Wrench, J., and T. Qureshi. 1996. "Higher Horizons: A Qualitative Study of Young

Men of Bangladeshi Origin." Research Study 30. London: Department for Education and Employment.

Young, Iris M. 1990. *Justice and the Politics of Difference.* Princeton, NJ: Princeton University Press.

Yuval-Davis, N. 1992. "Fundamentalism, Multiculturalism, and Women in Britain." In *Race, Culture, and Difference,* ed. J. Donald and A. Rattansi. London: Sage.

Zhou, M. 1997. "Social Capital in Chinatown: The Role of Community-Based Organizations and Families in the Adaptation of the Younger Generation." In *Beyond Black and White: New Faces and Voices in U.S. Schools,* ed. Maxine Seller and Lois Weis, 181–206. Albany: State University of New York Press.

———. 2005. "Ethnicity as Social Capital: Community-Based Institutions and Embedded Networks of Social Relations." In *Ethnicity, Social Mobility, and Public Policy: Comparing the US and UK,* ed. Glenn C. Loury, Tariq Modood, and Steven M. Teles. Cambridge: Cambridge University Press.

Previous Publications

An earlier version of chapter 1 appeared as "'Difference,' Cultural-Racism, and Anti-racism," in *Debating Cultural Hybridities: Multicultural Identities and the Politics of Anti-racism*, edited by Pnina Werbner and Tariq Modood (London: Zed Books, 1997).

An earlier version of chapter 2 appeared as "If Races Do Not Exist, Then What Does? Racial Categorisation and Ethnic Realities," in *The Racism Problematic: Contemporary Sociological Debates on Race and Ethnicity*, edited by Rohit Barot (Lewiston, NY: Edwin Mullen Press, 1996). Reprinted by permission of Edwin Mullen Press.

An earlier version of chapter 3 appeared as "Ethnic Diversity and Racial Disadvantage in Employment," in *Race Relations in Britain: A Developing Agenda*, edited by Tessa Blackstone, Bhikhu Parekh, and Peter Sanders (London: Routledge, 1998).

An earlier version of chapter 4 appeared as "Ethnic Differentials in Educational Performance," in *Explaining Ethnic Difference*, edited by David Mason (Bristol, UK: Policy Press, 2003). Reprinted by permission of Policy Press.

An earlier version of chapter 5 was published as "Muslims, Race, and Equality in Britain: Some Post–Rushdie Affair Reflections," *Third Text* 11 (Summer 1990): 127–34. Reprinted by permission of Third Text.

An earlier version of chapter 6 appeared as "Muslims, Incitement to Hatred and the Law," in *Liberalism, Multiculturalism, and Toleration,* edited by John Horton (London: Macmillan, 1993).

An earlier version of chapter 7 was published as "Multiculturalism, Secularism, and the State," *Critical Review of International, Social, and Political Philosophy* 1, no. 3 (October 1998). Reprinted by permission of Frank Cass Publishers, London.

An earlier version of chapter 8 appeared as "The Place of Muslims in British Secular Multiculturalism," in *Muslim Europe or Euro-Islam: Politics, Culture, and Citizenship in the Age of Globalization,* edited by Nezar AlSayyad and Manuel Castells (New York: Lexington Books, 2002). Reprinted by permission of Lexington Books.

An earlier version of chapter 9 was published as "Their Liberalism and Our Multiculturalism?" *British Journal of Politics and International Relations* 3, no. 2 (June 2001). Reprinted by permission of Blackwell Publishing.

Index

TARIQ MODOOD is professor of sociology, politics, and public policy, and founding director of the Centre for the Study of Ethnicity and Citizenship at the University of Bristol. He is also cofounding editor of *Ethnicities*.

CRAIG CALHOUN is professor of sociology and history at New York University and president of the Social Science Research Council.